Chinese Economists on Economic Reform – Collected Works of Chen Xiwen

I0124397

This book is part of a series that makes available to English-speaking audiences the work of the individual Chinese economists who were the architects of China's economic reform. The series provides an inside view of China's economic reform, revealing the thinking of the reformers themselves, unlike many other books on China's economic reform which are written by outside observers.

Chen Xiwen (1950–) has made major contributions to economic policy making on agricultural development and the rural economy. Born in Shanghai, he was one of the young people sent down to the countryside in the late 1960s to work in a production and construction corp. He has held a number of government and academic positions, notably director of the Rural Economy Research Department of the State Council and vice president of the Development Research Center of the State Council.

The book is published in association with **China Development Research Foundation**, one of the leading economic and social think tanks in China, where many of the theoretical foundations and policy details of economic reform were formulated.

Routledge Studies on the Chinese Economy
Series Editor
Peter Nolan, Sinyi Professor, Judge Business School,
Chair, Development Studies, University of Cambridge

Founding Series Editors
Peter Nolan, University of Cambridge and
Dong Fureng, Beijing University

The aim of this series is to publish original, high-quality, research-level work by both new and established scholars in the West and the East on all aspects of the Chinese economy, including studies of business and economic history.

Routledge Studies on the Chinese Economy – Chinese Economists on Economic Reform

Chen Xiwen

Chinese Economists on Economic Reform – Collected Works of Chen Xiwen

Chen Xiwen

Edited by China Development Research Foundation

Routledge
Taylor & Francis Group

LONDON AND NEW YORK

First edition of *A Collection of Chen Xiwen's Works on Economic Reform*
by Chen Xiwen
ISBN: 978-7-80234-209-5
published 2008 by China Development Press.

This edition published 2014
by Routledge
2 Park Square, Milton Park, Abingdon, Oxon, OX14 4RN

and by Routledge
711 Third Avenue, New York, NY 10017

First issued in paperback 2018

Routledge is an imprint of the Taylor & Francis Group, an informa business

© 2014, selection and editorial material, China Development Research
Foundation; individual chapters, Chen Xiwen.

The right of the editor to be identified as author of the editorial material,
and of the author for the individual chapters, has been asserted in
accordance with sections 77 and 78 of the Copyright, Designs and Patents
Act 1988.

All rights reserved. No part of this book may be reprinted or reproduced or
utilized in any form or by any electronic, mechanical, or other means, now
known or hereafter invented, including photocopying and recording, or in
any information storage or retrieval system, without permission in writing
from the publishers.

Trademark notice: Product or corporate names may be trademarks or
registered trademarks, and are used only for identification and explanation
without intent to infringe.

British Library Cataloguing-in-Publication Data
A catalogue record for this book is available from the British Library

Library of Congress Cataloging-in-Publication Data
Chen, Xiwen, 1950–
[Works. Selections. English]
   Chinese economists on economic reform. Collected works of
Chen Xiwen / Chen Xiwen ; edited by China Development Research
Foundation. — First edition.
      pages cm. — (Routledge studies on the Chinese economy. Chinese
   economists on economic reform ; 3)
   title: Collected works of Chen Xiwen
1. China—Economic conditions—1976–2000.   2. China—Economic
policy—1976–2000.   I. Chen, Xiwen, 1950– Chen Xiwen gai ge lun ji.
English.   II. China Development Research Foundation.   III. Title.
IV. Title: Collected works of Chen Xiwen.
   HC427.92.C35673813 2014
   338.951—dc23
   2013019548

ISBN 13: 978-1-138-59581-1 (pbk)
ISBN 13: 978-0-415-85748-2 (hbk)

Typeset in Times New Roman
by Apex CoVantage, LLC

Contents

Series preface

This series of books is authored by economists who were witnesses to and direct participants in China's 'reform and opening up' over the past three decades. Nearly three generations of Chinese economists are represented, for they include both older and younger economists. Articles that were selected display the characteristics of the period in which they were written. Most exerted a direct impact on China's economic-reform policies, whether they were policy recommendations, theoretical works, or research reports. Most of these works are being published for the first time.

The China Development Research Foundation organized and published this series in Chinese in 2008, to commemorate the thirtieth anniversary of the start of China's 'reform and opening up' and to further promote this historic social transformation. Authors and their descendants responded enthusiastically to the proposal. All the articles were edited and finalized by the authors themselves, except for those of the late Xue Muqiao and Ma Hong, which were edited and finalized by members of their families.

This series has been broadly welcomed in China. I am confident that this English edition will be helpful in giving foreign readers a better understanding of China's economic-reform policies.

I gratefully acknowledge the contribution of the World Bank, Ford Foundation, and Cairncross Foundation, who supported the translation and publication of this series in English. I would like to thank Justin Yifu Lin, Pieter Bottelier, Peter Geithner, David Dollar, and other experts for their valuable support and candid comments. My gratitude also goes to Martha Avery for her excellent translating and editing.

Wang Mengkui
Chairman,
China Development Research Foundation

About the author

Chen Xiwen was born in Shanghai on July 10, 1950; his ancestral home is Danyang, in Jiangsu Province.

In September 1968, Chen was one of the young people 'sent down to the countryside' to work in a 'Production and Construction Corps.' He was sent to rural Heilongjiang Province [in China's far northwest].

In 1978, he was admitted into the Department of Agricultural Economics of the People's University of China, having passed the first exam to be administered in China after the country reinstated the national college entrance examination in 1977. On graduation in 1982, he was assigned to work first in the Institute of Agricultural Economics of the Chinese Academy of Social Sciences and then, in 1985, in the Rural Development Research Center of the State Council. He became deputy director and then director of that center.

In 1990, he became deputy director and then director of the Rural Economy Research Department within the Development Research Center of the State Council. In 1999, he became a member of the Party Group of that Center, while continuing to serve as director of the Rural Economy Research Department. From 1994 to 1998, he was seconded to the Office of the Central Leading Group on Financial and Economic Affairs. Chen Xiwen was appointed vice president of the Development Research Center of the State Council in 2000.

Since 2003, Chen Xiwen has held a variety of positions, including deputy director of the Office of the Central Leading Group on Financial and Economic Affairs, member of the Central Rural Work Leading Group, director of the Office of Central Rural Work, and member of the [Communist] Party-building Directorate of the Central Committee of the Communist Party of China. He was a deputy to the 16th and 17th National People's Congresses, member of the National Committee of the 11th China People's Political Consultative Conference [CPPCC], and deputy director of the Economic Committee of the CPPCC.

Throughout his career, Chen Xiwen has been engaged in researching issues to do with rural economic theory and policy. Since the 1980s, he has participated in drafting most of the key documents in this area for both the Central Committee of the Communist Party of China and for the State Council. His published works have won the prestigious Sun Yefang Economics Award, and in 1992 he was honored with a special stipend from the government for his contributions and expertise.

Chen Xiwen's activities also include the following: member of the Evaluation Committee of the Sun Yefang Economics Foundation, member of the Board of Supervisors of the All China Federation of Supply and Marketing Cooperatives, and part-time professor in several institutions including the Party School of the Central Committee of Communist Party of China, Renmin University of China, China Agricultural University, Zhejiang University, Shanghai Jiao Tong University, Southwestern University of Finance and Economics, and Nanjing Agricultural University.

Author's preface

This year marks the thirtieth anniversary of the start of 'reform and opening up' policies in our country, and it has also been 30 years since we began rural reforms. Many are now looking back over this highly unusual period, reflecting on all that has happened and all we have learned, but most particularly those of us who have been involved in policy and research.

This spring I received a request from Mr. Wang Mengkui to participate in a series that the Development Research Center of the State Council is planning to publish on what happened over the course of these past 30 years. He asked me to select some of my writing that I myself felt should be included in one of the volumes. As president of the State Council's Development Research Center, comrade Wang Mengkui has been my leader and mentor for many years. I am honored that he has invited me and honored to be able to participate in this endeavor.

I have long been engaged in studying rural issues. Forty years ago, I was sent north to Heilongjiang Province as one of the 'intellectual youth' sent to the countryside to work in a 'Production and Construction Corps.' I was there for 10 years, and the experience is what led me to aspire to enter the agricultural economics department of Renmin University, once the college entrance examination system was reinstated.

It was my great good fortune to be a college student at a time when the Party held the epoch-defining Third Plenary Session of the 11th Central Committee [December 1978]. That event was held towards the end of my first year in college. It was prelude to rural reform throughout the country. Since this was my subject, and I was lucky enough to be studying it at a time of momentous change, I spent all my spare time doing surveys in the countryside and getting involved in policy debates. I started on the course that was to become my life's work: rural reform and development policy and research.

I have not been prolific in writing things over these years, so to assemble works that are worthy of inclusion in this thirtieth anniversary volume has not been all that easy. Nonetheless, I personally did experience the extraordinary process of rural reform over these three decades. I feel I have a duty and a responsibility to set forth a record of what happened from my own perspective. The course of rural reform in our country has been an extraordinary and greatly creative process. Led by the Party, hundreds of millions of farmers have sought to improve their own well-being, and much of the process has in fact been the creative work of the people themselves. Those of us involved in theory and policy have mainly tried to understand the hopes and needs of people at the grassroots level, to sum up their own successful practices, and then to make them more widespread.

Guided by a 'socialist system with Chinese characteristics,' what we have done has been to improve upon actual practices, as based on the realities of our country's socioeconomic development, to refine and elevate them so that they can have broader application and greater vitality. Over the past 30 years, people have written plenty of articles trying to advance rural development. They have touched on all aspects of the successes and the failures of reform. They have included works by theoreticians, policy makers, grassroots cadres, and farmers themselves. All my few articles can hope to do is present the subject from my own singular experience.

My hope is that these articles will lead people to reflect on how to take rural reform and development even further, and that they will encourage others to publish their own honest and forthright views on the subject.

The articles in this book are arranged in chronological order according to the time they were either written or actually published. Some were made public, but others have never been released and were used as 'internal materials' or policy recommendations at the time of writing. Included in this compendium, these latter have not been revised in any way, either in terms of their wording or their contents.

Chen Xiwen
June 2008

1   The rise of township-and-village enterprises and changes in national economic patterns*

(1985)

In 1984, the output value of all 'township-and-village enterprises' accounted for 13.3 percent of our country's gross output value, while industrial enterprises at the 'fifth level' of government accounted for 16.1 percent of the value of gross national industrial output. [Township-and-village enterprises, commonly referred to as TVEs in development literature, are simplified to 'township enterprises' in this article.] Last year [1984], the net value of fixed assets of enterprises at the township and village levels was already some 14.11 percent of the total net value of fixed assets owned by State-run industrial enterprises. (The State-owned figure incorporates only those that employ independent accounting and so that can be measured.)

In 1983, nonagricultural labor in townships and villages already incorporated some 62.67 percent of all nonagricultural labor employed in the State-owned sector. In 1984, township enterprises contributed 14.5 percent of the net increase in total State revenues that year, and 19.5 percent of the increase in State tax revenues. Of all energy produced by the country in 1984, 19.7 percent came from the raw coal production of township enterprises.

All of these statistics go to show that township enterprises are already playing a vital role in our economy, one that people should not take lightly. The standing and contribution of this rural economy is one that can no longer be thought of as confined to rural areas – it has national significance.

Township enterprises entered a period of rapid growth in the last few years. In 1984, gross output value increased by 40 percent over the previous year, and in the first quarter of this year it was up another 51 percent over the corresponding period last year. Such dynamic growth has become a focus of attention in the economic community. Naturally we need to evaluate the pros and cons of rapid development but at the same time we should understand the reasons behind it, especially as they relate to our overall model for economic development, including its mechanisms and its rationale. The subject involves judgments about how our national economy should grow from now on, and how we approach changes in its patterns of growth.

Therefore, although we appear merely to be analyzing the growth rate of township enterprises, we should realize that the subject is intimately related to the whole question of our national economy. I would like to share some preliminary thoughts on this subject in this article.

I

Compared to other countries, one important aspect of China's situation is that rural issues cannot be regarded as solely agricultural issues, even when talking in purely economic terms. The reason I bring this point up first is that we have in our rural areas an 'agricultural population' that vastly exceeds the number of 'farmers' needed to do 'farming.'

According to World Bank statistics, our country's population constituted 22.1 percent of the world's total in 1982. However, our urban population accounted for only 11.6 percent of the world's total urban population, while our rural population was 29.2 percent of the world's total rural population. People who are of working age in our rural population (between 15 and 64) represent 32.7 percent of the world's total working-age rural population. One of every three people in rural areas on this globe who is of an age to be working is therefore Chinese.

Our share of the world's natural resources is far less than that figure would seem to indicate, however, with the most notable case being the amount of arable land. Our country has 9 percent, or one-eleventh, of the world's arable land surface. Yet we have one-third of the world's working-age population of rural 'farmers.'

Limited farmland is one of the major problems confronting China's rural development. Clearly, we are going to need a fairly unusual 'path of development' if we hope to change this skewed allocation of material and human resources, and enable our population to become more prosperous.

Comparative analysis with other countries is helpful to understanding the problems facing our own rural development, but it is also useful in allowing us to keep a clear mind as we evaluate our options. The World Bank has gathered statistics from 126 countries, and from its 1982 figures on the economies of these countries, we can draw the following three conclusions.

1   Most countries that have reached a per capita national income of USD 800 have an agricultural labor force that constitutes less than 60 percent of their total labor force. This is with the exception of certain countries with rich resources and small populations.
2   In large countries,[1] when per capita national income exceeds USD 800, the agricultural labor force is less than 50 percent of the total, and the urban population is more than 40 percent. The percentage of people in agriculture is even less in superlarge countries that have reached a per capita income of over USD 800, and the percentage of urban residents is much higher.
3   Compared to superlarge countries[2] that approach ours in terms of population and national income, we have a notably higher percentage of 'agricultural labor' and a notably smaller amount of arable land per person.

One of our country's economic goals is to reach a per capita national income of USD 800 by the end of the century. The only way we are going to achieve that goal is to find a way to lower the percentage of people in our rural workforce, and to raise the percentage of people living in cities. Although each country that reaches a per capita national income of USD 800 may have taken a very different route and may have ended up with radically different conditions, all are similar in terms of the above-noted structure of the labor force and distribution of population. There is no reason to think China will be an exception to this universal experience.

However, if we can indeed decrease the percentage of our rural labor force while raising our urban population at the same time, the difficulties facing our rural development may not be as massive as they appear. We may also not be as unique as we think in terms of our path of economic development.

We adopted the Soviet Union's model of economic development for over 30 years. From Stalin's many comments about the 'scissor-like differential in exchange between industrial and agricultural products,' we can see that the Soviet Union very consciously adopted a certain model for economic development. Starting some 50 to 60 years ago, the Soviet government used agriculture to fund and support the growth of an urban and industrial economy, then in turn used that industrial foundation to help subsidize agriculture. Eventually this was achieved through technical assistance and absorption of agricultural labor into cities. If we disregard the suffering that this imposed on the rural population, we can recognize that this model did have one notable success. Starting in the 1960s, it was able to lower the percentage of agricultural labor in the country, from 42 percent of the total workforce in 1960 to 14 percent in 1982. During that same period, the urban population increased from 49 percent to 63 percent of the total. Clearly, our adoption of the Soviet model of economic development has not led to this same result. We have ended up with quite a different situation, in terms of the structure of our workforce and the distribution of our population. There are many reasons for this that should be analyzed elsewhere, but simple common sense tells us that one primary reason is that the Soviet Union never had to deal with a rural population the size of ours. It was the very size of this rural population that enabled us to mobilize funds for the process of industrialization, using our agricultural labor. To that extent, the Soviet model worked. However, the low efficiency with which our economic system has utilized capital investment in industry has prevented our State-run industrial system from providing sufficient employment for the natural increase in our urban population alone. As a result, we have had to diverge from the Soviet model, even as we followed its general line. In order to assure adequate employment of our urban population, and a rise in income levels that was comparable to what urban residents were seeing around them – a visible increase in State-run industrial development – we adopted measures that basically cut the countryside off from the cities. The new employment created by growth of our State-run industrial system was not used to lower the percentage of our rural workforce, but rather to maintain our existing urban workforce. Not only has that been a cause of the problems facing our countryside, but it has kept down the percentage of urban residents in our total population. At the same time, it has curbed increases in rural labor productivity.

For a long time, in the course of adopting the Soviet Union's economic development model, we overestimated the ability of our urban industrialization to improve rural employment. As a result, we were oblivious to the fact that we had to create another route to employing our rural labor, to transferring people off the land. In persisting with a clear urban-rural divide for over two decades, what we did was to build up a very large pool of surplus labor in the countryside. From this perspective alone, we should recognize that employment in rural areas is a greater problem than the issue of 'agriculture' in rural areas. It is true that the country put material and financial resources into supporting agriculture as it went about urban industrialization. If we are unable to decrease the amount of human labor per unit of tilled land, however, that investment is economically meaningless. Indeed, the materials, technology, and equipment for agriculture that modern industry provides are putting pressure on farmers to leave farming and get involved in other economic activities. Given that our system prevents their breaking through the urban-rural divide, however, for the past two decades all people could do was look for employment *in situ.* Prior to the Third Plenary Session of the 11th Central Committee [1978], finding employment *in situ,* where they were already located, was also impossible, given policy restrictions [on doing business], and given the relatively heavy burden of having to 'hand up' a certain amount of 'contribution' to the State. After the 'Third 11th,' political and economic changes have begun to enable farmers to realize their hopes in this regard. Reform of rural economic systems has been successful, State purchasing prices of 'supplementary farming products' have been greatly increased, and the underlying conditions have now been provided to our rural population for substantive change. The result has been the vibrant growth of township enterprises.

Given the way our system continues to enforce an urban-rural divide, developing township enterprises is without doubt the only way we are going to lower the percentage of our workforce involved in agriculture. By the end of 1984, the number of rural laborers working in township enterprises had reached 52.06 million, or about 14 percent of the total rural labor force. Within this figure, 49.24 million people were nonagricultural workers. This number is greater than the number of people employed in our entire State-run industrial system. In fact, it is 138.6 percent of the number of people who were employed by that system in 1983. Each rural resident 'supports' 1.91 people in our country. Using that figure, our nonagricultural rural labor force is already 'supporting' about 94 million people. The income being earned by this group of people also means that they no longer have to rely on agriculture for a living. Fifty-two million people, the number working in township enterprises, is roughly equal to the natural increase of our urban population between 1952 and 1976. If you add this number of nonfarmers living in the countryside to the number of people who have an official urban residency permit (*hukou*), we now in fact have a nonagricultural population in the country that constitutes some 32 percent of our total population.

The development of township enterprises also brings new hope to the future of our agriculture, since it has enabled an intensification of farming methods and an increase in operational scale. In statistical terms, the amount of land occupied by each member of our agricultural population has gone up by 13.7 percent, and the amount occupied by each agricultural laborer has gone up by 17.9 percent.

Through the development of township enterprises, we have found a way to lower our agricultural workforce that is quite different from the ways used in other countries. People can 'leave farming without leaving their ancestral homes,' and avoid a massive migration into cities. They can carve out their own path toward nonagricultural employment. Obviously, for a country such as ours with its huge rural population and ongoing need to subsidize urban residents, the rise of township enterprises has a far greater significance than indicated by just the phrase 'rural development.' The phenomenon is playing a direct and vital role in facilitating overall reform of our economic structure. It is going to be a major factor enabling us to reach a per capita income of USD 800 by the end of the century.

II

The dynamic development of township enterprises shows that our wealth of labor resources in the countryside is unwilling to be confined to working our 2 billion *mu* of farmland [One *mu* is equal to 0.667 square kilometers, so 2 billion *mu* is roughly 1.334 billion square kilometers]. People have a powerful desire to enter into the overall functioning of our national economic system. Enabling them to realize that desire is going to be a force for changing a number of existing structures in our country, including the pattern of agriculture and industry, the layout of urban and rural areas, the employment situation, and income distribution. Changing the status and role of 800 million rural residents in our national economic system obviously must be well aligned with our efforts to achieve certain economic goals by the end of the century. The development of township enterprises is therefore not merely a matter of 'farmers.' These enterprises have already shown their tremendous potential. Their development should be incorporated into the larger picture of China's economic development, and connected with changes in national economic patterns that have already occurred or will be occurring.

Most township enterprises are engaged in industrial production. In 1984, the gross industrial output value of these enterprises came to RMB 125.4 billion, nationwide. This was equivalent to the total output value of all State-owned industry in our north, northwest, and southwest. That is, it was equivalent to the industrial output of enterprises in 14 provinces, municipalities, and autonomous regions that operate under the system of 'ownership by the people as a whole.' (That total output figure is for 1983 and does not include the output of Sichuan.) In 1984, employees in industrial enterprises at the township and village level of government totaled 32.324 million. This was an astonishing 91 percent of all employees in the industrial sector that was 'owned by the people as a whole' in 1983. Clearly, with such an enormous 'workers brigade made up of farmers,' we are very quickly going to have to find an appropriate way for this economic sector to fit into our overall industrial system.

The experiences and lessons of many developing countries indicate that a number of other economic goals should accompany the transformation from an agricultural to

an industrial country, and the overall industrial development strategy should accommodate various other needs. Those include raising productive capacity, providing
for more employment, and forming a more rational distribution system in terms of
people's income. Not focusing on these things will make it hard to avoid the trap
of a 'dual economic structure.' Without setting up a series of large-scale modernized industrial enterprises, 'backward' countries will not be able to form their own
relatively independent industrial system. However, setting up large-scale industrial
enterprises frequently means that a country, while using its own basic infrastructure
and its own domestic talent, must also import advanced technology and equipment.
As a result, it is hard for such large-scale enterprises to develop anywhere except for
in cities or industrial areas. Moreover, the employment offered by these enterprises is
not in proportion to the huge amount of capital investment required. Therefore, while
such enterprises may become an important source of funds for industrialization, and
may guide the direction of technology in the nation as a whole, their strong suit is not
in providing employment. Nor does this strategy help balance income distribution
between urban and rural areas and among regions. Developing such large-scale modernized enterprises should not be equated to the larger process of 'industrialization.'

In this sense, 'backward' countries should aim to establish industrial systems
that allow for the coexistence of enterprises with different levels of technology
and different sizes of operations. Development strategies should assure that sufficient job opportunities are created as industry develops. They should make sure
that income distribution is relatively balanced between urban and rural areas and
among different regions.

Our country's township enterprises have already made a huge contribution to our
industrial system on the lower end of the spectrum in terms of technology and size.
There now needs to be a rational division of labor between what these enterprises
are producing and what urban State-run industrial enterprises are producing, so as
to avoid excessive direct competition in low-end products. Without such a division, 'big enterprises' and township enterprises will increasingly compete for raw
materials, energy, and markets, which not only will impact the potential for further
development of township enterprises, and their attendant employment possibilities,
but will continue to drag our urban State-run enterprises in the direction of producing low-end goods. That will make it harder to elevate our industry to the next level.
It obviously will lower the efficiency with which we use the basic infrastructure
of our cities, it will bring about irrational use of our best managerial talent and our
best technology, and it will thereby lower the caliber of our industry as a whole.

To bring about the necessary division of labor between these two kinds of
industrial systems, we must first bring the 'two skins' of these systems into contact with one another, integrate them into a complete industrial system within the
country through technology and through economic ties. Second, we should make
a rough evaluation of international and domestic market demand in order to determine processing capacity at different levels of technology, and which aspects of
our economy can best meet the different kinds of market demand. Then we must
differentiate among the different stages of product processing so that every link
on the processing chain can be equipped with the appropriate levels of technology.

The process of our country's 'industrialization' and the process of unifying its urban-rural divide can thereby be combined, as the two kinds of industrial systems play their different roles. Different sizes of operations and levels at which they are administered can be mutually complementary, so that we can maximize the efficiencies of each level of technology.

In summary, we should not underestimate the role of township enterprises, even if they stay at a low level of technology and operate on a small scale for a long time. Not only do township enterprises contribute enormously to increases in our national income, for which they should not be taken lightly, but, even more important, they provide employment opportunities that have the effect of leveling out income disparities between urban and rural areas and among different regions. This is an advantage that State-run 'big industrial enterprises' find hard to match. If growth of township enterprises is blocked, a very considerable rural population will have no alternative but to depend on agriculture for jobs and income. This will undoubtedly lead to constant increases in the cost of agricultural products. If we don't want to allow the gap in incomes to widen even further as that happens, we must either lower the actual incomes of urban residents or raise government subsidies to agriculture. That not only will put the same old burden back on our government but will present an enormous obstacle to systemic reform and change in our economic patterns. Our only solution is to allow township enterprises room to develop. That means that our State-run large-scale industrial system must put more effort into improving its technology and upgrading its products, so as to guarantee overall improvement of the industrial sector [while township enterprises take over the lower end of the spectrum].

III

In our former strictly controlled planned-economy system, township enterprises basically survived on the fringes of the system, outside the scope of plans. They grew within the 'cracks' of contradictions in the planning process. Once the idea of a 'commodity economy with a plan' was introduced [Translator's note: this is generally referred to as a 'planned commodity economy,' the term 'commodity' indicating a product produced for a market as opposed to being produced for planned distribution], it was hard to avoid a certain 'blind' and chaotic growth of township enterprises. Regulations were not yet in place and a rural population that had been living under a semi-self-sufficient economy was in any event unfamiliar with how to conduct legitimate economic activity. Solving these problems is a prerequisite to incorporating township enterprises into the overall system of our national economy. It is also going to be necessary for the ongoing health and stability of the enterprises themselves. The macroeconomic context in which we find ourselves is ideal for forcing township enterprises to undertake the necessary 'rectification' or restructuring. That context requires that we limit basic infrastructure investment and 'blind' expansion of consumption funds.

'Rectification' of township enterprises covers both micro operations and macro management.

At the micro level, township enterprises will have to pay closer attention to such problems as poor quality of products, goods for which there is no demand, and chaotic financial management. According to the statistics of competent authorities, the funds required to produce finished goods of township enterprises in Jiangsu, Shandong, Henan, Shanxi, and Hunan provinces account for about 42 percent of total fixed assets, while accounts receivables make up about 36 percent of all working capital. Although these percentages are high, they might be attributable to the combined effects of various factors, and slack sales and disorderly financial management are undoubtedly among these. According to the estimate of competent departments, two-thirds of total loans to enterprises at the township and village levels go into 'funds for producing finished goods' and 'all kinds of receivables.' As we are currently placing strict controls on bank loans, if enterprises do not improve the quality of their goods, organize their production according to market needs, lower their 'cost of finished goods,' and at the same time vigorously clean up their receivables, the working capital required for their operations will grow ever scarcer. For the normal operations of any township enterprise, this has to be an extremely serious problem.

At the macro level, we should focus on improving the [State's] 'management system' governing township enterprises so that it stimulates enterprises to comply with laws and regulations while promoting their development. It recently came to light that a few township enterprises had been producing and selling inferior counterfeit products, at the instigation of undesirable elements. Naturally we must strike back at the phenomenon of such people and such behavior, but we should also realize that their emergence is not an intrinsic part of the fact of the enterprises themselves but rather reveals the chaotic nature of how they are managed. Improving those systems includes striking back at undesirable elements but more important training entrepreneurs in townships and villages to respect ethical socialist behavior, and making sure that the growth of their business does not diverge from the track of our socialist economy.

Booming township enterprises have become one of the major sources of local revenue. Given this, we should be aware of two tendencies that are developing in the departments that govern the management of these enterprises in many places. First, such departments are 'blindly' approving the funding for new development 'projects' with no regard for the actual capacities of the enterprises or conditions of the locality. According to a survey of nine provinces and municipalities in the first half of this year, 7,196 township enterprise projects which were launched last year and are continuing on into this year, and another 9,917 new projects starting this year, are requiring loans and funding of RMB 2.83 billion for such things as working capital and equipment. This comes to approximately 57.8 percent of the total investment of these projects. The amount is 3.7 times the capacity of the nine provinces and cities to extend agricultural bank loans and credit cooperative support to new projects. The consequences of this kind of 'blind support' are that funds needed for investment are dispersed, the inability to fund worthwhile projects increases, and the number of unfinished projects and enterprises grows, imperiling the credit institutions making the loans. This also puts unexpected investment risk onto farmers. Second, many local governments, particularly at township or county levels, regard township enterprises as being their own captive companies or a kind of private bank, and they reach out their hands for money. Statistics indicate that, in 1984, 43.86 percent of the distributable net profits of enterprises at township and village levels went to those local authorities with direct supervision over the enterprises. This was 137.6 percent of the net profits meant to grow production, or 94.1 percent of the total loans made to township enterprises supposedly for equipment. Such exploitation has weakened the capacity of enterprises to accumulate capital. It has increased pressure on them to have to ask for further loans. Moreover, it increases the complexities of an already intricate system of vested interests, which in turn increases the difficulties of further reform of rural management systems and institutions.

Rectification at the two different levels in township enterprises, namely operational and management, should lead to having better enterprises with better prospects. It should lead to a decline in production of unnecessary goods and a decline in poor management and poor results. It is safe to say that without this necessary contraction of their operations and a more clearly defined orientation, rectification of township enterprises will not achieve much in the way of actual results. Therefore, 'contraction' and future growth should be seen as part of the same process in the course of rectification. At present, the future growth of township enterprises relates not just to a shortage of funds, but also to a lack of necessary materials even when existing funds are used effectively. According to a survey undertaken in Huangpo County in Hubei Province, the amount of electricity, coal, and steel allocated to township enterprises in 1984 could only satisfy a small portion of enterprises' needs, specifically 47.8 percent of electricity needs, 26 percent of coal needs, and 12.3 percent of steel needs. Basically the same situation exists in other places. The undersupply of materials is leading to increases in prices and production costs, decreases in profits, and a drop in employee incomes. Factories are running at less than capacity and workers sit idle. We must therefore address each situation according to its specifics, rectify enterprises with poor performance, and continue to support promising enterprises through various economic levers, particularly financial tools.

Another thing that has to be addressed in the immediate future of township enterprises is the shortage of funding. In 1985, only 2.8 percent of newly increased credit in the country was for township enterprises, naturally inadequate for entities whose output value is already accounting for 13.3 percent of the country's gross output value. It should also be recognized, however, that township enterprises have their own sources of internal funding on which they can draw. Our first task is to make rational use of the profits of enterprises, in terms of their distribution and reinvestment. In 1984, only 32 percent of the net profits of enterprises at township and village levels was used to expand production. The remainder was 'requisitioned by higher authorities or distributed out among people in the enterprise itself.' Obviously, there remains considerable potential to translate profits into reinvestment in production, if we have the necessary strict financial systems and bank supervision. Second, we should improve the system for depreciating fixed assets of township enterprises, and then use those funds in a rational way. If all enterprises were to draw a unified rate of 8 percent of depreciation funds, depreciation costs per year would account for about 60 percent of the total equipment loans for township enterprises, as based on a calculation of the net fixed assets held by the two levels of enterprises in the year 1984. This would be a very respectable source of funding for technical renovations, rebuilding, and expansions. Third, we should clean up the situation regarding accounts receivable, and reduce overstocked inventories of finished goods. If just one-third of the receivables could be 'cleaned up,' these three items alone would contribute three to four times what the State plan has allocated in loans to township enterprises in 1985. Fourth, we are going to have to control the speed at which wages in township enterprises are being increased, to within reasonable levels. Statistics indicate that the per capita annual wage earnings in township and village enterprises was RMB 621 in 1984, 14 percent higher than that of the previous year and already some 72 percent of the per capita annual wages of employees working in enterprises 'owned by the people as a whole' in the year 1983. The wage level was 101 percent of per capita annual wages of employees in urban service industries that are under collective ownership. Overall, total wages of township enterprises increased 25 percent in 1985 over the previous year, bringing the expected level of wages to some RMB 700 per year. Taking just 10 percent out of that wage level and applying it to reinvestment in the business will not impact the lives of employees in a major way, but it will increase funding to township enterprises by some 2 to 3 billion RMB. Looking at the overall situation of economic structural reform in the country as a whole, limiting increases in basic wages of township enterprises, to an appropriate degree, will be beneficial in moderating expectations about how much reform is going to benefit urban workers in the near term. It will help in reducing the level of conflict as we undertake urban reforms.

In our current macro-climate of strictly controlling the availability of State credit, township enterprises are going to have to rely on their own internal sources of funding for growth. This only addresses one side of the issue, however. How township enterprises capitalize on their own unique nature in making use of funds and in raising funds is an aspect to which we have not given adequate attention. In 1984, primary and secondary industries accounted for 96.9 percent of the gross output value of township enterprises, which means that agriculture, the 'primary industry,' is not a part of how township enterprises utilize and mobilize funds. Trying to have commingled funding for township enterprises and for agriculture, managed through a financial institution, may well negatively impact the growth of township enterprises. Even though agricultural banks are already handling loans to township enterprises in separate fashion, their primary role is to restrict credit and not to take the unique capital needs of these enterprises into full account. It is hard for agricultural banks to service the capital needs of township enterprises as they try to meet social needs for secondary and tertiary industry products. Owing to the internal production structure of township enterprises, their capital requirements are more similar to those of industry and commerce than they are to agriculture. Given that these enterprises are already quite large in size, we might want to consider separating out their financing needs, taking them away from the agricultural banks and gradually establishing banking systems that address their specific needs, either professional township-enterprise banks, or small-scale enterprise banks. At the very least, we should allow those departments in charge of extending loans to township enterprises a considerable degree of independence. We should also make sure that there is sufficient information flow between the institutions that fund township enterprises and the 'specialty banks' handling loans for working capital and infrastructure development in industry and commerce. Otherwise, we will not be able to break through the fact that the urban-rural divide restricts funding of commerce and industry in the countryside. We will not be able to make the orientation of investment shift away from the old situation. We will therefore not enable township enterprises to become truly incorporated into the national economic system.

As township enterprises develop, people are beginning to recognize the distinctions among the three concepts of 'rural areas,' 'agriculture,' and 'farmers.' They are beginning to understand the relationships among these three things as well. China's unique path of development is quickly distinguishing the concept of 'rural areas' from agriculture, and making 'agriculture' only one of the industries coming out of rural areas. A corollary to this is that China's farmers are having the opportunity to choose employment in rural areas that is not agricultural. It is quite apparent that the traditional concept of 'farmer' no longer applies to China's entire rural population. This change has been one of the consequences of the development of township enterprises, and has created a new economic pattern in rural areas. It has begun to change traditional patterns of income distribution, and as a result, is changing the traditional urban-rural divide in our country. It is not hard to imagine that ongoing development of township enterprises will be the stimulus for wholesale change in our national economy. That development will enable our economy to move all the more smoothly in the direction of the goals our nation wants to achieve by the end of this century.

Notes

* This article was published in the tenth issue of *Economic Research Journal* in 1985.
1 The term 'large countries' usually refers to countries whose populations are over 20 million.
2 This refers to Indonesia and India.

2 The key to economic development in rural areas is the correct treatment of farmers*

(1990)

Over the past decade, our country has made amazing and widely acclaimed progress in its rural economy. The situation began to get more complicated after 1985, however. That year saw a fairly large decline in grain production, and fluctuations in grain production then continued for the next few years, to the extent that people began to wonder about the present and future prospects of the rural economy. Exactly what are the lessons we should learn from these past 10 years of reform? What has brought on the recent problems and how can we address them and pull out of the situation as quickly as possible? How can we secure the development prospects for the countryside as we move into the future?

For the past five or six years, many cadres have been working on these very serious questions, including people in the theoretical arena and people actually working on the ground in rural economic departments. Their explanations and proposals, however, differ widely. This indicates that there are relatively substantial differences in methods and perspectives when people analyze issues. It also suggests that divergent opinions can be reconciled only when we address the root cause of problems rather than their superficial manifestations, that is, when we put the problems in a broader context.

I. Challenges facing the rural economy in recent years

The minute one starts talking about the rural economy, an image of extreme and bewildering complexity arises in people's minds. This is not only because that economy is indeed complex and multilayered, with intricate structural issues, but more important, because there are varying perceptions of it in our current economic system. Roles can be quite different, leading to radically different opinions on the subject.

The aspect of most concern to government departments is that annual increases in production of staple crops have come to a halt. Among others, those crops include grain, cotton, and oilseed crops. Since the highest historical production, grain production has declined by 8.5 percent, cotton by 37.7 percent, and oilseed crops by 20.4 percent. Given the pressure of ongoing increases in our population, it goes without saying that this presents the government with tremendous challenges as it tries to provide for the nation's people.

The government's concern is not shared by ordinary urban consumers, however. Consumption of the main food items continues to rise, with the exception of fish and shrimp. In comparing 1988 figures against those of 1985, fish and shrimp consumption declined by 0.02 kg per capita, but nine other main food categories saw increases to varying levels. Those included grain, cooking oil, vegetables, meat, poultry, eggs, sugar, cigarettes, and alcohol. At the same time, the Engel's coefficient in urban areas has gone down from 0.5225 in 1985 to 0.5136 in 1988. Expenditures on grain as a percentage of urban residents' annual living expense have gone down by 2.1 percentage points, from 8.95 percent to 6.85 percent. Clearly, even if we take inflation into account, the standard of living in cities seems not to be adversely affected by the weakened performance of basic farm products.

The sentiments of farmers are more mixed. First of all, in tandem with the poor production figures in farm products has come high enthusiasm for production of other kinds of products and an attendant increase in household income. 'Production-related' earnings contributed to 90.7 percent of farmers' per capita net earnings in 1988, compared with 88 percent in 1985, and the extra 2.7 percentage points were mainly accounted for by the rising net income derived from what are called 'household-based operations.' During the same period, the net income of rural households increased as a percentage of per capita income nationwide by 2.1 percent. There obviously has been no dampening of the enthusiasm to generate income by carrying on household operations. Second, we have to notice that there is a large discrepancy between the areas in which farmers are enthusiastic and areas on which the government is placing its hopes. This can be demonstrated by different growth rates of the per capita net income derived from different activities of a rural household. Again comparing data from 1985 and 1988, net income derived from agricultural activities (farming) increased by 16.0 percent (in current prices, same below), that from industrial production increased by 267.8 percent, from construction by 66.0 percent, from transport and other labor services by 55.6 percent, and 88.4 percent, respectively, and from wholesale/retailing, catering, and other service sectors by 86.0 percent. Over the three years between 1985 and 1988, agriculture contributed only 23.5 percent to the growth in a given household's per capita net income. During this same period, the government's price index for procuring grain went up by 36 percent, and the index for other cash crops went up by 19.1 percent. Clearly, agriculture was not a motivating factor behind the increase in farmers' incomes over these recent years. It is not hard to understand why there has been no great response on the part of farmers to the government's call to 'strengthen agriculture' and increase production of grain, cotton, and oilseed crops. Looked at overall, the main route to wealth these days for a farmer is not through farming. This phenomenon in rural economic development in recent years has long since come to people's attention.

This situation naturally is the result of highly complex social, economic, and historical factors, some of which I will attempt to analyze in what follows. One irreversible fact is that the situation is closely connected to the ongoing trend of less than bountiful harvests of grain, cotton, and oilseed crops. The phenomenon is absolutely not the result of desires on the part of government departments handling agriculture, or of farmers themselves, nor is it something that farmers themselves can change on their own. The appearance and the ongoing existence of this phenomenon is in fact causing severe problems for the greater portion of our country's farmers, as well as for all levels of government dealing with agricultural management.

Obviously, one cannot sum up the economic profile of our rural economy these days by saying it is either 'good' or 'bad.' On the positive side, urban residents are eating better in spite of a declining Engel's coefficient, and farmers' actual income continues to increase. Farmers are in fact getting richer. On the other hand, for several years now, because the government's annual increases in production plans for grain, cotton, and oilseed crops have not been met, we are having to import more, our stockpiles of grain are declining, and financial subsidies are rising dramatically since procurement prices are higher than those at which the government sells the products. Despite this, farmers themselves continue to feel that it is uneconomical for them to produce grain, cotton, and oilseed crops, and so their production keeps declining every year. It is hard to say, however, that this leads to a sense of insecurity about the entire rural economy on the part of farmers. The ones truly uneasy about the rural economy, given the overall picture of our current economic system, are government policy makers. Farmers themselves can always plant other things if income from grain, cotton, and oilseed crops is not so good. And if farming income is bad altogether, they can take up nonagricultural production. As we say, if the light isn't coming up in the east, it's lighter in the west. Farmers will always find a way to increase incomes and get by. As for urban consumers, the prices of basic farm products are set by the government and have little to do with agriculture. Urban residents are therefore unconcerned about good or bad harvests since it has little to do with them. Moreover, it has long been taken for granted that the government will not allow significant changes in the quantity and prices of basic farm products on the market. The government assumes almost all responsibility for the three main products, from production and supply to distribution. Farmers, urban residents, and distributors are far less concerned than the government about any of these things, and one of the key reasons is that people have now progressed beyond living at a subsistence level while at the same time there has been no fundamental change in the procurement system and pricing system for basic agricultural commodities. The result is that fewer and fewer people have any need to worry about the production of grain, cotton, and oilseed crops. Beyond the shadow of a doubt, our existing system will therefore not enable us to move away from the disconnect we face between 'production' and 'supply and demand.'

Economic restructuring is a process that takes time. In addition, it requires the adoption of correct transitional measures and a careful selection of the right 'entry point' [for a given policy]. One question should therefore be clarified at the outset: What exactly are the main challenges facing the rural economy? I will briefly review the thinking of others on this issue before presenting my own inclinations.

Correct understanding. The first prevalent theory is that we lack correct understanding of the issues. Cadres who hold this view feel that the lackluster performance of agriculture in recent years can be attributed to insufficient regard for the importance of agriculture among government officials and policy makers. They feel that in the face of the historic bumper harvest of 1984, certain officials and policy makers began to have a kind of blind optimism about what could be done by farmers. They reduced investment in agriculture and began to implement inappropriate procurement and pricing policies. This led to a dramatic decline in production of primary crops and years of unimpressive yields. This view holds that the ideal response is to raise awareness and proper understanding among senior government officials, and to increase investment in agriculture.

Benefits. The second prevalent theory is that our agricultural problems relate to comparative interests and benefits. People holding this view believe that the reason crop production is modest is that there is an imbalance in the 'interest relationships' or benefits of producing grain, cotton, and oilseed crops. Lower income has punctured the enthusiasm of farmers for growing crops, and has made rural communities shift their resources into production of other things instead. Rural communities are therefore increasingly distancing their economic activities altogether from farming, crops, and agriculture. This view holds that when the national policy changed in favor of holding rural households accountable for producing a certain amount of farm goods, and allowed them to keep and sell what was left over, those households essentially became independent commodity producers. As 'operating units,' they naturally now follow the laws of the market and of prices in making decisions about how to allocate resources. The fact is that prices of grain, cotton, and oilseed crops (as set by the government in procurement contracts) have been declining in recent years. Returns on resources put into producing grain are very clearly less than returns on the same resources put into other production. Therefore, this view holds, given that the terms of trade for these things are out of balance, it is unavoidable that production of grain and so on will fail to arouse farmers' interest. By the logic of this analysis, the only way to extricate ourselves from the situation is either to raise procurement prices to a great extent so that the government's contractual prices approach market prices, thereby giving farmers a greater comparative advantage in growing primary products; or to reduce contracted government procurement as much as possible, and allow more of farmers' surplus production to enter the free market. In the market, through higher prices and greater quantities, they can supplement the lower-priced amounts that they will still be obliged to sell to the government. Essentially, the two policy recommendations of people holding this view are that we should increase government procurement prices and also allow more production to be traded freely on the market. At the same time, as a supplementary measure, this view points out that we must concurrently change the distribution system. Otherwise, since government subsidies will suddenly increase in line with the increased prices provided to farmers, this reform will be accompanied by 'loss of assets' or 'flowing out of assets' [embezzlement of government funds by middlemen].

The two lines of thought as presented above encapsulate the main viewpoints that have been put forth by our theoretical community and by departments working in the field of agriculture over the past few years. Naturally, there have been many other opinions as well. I summarize the more influential of these below.

1. Ownership: This theory attributes the problems to issues of property rights

This view holds that after the policy changed to one whereby *households* contracted for production [as opposed to communes contracting for production to the State as the main accounting unit], questions relating to property rights, especially land rights, became more obscure rather than any clearer. Lines demarcating land rights are anything but clear, so long-term behavior on the part of farmers with regard to contracted land has not been conducive to good farming. This view therefore has a lot to say about land ownership. Policy recommendations include, first, that land be nationalized, or owned by the State, and second, that land be privatized, or owned by individuals, in part or in full.

2. Services: This theory attributes the problems to the poor services delivered by relevant government departments and the rural community itself

It holds that an improved farming service system is imperative. Policy proposals under this category vary greatly, however. Some advocate a stronger collective sector in rural areas and the combination of individual farming with collective unified operations (known as a dual-layer management system). Others criticize this. They say that relying on the old collective economy structures and taking up this kind of dual-layer management is equivalent to never having escaped the set rules of the people's commune system. That system constrained the autonomy of farmers. These people therefore advocate getting rid of the currently existing 'collective economy organizations,' of a 'community nature,' and instead cultivating 'rural cooperatives' as understood in the classic definition, built on the foundation of rural household economies [or businesses].

3. The 'nature of the economic eystem' issue: This theory holds that the main issue facing agriculture today is that it is done on too small a scale

This weakens the ability of the government to have any control over results. People who hold this view feel that an overly dispersed system of tiny household plots not only prevents technological advances but allows people to seek maximum profit at the expense of the greater good. Since rights to 'operate' or cultivate land have become so fragmented, the government and also rural collective organizations have lost the ability and the means to influence behavior on the part of farmers. They 'look only to the money.' In recent years, this tendency has led to extreme imbalances in agricultural production and to no further increases in yields on grain, cotton, and oilseed crops. Therefore, this view holds, the essence of the problem is in what 'nature' of economic system is best for agricultural production. The issue is one of principle in the sense of the correct 'path' that farmers should be encouraged to follow. From this lofty starting point, this point of view feels that the economic power of collective organizations should be strengthened. Means should be put in place to enable greater control, and the system whereby land is divided up among households for management should be changed right away. Major issues involving land use and use of investment funds should be made by the collective organizations. This will enable more effective government control and allow the government to realize the goal of raising yields again.

It is impossible to elaborate on the full spectrum of opinions on this issue. I will focus my analysis on the 'correct understanding' and 'comparative benefits' propositions, although when I describe my own views, I will at the same time mention my thoughts on the other three points mentioned above.

I think the 'correct understanding' and 'benefits' theories are both well grounded, although they do not go far enough in exploring the issues. The root of the problem is that only farmers can produce grain, cotton, and oilseed crops. If you get too far away from the essential element of 'farmers' themselves, you will never resolve the critical issues facing agriculture. My inclination, therefore, is to adhere more to the 'benefits' theory of how to tackle the problem. If nothing else, one self-evident truth should come from our four decades' worth of experience in handling the relationship between government and farmers. How well or poorly that relationship is handled provides a forecast of how well or poorly the rural economy is going to perform, and even how the national economy as a whole is going to perform. At the same time, abstracting out only one element of the issue and thinking the whole problem relates to procurement prices of agricultural goods is a gross oversimplification. It is an overly narrow interpretation of the highly complex issues currently confronting us. For convenience of the analysis and the presentation here, I am going to redefine the two issues of 'proper understanding' and 'benefits' as issues that relate to 'investment' and 'pricing.' This may not cover all aspects, but the two categories do incorporate the core substance of the two points of view.

II. On rural investment

It has long been commonly recognized by people who are involved in agricultural issues that a decrease in investment is one of the major reasons behind the current problems. Those problems include a decline in production to the point that the potential for future growth is being affected. Whether or not this means that the government is unconcerned with agriculture and therefore lowering its investment, or that the government has an inadequate understanding of agricultural issues, is questionable. In my mind, the logic is not at all that simple.

1. It is true that the government has lowered its investment in agriculture

Compared to the last three years of the fifth Five-Year Plan period, the government's investment in agriculture has definitely declined. This holds, whether investment is measured in absolute terms, or as a percentage of investment in 'basic construction' in all sectors of the economy (see Table 2.1). If the data in

Table 2.1 Central government investment in agriculture, and that investment as a percentage of all basic infrastructure investment in all sectors

Year	Agricultural investment (RMB100 million)	Percentage (%)
1978	53.34	10.6
1979	57.92	11.1
1980	52.03	9.3
1981	29.31	6.6
1982	34.12	6.1
1983	35.45	6.0
1984	37.12	5.0
1985	35.91	3.3
1986	35.06	3.0
1987	42.11	3.1
1988	46.17	3.0

Table 2.1 are depicted in graphic form, it is even easier to see the results of declining government investment not just on agriculture but on the sustainable, coordinated, and stable development of the entire economy. The severity of the problem lies not only in the fact that current investment in agriculture (not yet inflation-adjusted) is significantly lower than that of a decade ago. Even worse, the sharp decline in agricultural investment as a percentage of total government investment will be exacerbating existing structural problems in our national economy. This trend will be adding momentum to a growing wave. Changing such a situation is not going to be an easy matter. Taking 1988 investment in all sectors as a base figure, if we want to raise agriculture's share of that total investment by one percentage point, we have to increase the invested amount in agriculture by around one-third. If we want to raise the share of agriculture to 9 percent, not even thinking about our ambitious goal of doubling that amount to18 percent, we would have to invest an additional RMB 10 billion, two times our existing investment. Over the near term, this is one of the things that falls into the category of, 'it's not that we don't want to do such a thing, we simply can't.'

2. Overall investment in rural areas has consistently maintained steady growth

In marked contrast to the decline in Central government investment in agriculture, overall 'social' investment in fixed assets in rural areas has maintained a steady rise, whether in absolute terms or as a percentage of the total. (See Table 2.2.)

Given this phenomenon, and the undeniable fact that decreasing investment in agriculture is creating an unfavorable situation in the output of grains, cotton, and oilseed crops, we have to recognize that the problem is not one of inadequate capital overall but rather that the structure of the investment is increasingly unfavorable to agriculture. A glance at Table 2.2 will show the remarkable consistency of investment in rural areas, whether in terms of the absolute figures or the percentage of the

Table 2.2 Social investment [funds that are not allocated by the Central government] in fixed assets in rural areas and the percentage of rural social investment to total social investment[1]

Year	1981	1982	1983	1984	1985	1986	1987	1988
Social investment in rural areas (RMB 100 million)	250.01	329.92	415.70	553.94	677.66	820.17	1,061.06	1,321.97
As a percentage of the nation's total (%)	26.0	26.8	29.0	30.2	26.6	27.1	29.1	29.4

[1]National Bureau of Statistics, *Progress in Four Decades,* China Statistics Publishing House, 1989, p. 353.

total. The question we have to address is why, when overall investment is showing such strong and consistent increases, agricultural investment is showing such absolute and relative declines. This question has to be analyzed from two different angles: the degree to which the Central government is *able* to make allocations to agriculture, and the *returns* to farmers for differing kinds of investment.

3. A changing economic process is making fewer funds available to the Central government for its investing in society

One of the most notable economic phenomena to result from the restructuring of our economic system has been the decline in funds available to the Central government. Both local governments and local enterprises have received greatly expanded 'autonomy' or decision-making authority over their economic activities, including the ability to retain a greater amount of their earnings and the ability to decide on how to invest those earnings. The degree of control over investment decisions formerly made by the Central government has declined markedly in the process. This profoundly affects the investment system by which our agriculture is still being funded. Using data displayed in Tables 2.3 and 2.4, in what follows we analyze the current standing and the changes of the Central government's 'public finance' expenditures on agriculture and overall social investment into fixed assets.

From Table 2.3, we can see first that State appropriations for 'basic infrastructure' show a rapidly declining trend overall. Over nine years, they have fallen 17.2 percentage points in terms of total appropriations, or roughly 2 percentage points per year. Clearly, this trend has to have a major impact on the Central government's investment in agriculture. Second, the percentage of total appropriations being dedicated to agriculture is indeed declining, dictating a decrease in the absolute amount being invested in agriculture by the Central government. Third, the degree to which agricultural investments are declining as a percentage of the State's total expenditures on basic infrastructure [capital construction] is clearly lower than the degree to which basic infrastructure investments as a percent of all fiscal expenditures are declining.

Table 2.3 Investments in agriculture as a percentage of total Central government public-finance expenditures.[1] (Unit: RMB100 million, %)

Year	Total government expenditure	Government appropriation for capital construction		Capital construction investment in agriculture		Government appropriations for farm production and other undertakings in this sector	
		Amount	Proportion in the total expenditure	Amount	Proportion in government's capital construction appropriation	Amount	Proportion in the total government expenditure
1979	1,273.9	541.69	40.40	57.92	11.25	90.11	7.07
1980	1,212.7	419.39	34.58	52.03	12.41	82.12	6.77
1981	1,115.0	330.63	29.65	29.21	8.83	73.68	6.61
1982	1,153.3	309.15	26.81	34.12	11.04	79.88	6.93
1983	1,292.5	382.81	29.62	35.45	9.26	86.66	6.70
1984	1,546.4	488.93	31.62	37.12	7.59	95.93	6.20
1985	1,844.8	583.80	31.65	35.91	6.15	101.04	5.48
1986	2,330.8	671.82	28.82	35.06	5.22	124.30	5.33
1987	2,448.5	628.15	25.62	42.11	6.70	134.16	5.48
1988	2,668.3	619.49	23.22	46.17	7.45	155.10	5.81

[1]National Bureau of Statistics, *Progress in Four Decades,* China Statistics Publishing House, 1989, p. 423, 425, 355, 426.

A comparison between Tables 2.1 and 2.3 reveals two quite different pictures. According to Table 2.1, agricultural investment kept declining as a proportion of capital construction investment in all the sectors after 1984 and later stabilized at a low level. If we present, in graph form, the percentage data under the column 'capital construction investment in agriculture' in Table 2.3, a U-shape curve would be seen from 1984 to 1988 with the data in the two years very close to each other. Therefore, a decreasing government investment in agriculture, though contributing to the sector's smaller share of the aggregate capital construction investment in all the sectors, is by no means a fundamental cause. This is proven by the fact that the proportion of agriculture in the government's capital construction appropriations is markedly higher than that in the aggregate capital construction investment in all the sectors.

Therefore, even though the standing of agriculture has indeed been declining in terms of State 'public-finance expenditures,' that is not the main cause of decreased investment in agriculture. In the context of a steep increase in overall 'social investment' into fixed assets, the share that Central-government 'public-finance appropriations' holds in overall investment is declining swiftly. Investment in the 'basic infrastructure' of agriculture can fundamentally come only from public-finance allocations, which means that a similarly swift decline in agricultural investment is the natural consequence. That is, the decline in investment in agriculture is the natural consequence of the system we continue to employ for all investments into agriculture.

The situation reflected in Table 2.4 would seem to indicate that there has been quite a rapid rise in both 'social investment' and 'social financial strength' in recent

Table 2.4 Combined 'inside-the-budget' and 'outside-the-budget' revenues and total social investment.[1] (Unit: RMB100 million, %)

Year	State budgetary revenue	Extra budgetary revenue		Total social investment in fixed assets	Sources of fixed asset investment and their proportions									
		Revenue	Ratio to budgetary revenue		State budgetary		Domestic loan		Foreign investors		Privately owned funds and other sources		Social investment in rural areas	Private investment out of the total investment in rural areas
					Amount	%	Amount	%	Amount	%	Amount	%	Amount	Amount	%
1979	1,067.96	452.85	42.4												
1980	1,042.22	557.40	53.5												
1981	1,016.38	601.07	59.1	960.01	269.76	28.1	122.00	12.7	36.36	3.8	532.89	55.4	250.01	166.34	66.5
1982	1,083.94	802.74	74.1	1,230.40	279.26	22.7	176.12	14.3	60.51	4.9	714.51	58.1	329.92	198.53	60.2
1983	1,211.16	967.68	79.9	1,430.06	339.71	23.8	175.50	12.3	66.55	4.6	848.30	59.3	415.70	305.05	73.4
1984	1,467.05	1,188.48	81.0	1,832.87	421.00	23.0	258.47	14.1	70.66	3.8	1,082.4	59.1	553.94	379.11	68.4
1985	1,837.16	1,530.03	83.3	2,543.19	407.80	16.0	510.27	20.1	91.48	3.6	1,533.64	60.3	677.66	478.43	70.6
1986	2,184.52	1,737.32	79.5	3,019.62	440.63	14.6	638.31	21.1	132.16	4.4	1,808.51	59.9	820.17	574.82	70.1
1987	2,262.42	2,028.80	89.7	3,640.86	475.54	13.1	835.94	23.0	175.37	4.8	2,154.01	59.1	1,061.06	695.35	65.5
1988	2,457.82	2,270.0	92.4	4,496.55	402.68	9.1	914.54	20.6	254.51	5.7	2,874.81	64.7	1,321.97	865.23	65.5

[1] National Bureau of Statistics, *Progress in Four Decades*, China Statistics Publishing House, 1989, p. 427, 352.

years. A closer look, however, points to serious problems. First, what is called 'outside-the-budget' income is rising extremely rapidly for non-Central [local] levels of government, enterprise 'units,' and the departments that have direct authority over them. Over the nine years, this kind of non-Central-government income has risen by 19.6 percent, which is almost 10 percentage points more than the amount by which 'inside-the-budget' Central income has risen. 'Outside-the-budget' income is by now increasing at a rate that is essentially equal to the increase of 'inside-the-budget' State income. The total increase over these nine years of both kinds of income has been 13.4 percent, but State income, 'inside-the-budget,' has grown at 9.7 percent while non-State income, 'outside-the-budget,' has grown as stated above at 19.6 percent. Clearly this situation is contributing to the State's inability to control where investment funds are going.

Second, over this nine-year period, total 'social investment' in fixed assets increased by an average of 18.7 percent each year. Within this amount, however, the State's 'inside-the-budget' invested amount rose by only an average of 4.6 percent per year. This has led to a dramatic decline in the percentage of State funds being invested as opposed to other social funds, again leading to a radical decrease in the ability of the Central government to influence the structure of investment. Third, within this nine-year period, overall social investment in rural areas increased at a rate of 20.3 percent, which is higher even than the rate at which social investment increased overall. Roughly two-thirds of this investment in rural areas has been made by individual farmers, a figure that has remained fairly steady. These growth patterns of revenue and investment are distinctly unfavorable for ongoing investment in agriculture, which depends mainly on State funding. Such analysis from a macroeconomic perspective could lead us to conclude that either we are going to have to change the overall structure by which the Central government takes in revenues and makes investments, or we are going to have to find alternative funding sources for agriculture. Within the current framework of State income and investment procedures, there is very little room for maneuver when it comes to improving the situation with regard to investments in agriculture. Trying to change the structure of public-finance expenditures at the Central-government level in order to achieve any real improvement will be extremely difficult. I will address specific difficulties later, when I integrate them with a discussion of the Central government's procurement, sales, and pricing systems for agricultural products.

4. A great amount of 'social investment' is going into rural areas, but only a fraction of that is being applied to agriculture

In 1988, social investment in fixed assets in rural areas reached RMB 132.197 billion, which was 29.4 percent of total social investment in the country. However, 85.7 percent of the funds invested by individual farmers went into housing. Only 14.3 percent was spent on buying fixed assets for 'productive' uses of various kinds, and as can be imagined not much of that went into agriculture. In 1988, for example, only 9.8 percent of all investments made by rural collective economic organizations at various levels of government went toward farming, forestry, animal husbandry, and fishing. Some 69.1 percent went toward the industry, transport, and construction sectors. Housing will continue to claim the largest share of private investment in rural areas for some time to come. From 1984 to 1988, construction of new houses in rural areas resulted in additional 'floor space' for each respective year of 600 million, 700 million, 1 billion, 900 million, and 800 million square meters. There is no indication that this will be changing, so all we can possibly do is to encourage farmers to invest more of that 14.3 percent spent on 'productive uses' into the field of agriculture. From the perspective of rural collective economic organizations, at all the various governmental levels, the issue is how to change investment patterns and make sure than even more is invested in rural interests. Changing social investment patterns at the rural level is a highly complex and difficult thing to attempt. Not only are 'social funds' dispersed over 210 million households in over 740,000 villages and 45,000 townships, but these 'investment funds' do not belong to the [Central] government, nor do they belong to the entire system of the State-run economy. As compared to investment in urban areas, investment in rural areas is even more purely oriented toward profit. Therefore, the general belief is that the relative prices of agricultural goods have to be increased if we want to shift rural social investment in the direction of agriculture. Next, I will address the whole subject of pricing and just how feasible or unrealistic this kind of thinking might be.

III. On the pricing of farm products

There has been heated debate in the academic community for years about the pricing of farm products. Generally speaking, most cadres believe that the current procurement prices of 'supplementary farm products' are on the low side, which cuts farmers' motivation to produce these things. Many cadres believe that the changes put in place in 1985 were a 'blow' to the interests of grain-raising farmers in what we call the 'new commercial grain production areas.' The 1985 changes did away with the previous system of 'higher prices for production that exceeds the mandatory State quota.' Instead, they set up a system whereby a 'mixed' contractual price was established that was equal to 30 percent of the quota price and 70 percent of the above-quota price. This new price represented a significant loss to farmers. Such cadres go further in thinking that the recent years of poor agricultural performance can be attributed to this change in policy measures. They think it showed 'blind optimism' with respect to grain production and was the product of undervaluing the importance of agricultural issues. We feel that if the pricing of grain is not handled properly it can indeed result in serious harm to farmers' interests. However, the situation with regard to production of grain, cotton, and oilseed crops cannot be solely attributed to this one aspect of procurement pricing alone. Particularly under the economic system that our country currently employs, agricultural pricing is subject to a broad range of factors but in turn also influences a broad range of factors. Any discussion of agricultural pricing clearly has to be integrated with a discussion of the entire, very real, macroeconomic situation in the country.

1. Procurement prices of agricultural goods have shown a consistent increase over recent years, but the actual benefit to farmers has been minimal

[In 1978,] the Third Plenary Session of the 11th Central Committee of the Communist Party of China passed 'in principle' a 'draft' decision that was called *Decision of the Central Committee on Several Issues to Do with Accelerating Agricultural Development.* This provided that, from the summer of 1979 grain marketing period, the procurement price would be increased by 20 percent for amounts delivered under mandated quotas, and by 50 percent for amounts delivered above those quotas. Procurement prices for cotton, oil crops, sugarcane, livestock, and forest products were to rise similarly depending on their individual circumstances. These provisions were confirmed and set in motion in a January 1979 national meeting on pricing. In 1979, prices of supplementary farm goods rose considerably and continued to be adjusted upward every year over the next decade. Using 1978 prices as the base rate, or 100 percent, by 1988, the procurement price index for grain had risen 274.4 percent, that for cotton 176.1 percent, and that for oilseed crops 193.7 percent.[1] Using 1950 prices as the base rate, the overall procurement price index for supplementary agricultural goods had risen 217.4 percent by 1978; using 1978 prices as the base rate, the overall index had risen 244.5 percent by 1988. This shows that adjustments upward in the decade from 1979 to 1988 amount to more than the entire increase in prices in the 28 years between 1950 and 1978. Benefits received by farmers in the decade between 1979 and 1988 were very apparent: per capita net income rose by RMB 167.88 as a result of increases in farm prices, or 40.8 percent of the total net increase in per capita incomes in this period.[2] Naturally, as procurement prices for farm goods were rising, the overall price level was also on the rise and farmers had to increase their expenditures as well. That increase came to a per capita figure of RMB 155.21, or 92.5 percent of the per capita increase in that portion of income that could be attributed to higher agricultural prices. Under the economic system that we currently employ, therefore, while farmers did indeed benefit from upward adjustments in procurement prices, the extent of that benefit was miniscule in the face of other relevant factors. Over the entire decade, the direct benefit to the average farmer was a total of RMB 12.67; the average benefit per year was RMB 1.27.

2. Over the course of adjusting procurement prices upward, there has been a weakening of how much higher prices stimulate increased agricultural production

We can see from Table 2.5 that changes in the price indices of supplementary agricultural goods actually have exhibited the shape of a traditional Chinese saddle, or a 'U' shape, over the past decade. After the remarkable upward adjustment in procurement prices in 1979, prices continued to be adjusted upward but at an increasingly lower rate. Overall upward adjustments reached their lowest level in 1985 (especially for grain, cotton, and oilseed crops). After 1986, under pressure from renewed imbalances between supply and demand, upward adjustments every year began to increase again until the increases in 1988 were higher than any over the previous 10 years except for 1979. Most regrettably, the impact or material incentive of these upward adjustments was far less noticeable than it had been before 1984. This has to do with at least the following two factors. One is that investment in agriculture has been inadequate for years. This has led to a worsening of farming conditions so that any price stimulus cannot have a response in a short period of time. The second is that even though upward price adjustments improved the price level of farm goods, these were still in an unfavorable position relative to price levels of other goods that one might produce. Price incentives in the post-1986 period have simply not been strong enough.

Table 2.6 demonstrates the problem of achieving no apparent stimulus from price adjustments after 1986. We can see that the increased amount of per capita net income from farming comes from two sources: one is increased production and the other is the benefit of higher procurement prices. The stimulus played a considerable role in spurring production after the price increases of 1979. Between 1980 and 1984, the increase in farmers' net income due to increased production was clearly greater than the increase in income due purely to higher prices. After 1985, however, the situation was precisely the opposite. Increased income was due to higher prices rather than increased output. The situation reached an extreme in 1988, when an increase in production brought in more net income of only RMB 2.45 while a price rise brought in as much as RMB 60.23. In that year, 95.9 percent of the increase in net income of farmers was derived from increases in procurement prices. One cannot make simple comparisons between the two ends of this long period, since we were just beginning reforms of our agricultural system in the early part of the 1980s, and systemic change itself was propelling rapid growth in agricultural production. After 1985, the impetus of this systemic change was already slowing down. As the household-contracting system became more widespread and stable, systemic changes began to have an even weaker

Table 2.5 Nationwide procurement price index for farm products and for grain, cotton, and oilseed crops (the price of each previous year is regarded as 100)

Year	Combined index	Grain	Cotton	Edible vegetable oil and other oil crops
1979	103.9	100.7	112.0	104.3
1980	122.1	130.5	125.3	132.7
1981	107.1	107.9	116.2	105.5
1982	105.9	109.7	104.8	104.9
1983	102.2	103.8	101.5	101.5
1984	104.4	110.3	100.2	100.6
1985	108.6	101.8	97.7	104.3
1986	106.4	109.9	99.5	104.6
1987	112.0	108.0	104.7	106.0
1988	123.0	114.6	108.6	119.7

Table 2.6 Increases in procurement prices for grain, cotton, and oilseed crops, and changes in output of those crops (takes the previous year price and output as 100)[1]

Year	Grain		Oilseed crops		Cotton	
	Price	*Output*	*Price*	*Output*	*Price*	*Output*
1978	100.7		104.3		112.0	
1979	130.5	109.0	132.7	123.3	125.3	101.8
1980	107.9	96.5	105.5	119.5	116.2	122.7
1981	109.7	101.4	104.9	132.7	104.8	109.6
1982	103.8	109.1	101.5	115.8	101.5	121.2
1983	110.3	109.2	100.6	89.3	100.2	128.9
1984	112.0	105.2	101.2	112.9	101.1	135.0
1985	101.8	93.1	104.3	132.5	97.7	66.3
1986	109.9	103.3	104.6	93.4	99.5	85.4
1987	108.0	102.9	106.0	103.7	104.7	119.9
1988	114.6	97.8	119.7	86.4	108.6	97.7

[1]National Bureau of Statistics, *China Statistical Yearbook 1989*, China Statistics Publishing House, 1989, p. 198, 199, 706.

effect. We simply have to recognize the fact that even in the context of our current macroeconomic situation, and with farm productivity as it is, the ability of price adjustments to stimulate more production has very noticeably declined. We can go further and say that if we do not address the conflicts of interest between industries and sectors in the macroeconomic context, we cannot overcome our chronic problem of parity recurrence. In brief, it is getting harder to achieve any stimulative effect on production simply by raising the government's procurement prices for agricultural products.

3. The economic system that we are currently implementing puts the government in a bind when it comes to determining prices for agricultural goods

Our existing economic system makes the government the biggest buyer for basic farm products. These include the major crops of grain, cotton, and oilseeds. At the same time, our system makes the government the biggest seller of such products, in terms of urban consumers. Both farmers and urban consumers therefore have to be concerned about prices on only one side of the equation – once they know those prices, they can go ahead and plan their economic activities accordingly. As both buyer and seller, the government must take both sides into consideration. It must think of the optimum prices for the producers of agricultural goods, as well as for the consumers of those goods. Under the system we currently have, the role of the government effectively cuts off buyers from sellers, and severs a relationship that otherwise would moderate prices. In theory, under different economic systems and at different levels of economic development, the purpose of a government's handling things in this way can be as follows. First, if the government procures farm goods at low prices and sells for higher prices, this pricing system forces both farmers and urban dwellers to contribute to fund accumulation by the State as a whole. It makes both sides support the country's economic development. Second, if the government procures on expensive terms and then sells the food cheaply, its aim is to subsidize both farmers and urban dwellers. Third, if the government both buys and sells at high prices, it is just aiming to subsidize farmers. Fourth, if the government both buys and sells cheaply, it is on the one hand forcing farmers to provide funding for industrial development, through low pricing making them contribute to the State's development funds. On the other hand, it is also enabling a system of low wages for those employees who live in cities by keeping down their cost of living. It is thereby increasing the returns that enterprises pay up to the State, in the form of dividends and taxes, and again transforming those funds into the 'accumulated capital' needed for 'national construction' [for building up the country].

The procurement and pricing system for agricultural products that we use to this day in our country was formed in the early 1950s. Conditions at the time determined that we should follow the fourth in the list of policy options above. We buy cheaply from farmers and we sell cheaply to urban residents. The conditions at the time that determined this policy included the nature of our social system, the goals for economic development that we set at the time, and the constraints of our actual level of economic development. Through measures that included low-priced procurement of agricultural products and low-priced sale of those products, to the greatest degree possible, the government took 'surplus economic value' that had been created by both farmers and urban enterprises and applied it toward the enormous investment needed to industrialize the country. It must be said that our government had little alternative but to adopt this strategy and it cannot be criticized too much today. Given the domestic and international political situation in the early years of the country, and the economic conditions that had to be faced, such a system was necessary in order to accumulate funds for industrialization. It also should be recognized that our country basically relied on its own forces to create the foundations of an industrialized nation. Nonetheless, it must also be noted problems inherent in the system from the beginning were bound to get worse once the system became increasingly entrenched. Contradictions were bound to sharpen. Urban residents had to pay a serious price for a system in which both farm goods and wages were kept low, which meant that times were very hard. Living standards improved only very slowly. On the other hand, urban industries grew extremely fast, which was the payback to a degree. The system assured expansion of the scale of national industry and it provided city dwellers with adequate employment. This helped to dissolve the contradictions that otherwise might have developed in society under a system of such low wages.

Between the years 1953 and 1978, real wages per employee throughout all enterprises in our country increased at the rate of only 0.38 percent each year, while the gross value of industrial output grew at the rate of 10.71 percent per year. At the same time, the number of employees grew on average by 6.73 percent each year, including those in enterprises owned 'by the people as a whole,' or 'State enterprises,' and those owned by collectives in cities and towns. As a result, the per capita consumption of urban dwellers rose by an average of 2.49 percent each year during the 1953–1978 period.[3]

The situation in rural areas was altogether different. The economic surplus created by agriculture essentially funded the industrial development of urban areas. The mechanism for doing this was known as the 'scissor-like differential,' in that what was contributed by agriculture, through low pricing, became value to industry, and the more one was pushed down, the more the other went up. Accumulation of funds for agriculture itself was minimal, as well as any increase in capacity for secondary production by the agricultural sector.

The average overall increase in gross agricultural output between the years 1953 and 1978 was 2.68 percent.[4] At the same time, the rural labor force grew by 2.01 percent[5] per year during this period. The area under cultivation in the country grew by an average of 0.23 percent each year.[6] Starting in the late 1950s, a 'leftist' line of ideology and government policies began to influence what farmers could do for a living in the countryside. This ideology reached an extreme to the extent that farmers were strictly forbidden to engage in any nonagricultural production, and they had no alternative employment beyond tilling the land. Since resources available for developing agriculture were greatly outpaced by increases in the rural labor force, due to population growth, a large part of the rural labor force was in fact engaged in what we call 'disguised unemployment.' (At the time, 'developing agriculture' primarily referred to increasing the acreage under cultivation.) This disguised unemployment led to a very slow improvement in levels of consumption and standard of living. Between 1953 and 1978, farmers' per capita consumption grew by only 1.71 percent,[7] which was one-third lower than the same statistic for urban dwellers. The rural-urban consumption ratio rose from 1:2.4 in 1953 to 1:2.9 in 1978.[8]

From the above, it can be seen that the rural economy has paid a double price for the system by which farm products were purchased by the State at low prices. Rural areas paid the price of damaging their own ability to accumulate funds and increase productive capacity, and they paid the price of a very slow rise in farmers' standard of living. The system of low-priced procurement may have been necessary in the early days of our country's industrialization, but as industrial systems were set up and strengthened in cities, it should have been adjusted as time went on. The cost of not doing so was very high. It resulted in an agriculture that lacks vitality and farmers that lack any motivation to produce. Extended over a period of time, such a situation leads to, and indeed has led to, severe problems. What's more, once the economic pressure of such a system exceeds the ability of farmers and agriculture to endure that pressure, and the rural economy is on the brink of collapse, urban industry is also not immune from the consequences.

During the 'period of hardship' during the late 1950s and early 1960s, the following situation actually came to pass: The total population in rural areas in our country fell from 552.73 million in 1958 to 531.34 million in 1960. This was a decline of 21.39 million people in the space of those three years.[9] Following on that, the number of staff employed in units 'owned by the people as a whole'

[State-owned] went from 50.44 million in 1960 to 32.93 million in 1963. This was a decline of 17.51 million in the space of those three succeeding years.[10] In the same period of 1960 to 1963, the total population in urban areas in the country declined by 14.27 million people.[11]

We are not saying that the period of hardship as described so graphically by these figures can be attributed to the system of low-priced procurement of farm products. In presenting these shocking figures, we simply hope to focus attention on and clarify a critical problem. If rural society and rural economic development lag behind urban development and industry for a long period of time, that situation places the very foundations of national economic stability in a very vulnerable position. The moment any kind of unusual problems appear, calamitous consequences have the potential to undermine the entire economy and not just the situation in the country's rural areas.

In order to deal with the 'unusual problems' of the early 1960s, the government took measures on a number of different fronts. One was to radically increase the procurement prices for farm products. Grain prices were increased by 73.4 percent in 1961, over 1960 prices. For the same period, oilseed crop prices went up 18.59 percent, hog prices went up 26.39 percent, egg prices went up 38.5 percent, and aquatic-product prices went up 26.2 percent. These measures drove the combined procurement price index for farm products up by 28 percent. The extent of the price increases in that year have not been seen before or since in the history of our country, in all of its 40 years since our Republic was founded.

In 1962, in spite of extreme hardship, the government decided that procurement prices for grain, oilseed crops, and livestock should be increased further, by 5.6 percent for grain, 1.2 percent for oilseed crops, and 2.10 percent for livestock.[12] This decisive measure played an absolutely vital role in restoring our rural economy. From 1962 to 1965, grain output grew by 31.88 percent, cotton output grew by 162.25 percent, and peanut and rapeseed output grew by 111.13 percent.[13] Even though such rapid growth of primary farm products over these four years was undeniably of a 'restorative' nature, simply getting back to where we were before, it nevertheless established the material foundation that enabled our nation to come through a period of extreme economic hardship.

In the early 1960s, our rural economy essentially recovered within four short years. It went from actual collapse to the highest production figures in the country's history for most agricultural products. It should be said that this is a mark of the superiority of our socialist system. Among measures taken by that system, raising the prices of agricultural goods was clearly the most effective. At the same time, increasing prices in that way put a considerable strain on our country's public finance. The price that had to be paid for agricultural recovery was, specifically, as follows. Between the years 1961 and 1965, the government paid RMB 18.67 billion (at 1960 prices) for grain, cotton, oilseed crops, and hogs delivered by the farmers. During the same period, total government revenues were reduced by RMB 97.67 billion and expenditures went down by RMB 139.33 billion.[14] It is not hard to imagine just how difficult it was to carry out policies that raised farm procurement prices in such a distressed economic climate. Over a five-year period, the increased outlays from such policies came to RMB 10.1 billion, while increased revenues from raising consumer prices to a degree came only to RMB 2.08 billion.[15] The difference between these two figures was made up for out of the budget.

The purpose in looking back at this period of history is to clarify one specific issue. Faced with extreme difficulty at the time, the Party and the government adopted correct measures, the national economy was able to get through a crisis, agriculture revived and began new growth, urban residents were again able to live calm lives, and so on, but this entire process only further distorted the price relationship between purchase and sale of agricultural goods. It also formed a set pattern: No matter how the government raised procurement prices on itself when buying from farmers, the sales prices of agricultural goods in cities only rose modestly, it did not increase to a comparable extent. Every increase in procurement prices therefore signified an increase in subsidies. An increase in subsidies signified an increase in the budgetary deficit. The government placed itself in an increasingly difficult dilemma. If it did not raise procurement prices, farmers would have little incentive to raise more food and there would be no assurance that crop production would advance; each increase in prices put an additional burden on the budget, however, since it was impossible to impose corresponding increases in food prices. Once the trend was started, it simply became worse. By now, the current situation has become untenable. The financial burden is too heavy.

We have run a budgetary deficit in 10 of the 11 years since 1979 and the intense rise in the cost of subsidizing the procurement of farm goods has played a major role in those deficits. That whole side of the issue should not be underestimated. In addition, however, and over the long run, the policy itself, of asking farmers to make a 'contribution' to the nation in the form of what is known as a 'contribution tax,' has gradually lost its economic rationale. The economic surplus derived from farmers and shifted out of rural areas has increasingly been used simply to subsidize consumption of urban residents. Looking back over the medium and even longer term, it has not been put to industrial development as originally conceived. Carrying on in this manner for much longer will inevitably lead to serious social problems.

Between 1978 and 1987, total public expenditures on price subsidies in general came to RMB 272.593 billion. Most of that was for basic agricultural commodities. This was 19.04 percent of government revenues during that period. During this period, price subsidies as a percentage of total revenues went from 8.37 percent in 1978 to 24.64 percent in 1984. While revenues rose by 4.99 percent each year between 1979 and 1984, price subsidies rose faster during the same period, by 25.69 percent.[16] Given that, by 1984, nearly one-fourth of our government revenue was being spent on price subsidies, and given that the gap between revenues and the accelerating cost of subsidies was growing, the appearance of policies to change the situation should not be viewed with surprise. Price reform measures proposed in 1985 were very definitely not 'blind optimism about the grain situation.' Behind them lay very real financial considerations.

In fact, price subsidies are far from being the only financial subsidies in our country. Another large component of subsidies is created by the way in which distorted pricing accommodates or makes allowances for the losses of State enterprises. In addition, direct subsidies to enhance the income of urban consumers have risen dramatically in recent years (these include subsidies for such things as pork, which started in 1985, and for meat, eggs, sugar, vegetables, and other food nonstaples, which started in 1988). By 1986, our nationwide subsidies came to 25.8 percent of revenues that year and the percentage rose to 32.2 percent in 1988 and is expected to rise to 32.6 percent this year [1989]. The total subsidy amounts were RMB 58.226 billion in 1986, RMB 76.278 billion in 1988, and a projected RMB 93.117 billion in 1989.[17] Given that consumer prices for these commodities are inelastic, the government will be assuming an increasingly heavy burden if it continues with the same traditional way of handling the problem. Moreover, persevering in the same manner will put enormous constraints on the economy as a whole, not to mention the way in which existing policies have a profoundly negative influence on agricultural development.

At this point, it would be good to analyze the relationship between the government's subsidies for agricultural products and its investment into agriculture, since this in fact is one major problem affecting prices. Between 1952 and 1988, farmers 'handed up' a total of RMB 371.222 billion in taxes.[18] This was 9.5 percent of the total sum of national income from agriculture in that period,[19] or 12.24 percent of the total sum of government revenues in that period.[20] The agricultural tax is only one part of what agriculture provides to the State, however. The greatest part of what farmers provide is in the form of what is known as the 'contribution tax' that is de facto paid by them as a result of the 'scissor-like differential' in the valuation of agricultural and industrial products. According to estimates of authoritative sources, farmers have provided a sum in excess of RMB 690 billion to the State in this latter form of contribution. That figure includes the years between 1949 and 1988, and is approximately 185 percent of the official 'agricultural tax' paid by farmers in this period. Summing up the two different kinds of taxes, the explicit as well as the disguised, comes to a figure of around RMB 1.1 trillion in all – this is the contribution that farmers have made to the national treasury since the founding of the country.

Turning to the investment side, between the years 1953 and 1988, the State has invested a total sum of RMB 107.051 billion in agriculture.[21] This is roughly one-tenth of the sum of taxes and 'contributions' derived from farmers. If one also adds in other State funding on behalf of agriculture (mainly in the form of expenditures in support of agricultural production and various agricultural undertakings), between the years 1950 and 1988, total appropriations for agriculture have come to some RMB 312 billion.[22] This is a return to farmers of roughly 30 percent of the taxes and 'scissor-like differential' that they themselves have paid up to the State. The remaining 70 percent represents a pure contribution on the part of farmers to urban development and the industrialization of the country. As shown by this data, the 'scissor-like differential' between agriculture and industry, that is, the different ways in which the two sectors have been handled, has been of ultimate importance to the country's industrialization and its urban development. Only the agricultural tax, paid by farmers over the past 40 years, has been returned to agriculture in the form of government appropriations (this has changed somewhat in the last decade, as the amount of appropriations has exceeded the amount paid in taxes, and the discrepancy is widening.) To reiterate, it is clear that the 'economic surplus' that the government has derived from rural areas has been in the form of a hidden or disguised 'scissor-like differential,' rather than in the form of the agricultural tax.

Given economic systems and processes that work in this manner, the government has to adhere to two conditions to achieve the desired results. First, it has to assure that a substantial difference between industrial pricing and agricultural pricing is maintained in order to get the benefit of the difference. Second, it has to assure that the 'surplus value' derived from that scissor-like pricing flows to the government as public revenues and is not retained by industrial and commercial enterprises. Only then can the government assure not only that industrialization and urban development are indeed the beneficiaries of the policy, but that the policy has the capacity to put a certain investment back into agriculture. Since 1979, these two conditions have demonstrably changed. First, prices of supplementary farm products have been rising constantly, as noted above. The procurement price index has gone up by 144.5 percent in the period 1979 to 1988. These price increases have mainly been initiated by the government and also funded by the government through public finance expenditures. If the government is unable to increase revenues significantly, its capacity to keep paying out is necessarily going to decline. During this same period, the prices of industrial products have also been rising, but these price increases have been instigated by enterprises themselves and the returns off sales have been garnered by the enterprises as well. Due to the increasing autonomy of enterprises as a result of reforms, enterprises are mostly retaining their earnings. The benefits of higher prices are not being paid up to public finance.

An imbalance has been developing, therefore, between public expenditures and public revenues, even as prices have risen for both industrial and agricultural products. In the period between 1979 and 1988, State revenues increased at an average annual rate of 8.73 percent. During that same period, State expenditures increased at a rate of 9.16 percent.[23] This has placed an enormous financial strain on the government. A second aspect of this situation is that, as enterprises retain more of their earnings, consumption funds are rising faster than national income. National income grew an average of 19.1 percent each year between the years 1983 and 1988, while the monetized income of citizens overall grew at an average rate of more than 22.9 percent. That is a difference of 3.8 percentage points.[24] Since the additional government revenue that can be derived from price increases in industrial products is relatively small, any decision to increase procurement prices is a decision to increase net expenditures of the country. For example, the amount by which government revenues increased between 1986 and 1987 was RMB 8.637 billion. The amount by which subsidies increased was RMB 8.728 billion. Even though all of the increased revenue was used for the increased subsidies, there was still a shortfall of RMB 91 million.[25] This unavoidably impacts the government's ability to make direct investments in agriculture. If we take into account the fact that prices for farm products to consumers have basically changed very little in recent years, we can easily see the predicament that the government is in with respect to the investment-price cycle in agriculture. The government's investment in agriculture can earn no direct returns and basically cannot be retrieved under the existing economic system. Agricultural goods increase as a result of investment, but then have to be procured at higher prices due to a variety of reasons. Meanwhile, consumer prices are also constrained by a variety of reasons and cannot be raised. The ultimate result is that government subsidies to agriculture increase in line with government investments in agriculture. The simplest way to describe this entire process is that the result of any investment is an ongoing increase in price subsidies for agricultural products.

Beyond the shadow of a doubt, this is not a sustainable economic process. If we do not reform the way we currently price agricultural products, not only will it be unrealistic to think we can continue to keep on raising the government procurement prices for farm products, but a more serious problem will present itself. Even if the government does what it can to deal with the problem in the short run, the irrationality of the economic process will inevitably begin to drag the entire economy into an extremely grave situation. In brief, we do not feel there is much potential left at all in what has been our normal procedure, namely, increasing subsidies in order to raise the procurement prices of agricultural products. We feel this way not just because of the budgetary crisis in recent years, but because it is so clearly counterproductive behavior on the part of the government. It is counterproductive if we want to achieve our goal of sustainable, stable, and well-coordinated development.

IV. The crux of the matter is to treat farmers correctly

In the above, we have analyzed the problematic nature of relying on public finance to put ever more large-scale investment into agriculture while at the same time increasing procurement prices for farm products. This is not because we do not approve of measures by which the government redistributes income to agriculture, to the extent it can. On the contrary, we believe that this is precisely one of the government's duties. What we want to emphasize is that it is simply unrealistic to try to resolve the problem in this way in either the near term or on into the future. Resorting to ever-higher government investment and price-support subsidies will not only exceed the capacity of our public finance, but will exacerbate what are already severe structural problems in our economy. Such a course of action will have seriously negative consequences for any ongoing reform of our economic system and for our hopes of achieving sustainable, stable, and coordinated economic growth.

We believe that any remedy to the current agricultural dilemma needs to start from the need to guarantee long-term and stable growth of the economy. An approach that adjusts the price of grain a little here, then of hogs there, oilseed crops here, then cotton there, that then has to reset the prices for industrial inputs the minute agricultural prices are fixed, a kind of 'first a little more flour, then some more water,' is useless. Not only does it *not* contribute to pulling agriculture out of its problems but it destabilizes the national economy by inciting overall systemic volatility. As an urgent response to crises, the government may be able to cut back on construction projects and other expenses in the short term, substantially increase funding for agriculture, and hike up its subsidies for procurement. This was done in the early 1960s and late 1970s. (In 1960 and 1978, appropriations for agriculture increased dramatically by 55.4 percent and 39.3 percent, respectively[26]; in 1961 and 1979, the combined procurement price index for farm products rose sharply from the previous year, up 28.0 percent and 22.1 percent, respectively.[27]) We need to keep in mind that these measures were taken at a time when the economy was on the brink of collapse, however, and the government had no alternative. More important, adopting such extraordinary measures had no effect on the way in which agriculture has a cyclical destabilizing effect on our economy.

The reasons for this naturally are extremely complex, but if one were to simplify, two factors at the least should be taken into account. One is that we have never integrated agriculture and rural development, as organic components, into our economic development strategy. It is true that every Five-Year Plan sets goals for agriculture in the form of concrete targets for grain, cotton, oilseed crops, meat, and so on, but the measures by which these things are to be achieved are vague in the extreme. There is little discussion of where the economic resources are going to come from to achieve these targets, such as funding, material resources, energy, science, and technology. If plans for agriculture are vague, those for rural development are even more so. There is no mention of how we are to increase investment in human capital in rural areas, how we are to address the worsening issue of employment, how we approach education, culture, hygiene, and so on in rural areas. None of this is made explicit in terms of concrete measures, nor even in terms of general goals. As a result, coordination of agriculture and rural development with the overall national economy becomes rather difficult. Problems that result from such lack of coordination accumulate until they eventually reach a tipping point at which they require massive governmental intervention. Measures are then aimed at addressing short-term imbalances and the immediate situation, however, rather than at any kind of long-term resolution. Underlying structural problems and the contradictions between cities and countryside, industry and agriculture, remain exactly as they were before. Every few years it becomes hard to avoid yet another agricultural crisis.

The second factor that should be taken into account is that while [our policy makers] emphasize the supply of agricultural products, they overlook the issue of farmers themselves. Farm goods are the product of the labor of farmers, and without adequate methods of motivating them, in an effective way, ongoing stable supply of agricultural products will naturally lack any real foundation. As we have seen throughout Chinese history, we will also then lack the basis for 'long-term rule and enduring peace.' Starting in the 1950s, we have instituted systems for centralized procurement of the main farm goods, we have roped all farmers into a system of collectives, we have segregated farmers from urban areas via a strictly controlled system of household registration, we have forcefully prevented rural areas from carrying on any kind of sideline business by regarding that as 'capitalist tails' [to be cut off], and so on. If one analyzes these things from an economic standpoint, one discovers that the entire purpose of these things has been, to the greatest possible extent, to guarantee supply of agricultural products as needed by the government. That is to say, the focus of all these arrangements has been basically on the supply of those products and not on advancing the modernization of rural areas or the status of farmers themselves. If this were not our focus, it would be hard to explain why, in the course of our country's urbanization and industrialization, even as the value of our agricultural production went from 45.42 percent of gross national output in 1952 to 19.65 percent in 1988,[28] our rural laboring population went from 180 million to 400 million.[29] Between 1965 and 1980, our country's urban population increased by only 2.6 percent.[30] This is notably lower than the average 3.5 percent of low-income countries, specifically 42 other countries looked at over the same period, and it is lower than the 3.8 percent of 35 medium- to low-income countries looked at over the same period.[31] Between 1965 and 1987, our nonagricultural population in cities rose from 14 percent to 17.7 percent of the national total,[32] up 3.7 percent over 22 years. This 3.7 percent is significantly lower than the 13 percent growth over that period of 42 low-income countries and the 12 percent growth in 35 medium- to low-income countries.[33]

The necessary consequence of the above facts, the way in which urbanization has not proceeded in line with industrialization, the rate at which agriculture's share in the economy has declined, and the decline in the economic role of farmers themselves, is that farmers have lost the opportunity to participate in national development. This cannot help but influence the stability and sustainability of our country's supply of agricultural products.

The first factor described above, our inability to integrate agriculture into the nation's economic development strategy, has been extensively discussed in the academic community. Therefore, we would like to focus on a further exploration of the second factor, the relationship between the supply of agricultural products and the development [human development] of farmers themselves.

Our overall situation puts severe constraints on the speed at which we can increase the supply of agricultural products. These constraints include a vast population, limited arable land, and very low per capita availability of natural resources [such as water] for agriculture. This forces our government to place an intense emphasis on guaranteeing the national supply of and the distribution of farm goods. When taken to an extreme, though, sole focus on supply, without commensurate focus on the necessity of rural development and the necessity of benefitting farmers themselves, leads to undercutting the foundation of that supply. At this point, we need to raise an important question, namely, 'What is the focus of our work in rural areas?' Can we reduce the issue of 'rural areas' to one of simply 'agriculture,' and even further to that of simply 'farm products'? Few people would indeed equate the issue of the countryside to one merely of farm products. Nonetheless, prior to the Party's 'Third 11th' [1978], it would be very hard to say that our rural economic policies did not aim for guaranteeing a supply of farm products at the expense of farmers themselves.

After that Third Plenary Session of the 11th Central Committee of the Communist Party of China [December 18–22, 1978], the Party's guiding ideological line of 'seeking truth from facts' was restored and the impoverished situation of farmers and rural areas was given recognition as being 'reality.' This provoked those who were now making policy into concerted action. The idea of the rights and interests of farmers themselves was revisited and was then elevated to a position higher than that of simply meeting targets for requisitioning agricultural output. At the Fourth Plenary Session of the 11th, a Decision was passed on September 28, 1979, titled *Decision on Certain Issues Regarding Accelerating Agricultural Development.* It sums up certain lessons that we have learned from our experience, and that we must keep firmly in mind.

'The first and important issue is a clear understanding of what is included under "socialism" and what is included under "capitalism." *Diversified operations* of communes and production brigades are part of the socialist "economies." Private plots, private livestock holding, household sideline businesses, and rural markets both supplement and are a subordinate part of socialist "economies" and we absolutely cannot allow any criticism of them or rejection of them due to the claim that they are "capitalist." Distribution according to labor and higher pay for a greater contribution is the socialist principle of distribution and it is absolutely forbidden to oppose it as being instead a capitalist principle. The principle that upholds the "three levels of ownership with the team as the basis" is one that is appropriate to our current level of development of agricultural productive forces. We absolutely do not allow any arbitrary change, or any so-called "poor transition." Policies that have been proven effective through actual practice must absolutely not be changed lightly. Otherwise, the people lose confidence in their government and farmers are not motivated to produce. At the same time, we must determine to modify and correct all incorrect policies that are not beneficial to agricultural productivity or to the enthusiasm of farmers. In formulating national economic plans, we must follow the correct order of priorities: first agriculture, then light industry, and last heavy industry. We must strike the correct balance between agriculture and industry. Each and every basic infrastructure development project must first take into account the capacity of agriculture to carry that specific burden.'

The *Decision* went on to say,

'Our leadership in the field of agriculture must proceed from actual conditions, and must be managed in accordance with both natural laws and economic laws. We must manage things in a way that serves the interests of the people, we absolutely must adhere to the principle of democratic management of communes, and we must respect and protect the democratic rights of commune members. We absolutely must not rule willfully through administrative fiat, or "blind commands," or with disregard for the complexity of situations in trying to make one solution fit all problems.'

The *Decision* also stipulated the following:

'The uniform [centralized] procurement price for grain is to be raised 20 percent from the time summer grain goes to market, and any delivery above the mandated quota amount is entitled to an additional price increase of 509 percent. Procurement prices for cotton, oil crops, sugar crops, livestock and aquatic products will also rise gradually depending on their specific circumstances.'

'From now on and for some time to come, the mandatory procurement quotas for food grains will be kept a stable level based on what they were between 1971 and 1975, and once they are set they will remain unchanged for five years. Moreover, starting in 1979, quotas will be reduced by five billion *jin* [or 2.5 billion kg], to lower the burden on farmers. Rice regions with a per capita grain ration that is below 400 *jin* [200 kg], or miscellaneous grain regions [areas that grow grains other than wheat and rice] with a per capita ration below 300 *jin* [150 kg] are exempt from having to supply grain to the government. Extra grain procurement [by local officials or others] is absolutely forbidden.'

The promulgation of this *Decision* enabled sweeping rural economic reform, and the tremendous growth in our agricultural production between 1979 and 1984 took the whole world by surprise. Nonetheless, within the space of less than one decade, the lessons of how we were able to and why we *had* to reform agriculture in the late 1970s had already faded in the minds of some cadres.

We are again confronting another shortage of agricultural goods and another crisis in the relationship between supply and demand. Instead of looking for the reasons in our current economic system, and seeking solutions while continuing to push for ongoing reforms, some of our cadres are looking backward for solutions. They are maintaining the old attitudes toward farmers and the old approach in how to handle them. We must be aware of the fact that certain local authorities are already stirring up resentment, unease, and even hostility among farmers as a result of their attitudes toward the household contract responsibility system. They are stirring up opposition to how they are implementing procurement policies of basic farm products, as well as their approach to township enterprises and [not wanting] the rural labor force to shift to nonagricultural sectors. If these local authorities do not pay adequate attention to the issue, the relationship between 'the Party and government,' and 'farmers,' will not be immune to the possibility of serious deterioration. If we return to the old ways used prior to the Party's Third 11th, which were an injustice to farmers, we can be sure that those old ways will not save agriculture from its current problems. Hurting farmers just to gain a little more in the way of procurement of farm goods may indeed result in one or two years of a little more grain, cotton, and oilseed crops, but the price we will have to pay for that in the end, the real consequences, are unthinkable.

In the early 1960s, faced with a national economy that had sunk into dire straits, comrade Mao Zedong began to reconsider his previous ideas in many ways. He said,

> 'In 1960, what we had was both a natural disaster and a manmade disaster, if we put aside the destruction also perpetrated by our enemies. We ourselves made mistakes in our work. Examples – we did too many water conservancy projects, too much industrialization, too much mobilizing of human labor.'

He went on to say that the first Lushan Conference brought on the negative consequences of 'overestimation of grain production, overly high procurement quotas, and overly high distribution, and it is worth our while to remember and learn our lessons from this.' In analyzing the fundamentals of these 'lessons,' Mao Zedong summed things up as follows,

> 'In the process of socialist construction, we often act blindly, since much about socialist economies remains largely unknown to us. I, for example, understand little of the economics of national construction. Industry and commerce, I don't understand much. Agriculture, I understand a little.'

He went on to say, 'What I focus on more are systemic issues, issues to do with the "relations of production" [i.e., human interactions in the economic sphere]. When it comes to the means of production, I know really very little.' He also believed, 'We now know a little but still not very much about socialism. We are learning as we go along.'[34] In the midst of the great disaster, Mao Zedong not only tried to sum up the general lessons to be drawn from China's experience of socialist economic construction, but he focused especially on the government's treatment of farmers. In this respect, his understanding was more sharply defined and he was much more emphatic in his comments. In 1961, he said to high-level Party cadres, 'China has 500 million farmers. If you do not unite with them, no matter how strong your industry is, how big your Anshan Iron and Steel Company is, *you will be overturned.*' [italics added] He also concluded that it was pointless to even think of doing anything in the country if the government distanced itself from farmers.[35] Thirty years have gone by since these truths born of hard experience were uttered by Mao Zedong, but they still have considerable force and relevance today. Naturally, the difficulties we are facing are nowhere near as hard as three decades ago. Nevertheless, the fundamental lesson is fully applicable today: The government cannot inflict injustice on farmers with impunity. We have had two successful occasions on which we emerged from disaster, in the early 1960s and in the late 1970s. From these, we can draw the following lesson: The worse the economic situation, the more we must protect the rights and interests of farmers, and the more we must avoid any tendency to turn 'farmer' problems into mere problems of 'agricultural products.' In difficult times, we need to look beyond any superficial conflict between supply and demand of agricultural goods. We need to examine the system or policy that led to the problems. Through furthering reforms, we should search for effective measures that motivate farmers and develop their productivity. This is not just in order to enable a stable and sustainable agriculture. It is to create the foundation for establishing any kind of 'long-term rule and enduring peace.'

In the course of this process, naturally economic adjustments are necessary that might increase investment into agriculture and that might increase subsidies for higher procurement prices, but everyone should be quite clear on the fact that holding overly high hopes for these interim measures is unrealistic. At the end of the day, the whole issue of a 'correct approach to farmers' means restoring rural development to its rightful place in our national economic strategy. It means setting up a series of rural economic systems that are welcomed by the great mass of farmers. Using the significantly descriptive phrase we have been using over the past decade, it means 'relying on sound policies.' We must rely on such policies to relieve farmers' anxieties, and to be willing themselves to invest more of their economic surplus into agriculture. People may argue that this is 'looking to far-away water to resolve an immediate thirst,' but we feel it is better than 'drinking poison to stop our thirst.' In other words, we feel it is better not to rely on solutions that, despite their immediate effect, will fuel resentment among farmers in the long run. For a country with such low per capita natural resources and low economic and technological development, fully addressing agriculture is going to be a very long process. Therefore, we need to look to the future and prepare ourselves mentally for a long battle. We have to be realistic as we lay the groundwork in the immediate future, realize that we are building systems and organizations. We must make sure that they take advantage of our accumulated experience and handle the relationship between industry and agriculture in a more rational way, as well as the economic relationship between cities and countryside and among the various departments [economic sectors] working in the countryside itself. Agricultural development has to proceed on the basis of adherence to economic laws and firm reality. If we can effectively implement this approach over a long time, say 5, 10, or even 20 years, there should be no grounds for pessimism about what agriculture can achieve.

In what follows, we present some initial thoughts on several important relationships that shape our policies on 'how to treat farmers correctly,' with the hope that they will stimulate further debate on the issue.

1. The relationship between farmers and the land

The relationship between farmers and land has long been of primary importance in defining the government's policy with respect to handling farmers. If this relationship is mishandled, it becomes the most direct cause of agricultural slowdowns. Examining this relationship is obviously necessary in any discussion of how best to handle the situation of farmers.

In the 40 years since the founding of the country, the relationship between farmers and land has already experienced several tremendous changes. Land reform 'rooted out and eradicated' a feudal land system that had persisted in our country for over 2,000 years. By the winter of 1952, more than 300 million formerly landless farmers had each received a portion of the 700 million *mu* of farmland that was confiscated from rich farmers or landlords. This was then divided up for reallocation. This released farmers from the heavy burden of handing over grain as rent to landlords, an amount that came to 70 billion *jin* each year [35 billion kg].[36] For the first time in Chinese history, the centuries-old dream of having 'tillers of the land own their own fields' became a reality. Just before the end of this land reform, however, the Central Committee of the Communist Party of China formulated what was called a *Resolution on Mutual Aid and Cooperation in Agricultural Production (Draft).* This was formulated in December 1951 and officially adopted in February 1953.

In December 1953, the Central Committee then adopted the *Resolution on Issues Relating to Developing Agricultural Producers' Cooperatives.* In October 1955, the Central Committee adopted the *Resolution on Issues Relating to the 'Cooperativization' of Agriculture.* In November 1955, the Central Committee put out what was called a *Model Example for Articles of Association of Agricultural Cooperatives (Draft),* and in June 1956, it put out a *Model Example for Articles of Association of High-Level Cooperatives of Agricultural Producers.* By the end of 1956, 120 million rural households were participating in such cooperatives nationwide, or around 96 percent of all rural households. This marked the end of a very brief period in history when Chinese farmers were themselves small-time landowners.

From the end of land reform in 1952, to 1956 by which time coverage of the so-called high-level cooperatives had been extended throughout all rural areas, the relationship between Chinese farmers and land had gone through changes that can be described as follows.

Privatization of land was followed by a dividing up of land for independent operations by households. During this period, swapping of labor and swapping of the means of production was carried on in a kind of mutual aid process. In the next period, land shares as held by households were now entered into 'cooperatives.' Unified operations were carried out not individually, by households, but by the cooperatives, with farmers participating in collectivized labor. Results in the form of actual crops and also dividends on the land [which was still in the 'possession' of farmers] were distributed according to the principle of 'distribution according to labor.' This stage in the evolution of our relationship between farmers and land was known as the period of 'primary-level cooperatives.'

In the next period, land was 'transferred out' to ownership by the collective itself for no compensation to the individual farmers. The main means of production [farm implements] were sold [by farmers] to the collectives at highly discounted prices. Unified operations were now carried on with collectivized labor but distribution still followed the principle of 'distribution according to labor.' This stage in the evolution of our relationship between farmers and land was known as the 'period of high-level cooperatives.'

In the course of this four-year process, not all farmers went through all stages. A very substantial number of the high-level cooperatives were created directly out of the 'mutual aid' organizations. Individual farming operations were transformed directly into high-level cooperatives in a process that was called 'ascending to heaven in one step.'

In August 1958, the CPC Central Committee passed the *Resolution on Issues of Establishing People's Communes in Rural Areas.* This required the formation of 'generally one commune per township, each commune to include around two thousand households.' The salient characteristic of people's *communes* as distinguished from *cooperatives* was described by the phrase, 'first big, second public.' In other words, they were larger than the former 'high-level cooperatives,' in size equaling around 20 or 30 combined cooperatives, and they were more 'public.' That is, the degree of public ownership of the means of production in communes was higher. The process of combining 'high-level cooperatives' into communes was described by the August 1958 *Resolution* as follows: 'When several cooperatives are consolidated to form a larger commune, the assets and liabilities that each cooperative formerly possessed will naturally be different, including both internal and external debts. In the process of combining them, both cadres and the masses should "be infused with the communist spirit." People should not be too fastidious about small details. They should accept that there will be differences, and they should not try to account for every *jin* of grain.' The *Resolution* also noted that, 'generally speaking, private plots can be turned to collective management in the course of consolidating cooperatives.'

When people's communes were established, all means of production became communally owned, with no exceptions. Commune members received wages plus rations, and for a while everyone even had to eat in public canteens since the concept of eating in a household was 'negated' as being against the communal spirit. The communal 'significance' of the people's communes as described by the *Resolution* is scarcely believable to people today. The *Resolution* held that,

> 'The realization of communism in our country is not a distant dream of the future. We should be zealous in making use of the [social] "form" of the people's commune as we feel our way forward in this transitional stage to communism.'

In December 1958, a *Resolution on a Number of Issues Concerning People's Communes* was passed by the Sixth Plenary Session of the 8th Central Committee of the Communist Party of China. It went a step further not only in confirming the August 1958 *Resolution,* but in describing in highly imaginative terms the future prospects and the 'nature' of people's communes, while narrating how they had developed over the previous three months. It said,

> 'In 1958, a new form of social organization arose like the early-morning sun over the broad horizon of East Asia. Large-scale people's communes in the countryside unify government and society, and integrate all the "faces" of industry, agriculture, commerce, intellectuals, and soldiers.'

'Within just a few months' time, all 740,000 agricultural cooperatives that existed nationwide were transformed and reorganized into more than 26,000 people's communes. Over 120 million households participated in the process. This figure includes more than 99 percent of all [rural] households of all ethnic groups nationwide.' In describing the distribution system [i.e., in this case meaning the payment system] employed by communes, which combined a wage system and a 'system of rations,' the *Resolution* asserted,

> 'In the past, [people were] always anxious about enough to eat, enough to drink; they were worried about fuel, oil, salt, soy sauce, vinegar and tea. Now, families that used to struggle to make both ends meet may rest assured, since they can "eat for free," which is to say that they are receiving the most fundamental kind of social security.'

The *Resolution* concluded, 'The rationing system of the communes is seeing the first budding of the communist principle of "distribution according to need." '

Clearly, the idea behind setting up people's communes included more than just reaffirming the abolition of private property, which had already been implemented by the high-level cooperatives. The purpose in setting up the communes was also to weaken the connection between a person's income and how much work he put into his land. Since total income was now to be distributed equally over 2,000 households, the need for and the chances that anyone could calculate how much work had gone into land were greatly reduced. To an unprecedented degree, farmers became divorced from the land, in terms of seeing the direct economic benefit to them of their labor. This was a major change in our 'relationship between farmers and land.'

The establishment of people's communes took place over the autumn and winter of 1958. Severe problems emerged over the next several years. By March 1962, the Central Committee of the Party therefore issued a new *Directive*. It was called *Directive on Issues to Do with Changing the Basic Accounting Units of the People's Communes in Rural Areas.* This *Directive* required that the basic accounting unit be 'passed down further' [in organizational terms] to the level of production teams, rather than communes. It stated that under the new situation, 'generally speaking, a team of some twenty to thirty households should be involved.' The *Directive* now asserted that,

> 'taking the "production team" as the basic unit of accounting is more appropriate to the level of productive forces in our country's rural areas. It is more in line with the degree of [ideological] awareness of our farmers, and it is more in line with the managerial ability of grassroots level cadres.'

The *Directive* also explicitly stated that,

> 'Using the production team as the basic accounting unit within the people's communes in essentially all parts of the country will not be [the policy] for just a short period. It will be the underlying system that we implement for at least the next thirty years or so.'

The system did indeed stay relatively unchanged for the next 20-some years, until it was replaced by the 'household contract responsibility system.' The 'household contracting system' was put in place throughout rural areas in the early 1980s. There is no doubt that, in 1962, switching to an accounting system based on 20 to 30 households made it easier for people to figure out how much income they should receive based on how much investment of labor they had put into the land. The 1962 *Directive* therefore strengthened the relationship between income and quantity of labor. Compared to how things had been before, things such as the calculation of labor, supervision over amount of labor, evaluation of labor, and so on were now easier to quantify. This *Directive,* and the whole sequence of related documents from the Party's Central Committee that were to follow, did in fact play a role in the economic recovery of the early 1960s.

However, it should also be recognized that this *Directive* made us miss an important opportunity. Together with such further documents as the *Revised Rules on Rural People's Communes (Draft),* and the *Decision on Further Strengthening Collective Ownership of People's Communes and Developing Agricultural Production,* passed by the Tenth Plenary Session of the 8th CPC Central Committee [September 1962], the *Directive* deprived the countryside of a chance to adjust the relationship between farmers and land.

The reason this might have been such a key opportunity was that during this period, in 1961 and 1962, farmers were themselves spontaneously initiating a process of 'contracting production down to the household level.' This marked the reemergence of a practice that had actually been tried once before. (The first time had been when high-level cooperatives were just being established, from the autumn of 1956 to the spring of 1957. At that time, the experiment encountered resistance.) In 1961, many farmers and grassroots cadres throughout much of the countryside began practicing a form of 'contracting production down to the level of the household' by secretly dividing up land while appearing to keep it undivided. Out of concerns for their own interests, farmers were dissatisfied with the mere 'adjustment' that made production teams the basic accounting unit. They now wanted a clearer and more direct claim on land. They wanted greater clarification of their economic relationship to the land. In the spring of 1962, Mao Zedong sent his secretary, Tian Jiaying, on a fact-finding mission to Shaoshan and other places in Hunan Province. As head of a delegation, Tian Jiaying arrived in Mao's hometown where he met with many commune members. These people told him in no uncertain terms that they wanted farmland to be contracted to individual households. This was absolutely typical of the sentiment among farmers at the time throughout the country. After his investigation in Hunan, Tian Jiaying delivered his conclusions first in Shanghai and then in Beijing, both to Mao Zedong and to Central Committee leaders.

It was Tian's belief that contracting production to households did have advantages, given the amount of hand labor required by farming, as well as the need to 'come through' the current intense difficulties the country was experiencing. His stated belief was that 'collective operations will be hard to maintain at present.' Therefore he too had the idea that it would be best, in this transitional period, to divide land up by households and contract production directly to them. Chen Yun read the delegation's 'adjustment reports' in Shanghai and commented that he regarded its point of view 'refreshing.' He gave it strong support. Zhou Enlai went further in getting Yang Shangkun in Beijing to make a telephone call to Tian Jiaying in order to ask him, 'Would it be possible to make the self-owned portion even broader?' [i.e., relax controls on private ownership even further in rural areas]. Once Liu Shaoqi and Deng Xiaoping had heard of Tian Jiaying's report in Beijing, they too expressed support for his recommendations.

The possibility of a transformation in farmer-land relationships of a far more sweeping nature therefore was on the horizon in 1962. It would have changed economic relationships profoundly in the countryside, and gone far beyond a mere adjustment of the accounting level of agricultural production. Mao Zedong was, however, strongly opposed. He felt that the outer limits to what he could accept had already been reached by making the accounting unit for production the lower-level 'production team.' After hearing Tian's report in Shanghai, Mao decisively announced,

> 'It is true that we need to follow the mass line [i.e., do what the people, or the "masses," feel we should be doing] but there are also times when we cannot just blindly listen to the masses. For example, we cannot accept this idea of contracting production on down to the level of the household.'

At the Party's Central Committee Working Meeting held at Beidaihe in August [1962], Mao Zedong started right off with a criticism of the idea of contracting production to households. He yet again brought up the 'sharp efficacy of class struggle.' He felt that if production was indeed contracted to households, within one year the country would start fragmenting into different classes. There would be more corruption, high interest rates on loans, purchasing of land, and such behavior as the taking of concubines. All of these things would be done not only by normal people but by Party members and even the heads of Party branches. On the other side of the matter, there would be bankruptcies among the less fortunate. Those less fortunate included the 'four kinds of dependents,' namely family members of the military, workers, martyrs, and cadres, and the 'five kinds of guaranteed households' [people requiring State support].

By the time of the Tenth Plenary Session of the 8th Central Committee of the Party in September [1962], Mao Zedong was going a step further in propounding his view that class struggle had to be carried on all the time.[37] As a result, the call for contracting production at the household level was silenced for close to another 20 years.

The purpose in narrating this condensed history is to make us recognize more clearly the link between 'farmers and land' and the success of 'agriculture.' It is to make us see how changing the relationship between farmers and land takes agriculture in the direction of growth or decline. And it is to remind us of the extreme importance of this matter. Addressing it properly will be critical to the rural economy not just now but for a long time to come. Even more important, however, I want to use the lessons of history as evidence that we can only change and improve the household-based land contracting system incrementally. We cannot overthrow it all at once.

Since the Third Plenary Session of the 11th Central Committee of the Communist Party of China, we have been implementing the household-based contracting system for 10 years in certain places and, in more recent locations, for 5 years. The system has generated tremendous debate among all parties, theoretical circles, actual practitioners in rural areas, and farmers themselves, partly because of the slowdown in agriculture in recent years. The greatest concerns, or one could say still unsettled considerations, focus on three issues. These are the land ownership system, the system governing 'usage rights or operating rights to land,' and the optimum size of farming operations. Needless to say, each of these is intimately related to the interests of farmers themselves.

1. The issue of land ownership. In recent years, there have been three distinct kinds of policy recommendations with respect to land ownership systems. These have been private ownership, ownership by the State, and an improved version of community-based collective ownership. I believe that each of these can be pursued further in theoretical terms, but a very practical consideration has to be taken into account. We have to deal with the existing situation, no matter what approach we might want to adopt in theory. This basic fact trumps everything else. The situation is that some 2 billion *mu* of tillable land is being farmed by around 200 million farming households [an average of 10 per household]. Any attempt to transform the current situation in the short or medium term will encounter strong opposition from farmers. If measures are forcefully implemented, it will lead to extreme disturbances in our rural socioeconomic situation. If a new system of ownership is instituted, but the current situation of dispersed land operations by farmers is left as it is, one has to question the rationale for changing the system of land ownership. Those who are advocating either State ownership of land or private ownership of land believe that the main purposes of a new system would be as follows.

First, it would strengthen management over farmland in order to prevent its ongoing loss [to construction and other industrial purposes]. Second, it would increase investment into land in the medium and long term, thereby improving basic infrastructural development of the land. Third, it would stimulate a market for land, with the hopes of realizing 'economies of scale,' that is, larger-scale farming operations.

Let us look first at the 'State ownership' proposal. When you get right down to it, our country's farmland is currently managed by organizations and cadres at the 'village' level of government. For the near and medium term, that situation is going to be very hard to change. Therefore, if we were to nationalize all land, make it State-owned, we could indeed place restrictions on the authority to 'occupy' or 'use' land, but we still could not have the State actually 'manage' the land. In reality, the State cannot get around the authority of village organizations in the direct handling of land affairs. Making land State-owned would not in fact resolve problems of land management. Making land State-owned would also not resolve the problem of needing more medium- and long-term investment in land. The pattern of land renting to farmers has long since been fixed. Before that pattern is changed in its very essence, the State cannot simply take in farming income based solely on its new legal authority over land, and without deriving more income, it will not have the economic basis for plowing in greater investments. The main investment into land is still going to come from farmers and rural collective organizations. As a result, merely announcing the nationalization of land will also not contribute to putting greater investments into land. With respect to the policy objectives of greater transferability of land and greater consolidation, those too would not be achieved by nationalization. If land were to become State-owned, naturally the State would have the authority to determine who can contract for what land, who cannot, what kind of person can get more and what kind less, so that, in theory, the State could use administrative means to see that land is more transferrable and begins to be consolidated for greater economies of scale. The crux of the matter is that, right now, land is not only the 'means of production' for farmers but also their social security. It is their safety net. Before we change this double-layered function of land, it is in fact impossible for the State to dictate that some farmers can contract for farming land while others cannot. Consequently, the whole issue of making land-use rights more transferrable and consolidating farmland for greater economies of scale is also not going to be resolved by setting up a system of State ownership. Given that such a system will not resolve the issues, it would seem to be unnecessary either at present or in the medium term.

Then we come to the privatization proposal. First, instituting a system of privately owned land does not in fact tie in directly to better management of land. Second, privatization may indeed encourage farmers to pursue a long-term approach to land and to put long-term investments into land, but that does not at all mean that the investment will be into land for farming purposes. The price of products coming off the land is a major factor in the decision making of farmers. Their investment behavior is determined not only by a clarification of rights over land, but by how much they can make off the land. Relatively speaking, prices of farm products are on the low side. In a macro-environment in which grain, cotton, and oilseed crops in particular are underpriced, it is highly unlikely that demarcating property rights over land will result in any great increase in long-term investment into agricultural production. Third, in theory it might appear that clarifying property rights will contribute to developing a market for land. One might [in theory] base an argument for instituting a system of private ownership of land on this idea that it will lead to greater transferability of land. Our actual situation, however, is that the average amount of land per capita is extremely small. Instituting such a privatized system of tiny land holdings, in our society, should be viewed with very great concern if the objective is to keep land in farming. The reason is that our society is also in the midst of industrialization [and industry returns more on land than farming]. Instituting such a system would necessarily lead to soaring land prices and the quick realization on the part of farmers that their land is their primary asset. That would then impede the development of a land market for agriculture, and it would impede the consolidation of small plots into larger tracts for farming. Similar examples may be found in a number of Asian countries that have small per capita land resources and that have instituted a privatization system. Therefore, even if we put aside any ideological considerations, restoring land privatization would not address the crux of the issues in our country.

Given the above, we recommend that we stabilize the existing system of land ownership. That is, we recommend that we make improvements to the existing system of collectively owned land of rural communities. The system's greatest virtue is that it gives farmers a basic sense of security. Most of the problems that relate to this existing system arose after we instituted the household contracting system. A great number of places failed to carry out organizational reform as a response to changing economic relations. As a result, in many places collective ownership exists in name only. This has greatly undermined proper management practices with respect to farmland.

Improving the situation will call for the following kinds of action.

(1) *Clarify ownership of land that is held collectively.* We need to be more explicit in confirming that the 'owners' of 'collective land' are those grassroots economic organizations in rural communities that were the basic accounting units at the time of the original people's communes. In most places, these are economic organizations at the governmental level of rural villages, namely, villagers' teams or 'small groups' [in Chinese, *cunmin xiaozu*]. As to whether or not, or just how, these 'owners' of collective land can evolve into economic organizations at the village administrative level will depend entirely on the desires of the farmers themselves and the state of the village economy. We surely cannot make arbitrary changes to the ownership rights of collective land at the village level. That would bring about unnecessary chaos both in local economic interests and in the psychological state of farmers.

(2) *Expand the right of 'owners' to revenue from collectively held land, and make that right to revenue more explicit.* The current situation is absolutely untenable over the long term. Right now, farmers who have contracted for land pay up what is called a *ti-liu* or a sum of money to the collective organization. The economic relationships involved in this process are extremely murky. Amounts that must be paid are highly arbitrary, depending on who is in charge. We need clear stipulations that community-based economic organizations, as land owners, are entitled to specific levels of rent. This will not only define and clarify economic relationships but will help standardize appropriate amounts of rent. The taking in of rents by legitimate organizations can help in the transition between what is now a 'land contract system' and [what in future will be] a 'land rental system.' Rents can be collected from farmers directly, or indirectly via a township authority, in the form of a surtax. Once such 'land rents' are collected, in addition to agricultural taxes, depending on specific circumstances, they can be rebated back to village-level economic organizations. Rents obtained by village-level economic organizations should be used primarily to fund agriculture-related projects, such as irrigation systems, and to strengthen and improve administrative handling of land use. Such funds would need to be kept in special designated accounts at the Bank of Agriculture account or

in pooled accounts but under a specific line-item title. With the help of the Bank of Agriculture, the township government should exercise regulatory supervision over the village land rents, and should make public, to farmers, the actual uses to which funds were put after examining and verifying such use. In addition to land used for farming purposes, land rents should gradually be instituted on land used for nonagricultural purposes by 'nonfarming entities,' as well as that allocated to households for their residences.

(3) *Expand the rights of owners of collectively held land to dispose of [i.e., transfer certain rights to] that land.* In principle, it should be recognized that 'owners' of collectively held land have the right to sell it, to rent it, to turn it into shares as shareholding operations, and to use it as collateral for loans. Owners do not have the right to sell land to private individuals. Moreover, such actions with respect to land can be undertaken only after a process of democratic discussion and determination within the 'ownership' body. However, when farmland is transformed into land for nonfarming purposes, the 'rights' listed above can [or should] become effective only after being approved by the government's land management departments. In this regard, it would be beneficial and indeed it is quite necessary to improve the current situation.

Strengthening and improving the delineation of collective rights to rural land will be positive in a number of ways. It will help stabilize the household contracting system, will enhance administrative management of land, will improve basic infrastructure inputs into land, such as irrigation projects, and will enable rural economic organizations to better serve farmers.

2. The issue of 'land-use rights' and operating rights. Based on the evolving relationship between farmers and land since the founding of the country, we must first of all acknowledge the equal rights of all farming households living in the same community to contract (or rent) land that is held collectively within that community. Such rights derive from the 'right' that any farmer has to work, and also from the rights that all rural residents have to the most basic form of social security provided by the State. Only starting from that premise can we begin to think of any adjustments to the existing land use and operating rights to rural land. Any changes have to be based on the actual state of economic development in a given location, and on the desires of local farmers. Some areas have already begun to implement new ways of handling land-use rights that will no longer be adjusted according to changes in the 'registered population' of the locale. They have announced that such changes will begin from a certain point in time. It should be said that this has a very positive and practical significance in terms of preventing farmland from further fragmentation, division into ever tinier parcels. It should help in terms of curbing ongoing 'blind' growth in the rural population, and it should encourage farmers to invest in improvements on land they are farming. This should be integrated with a process of ensuring that the 'owners' of collectively held land have the right to income off that land. Households who are 'contracting' for land can gradually switch to a system of 'paying rent' for the land, which will allow for straightforward payments for renting the land rather than what is now an extremely vague and nontransparent practice of paying into a 'collective reserve' for collectively held land. In general, terms for renting land should be no less than 10 years, but the rental contracts should not be divisible or inheritable. Farmers who want to transfer their rental rights to land should receive compensation from the community-based economic organizations; any assignment of leases should first receive the approval of those organizations. For the near future, our goal should simply be to reassure farmers who are either contracting for or renting land – we want to 'stabilize' their expectations. Readjusting economic relations can come later, in terms of changing the usage rights to land on a more long-term basis and making such adjustments part of a nationwide rural policy.

3. The issue of larger-scale farming operations on larger parcels of land. We have to recognize that eventually our country's agriculture must move in the direction of fairly large-scale agricultural operations. Such operations must be built on the basis of an entire economic and technological system, however. Until we come to a more fundamental resolution of the problem of nonagricultural employment of our huge rural labor force, until we become a more urbanized and a far more industrialized nation, and until we have better marketing systems and services for our agricultural goods, it must remain a distant illusion.

For the near and medium term, therefore, operations of scale in agriculture will apply only to a very limited number of rural areas that truly have the right conditions for it. We should apply such policies only where they can be effective, and should not indiscriminately talk about 'large-scale operations' as our basic economic policy. It would be very easy to create alarm among the majority of farming households, which would be detrimental to stabilizing and improving our basic agricultural policy of the 'household-based contract responsibility system.' At the moment, we should prevent abuse of administrative powers, actions taken under the pretext of following an ostensible policy of greater economies of scale in agriculture. We cannot allow any kind of arbitrary infringement of farmers' rights over the land they have contracted, or actions that contravene both economic realities and farmers' wishes. We must guard against reverting to a tendency to rule by 'blind' fiat.

It is realistic to think that our basic economic policy in rural areas can apply only to the majority of cases. Among 800 million farmers, there are bound to be exceptions. Exceptions and special circumstances should obviously not be taken as the basis for our fundamental agricultural policy. Rather than focusing right away on accelerating a move toward economies of scale in agriculture, we should put our efforts into researching how to prevent further fragmentation of land into smaller and smaller parcels. In policy terms, this is both more realistic and more urgent. Therefore, it is not wise to lead everyone's attention in the direction of economies of scale, whether that 'leading' be done by our theoretical circles, rural affairs departments, or farmers themselves. Naturally, when conditions are conducive to larger operations, we do not oppose them, whether those are moving toward a 'dual-plot' system of contracting, or to unified operations of farms. Those not only can but should be undertaken, especially in cases of large tracts of newly reclaimed land. These situations apply to a very small number of areas, however. We must not discuss them as though they were on a par with our basic policy of household-based operations. We definitely want to avoid misunderstandings and anxiety among rural cadres at the grassroots level and among farmers.

2. The relationship between farmers and the market

In theory, we have never used 'command-type' [mandatory] plans for the rural areas, and therefore farmers have theoretically never been completely insulated from the market, but in fact our government procurement plans for basic farm products have been mandatory. As a result, the relationship between farmers and the market has been distorted for a long time. After the Third Plenary Session of the 11th Central Committee of the Communist Party of China, incremental reforms of our circulation and pricing systems are gradually bringing farmers into closer touch with the market. Reliable sources estimate that the value of farm products sold independently by farmers was already 60 percent of the total by the end of 1988. Although government procurement prices are usually lower, which skews the above figure, it is undeniable that farmers now have far greater opportunities to sell their products through a 'market,' and can plan their production accordingly.

That remaining 40 percent of farm goods, however, is made up of the basic commodities that are essential to our national economy and everyday life. They include grain, cotton, and oilseed crops. If we cannot apply market mechanisms to these necessary commodities, it will be hard to stimulate 'contracting households' to put more resources into growing those things and it will be hard to increase their supply. Applying market mechanisms, however, will mean that the cost will soon surpass the government's current financial capacity to pay (i.e., the capacity of urban residents to pay). We therefore face a serious dilemma. It is hard for us to resolve our current macroeconomic problems in any fundamental way at the moment, since they are structural. This has led to an inadequate supply of staple crops that is severe. As we say, we have 'an excess of eaters and a shortage of producers.' If the situation continues, it will lead to inestimable consequences. Therefore, despite the considerable difficulties of changing our existing system of procurement and controlled prices, we absolutely must persist in achieving progress on reforms in the near future. We must align farmers with market forces in terms of basic commodities, so as to assure their economic interests.

1. Reform the grain procurement system. In recent years, the quantity of grain sold to urban consumers at subsidized prices has come to around 80 billion jin of grain [40 billion kg]. If you add in other grain supplies that the government must guarantee [for military and so on], food security is threatened if the government does not have direct control over 160 billion jin of grain [80 billion kg]. In recent years, around 30 to 40 billion jin of grain has been sourced on the international market [15 to 20 billion kg]. The rest has been purchased domestically. Generally speaking, there are now two proposals on the table for reform of the grain procurement system.

First: Keep the amount of grain purchased under contracts with farmers at the existing level, which is 100 billion *jin* [i.e., 50 billion kg, which is purchased at lower prices]. This amount would include the so-called public grain that is requisitioned as an agricultural tax. Allow any amount purchased by the government *over* that level to rise to market prices. This proposal would minimize social repercussions of reform of the system, and ensure a smoother transition from the old system to the new. The problem is that it would considerably increase the cost of government subsidies. At a rough estimate, the increased cost to public finance would be RMB 10 billion.

Second: Set the total amount of government procurement at a level of 120 billion *jin* [60 billion kg]. At the same time, institute reform measures to increase taxes, raise prices, and [huan gou? MA check pg 56]. Taking each of these in turn would be as follows. First, with respect to increasing the agricultural tax: Increase the 'public grain' [tax] to 40 billion *jin* [20 billion kg], which would be an increase of 60 percent. Of this amount, the actual grain producers would be responsible for no more than 30 billion *jin,* while the rest would be paid by nonagricultural businesses that carry on operations on rural land. Their contribution would be either in kind or in cash, and the prevailing market price would apply. Second, with respect to increasing prices: Reduce the quantity of grain purchased under 'quota' requirements, but at the same time raise prices on the remaining quantity of grain that is purchased under such contracts. Lower the contracted amount to 40 billion *jin,* or a decrease of 47 percent from the previous quantity under contract. Put the savings on the amount made from the 'public grain' tax toward the higher-priced contracted amount. Doing this will allow us to raise prices by around 30 percent. Third, change our current method of swapping chemical fertilizers for procurement of grain. Consolidate 20 million tons of chemical fertilizer (which accounts for around one-fifth of our total chemical fertilizer sales) and, at a ratio of 1:1, exchange it for 40 billion *jin* of grain while settling out price differentials separately.

We would accomplish three goals through these measures. First, we would change the comparative advantage of growing basic crops in the countryside and allow farmers to reallocate resources in the direction of grain production. Second, we would enable the contracted price for grain to begin to approach market prices and make government procurement behavior begin to simulate a market. Third, we would insulate farmers from inflation by using material goods, namely chemical fertilizers, instead of cash payments for grain. At the same time, we would to a degree resolve our problem of 'losing' a certain percentage of profit to intermediaries in the process of supplying chemical fertilizers. If government needs exceed the limit of 120 billion *jin,* then it should buy at the prevailing market price and contract for that grain through separate negotiations. This entire proposal is tied in to other systemic reforms that are currently underway, and implementing it would be quite difficult. Its virtues are that it would not demand too much more from our budget, and it would help cultivate elements of a new system.

However we proceed with reform of our grain procurement system, and whichever proposal we eventually adopt, two points need to be made clear. First, the government must have control over access to a considerable quantity of grain for some time to come, and this must be explained in no uncertain terms to farmers. This excludes the possibility of fully marketizing our grain procurement system in the near or medium term. Second, any reform of our grain procurement systems must be done in conjunction with reform of how grain is sold. Otherwise, the consequences of distortions in the pricing of grain will be borne solely by the government and farmers, and reform of the entire system of grain procurement will not get very far. In short, the aim of our reform is to enable the government to buy as little grain as possible at distorted prices, and to enable farmers to sell as much grain as possible at market prices. For the near and medium term, our aim is to encourage farmers to reallocate resources in the direction of grain production, by using market-driven forces.

2. Reform the procurement system for cotton and other cash crops. The system needs to move gradually in the direction of setting up several kinds of markets, including auction, wholesale, and a futures market. Certain key cash crops can be and indeed should be subjected to exclusive procurement and sales. Such a system, however, should not insulate farmers entirely from the market. In particular, we need to encourage the development of cotton agents or brokers who would engage in market transactions on behalf of cotton growers. Going through professionals for 'marketized' exchange should help make supply and demand more transparent and reduce the number of intermediaries involved, so as to safeguard farmers' interests.

Agricultural production in our country is dispersed among more than 200 million farming households. Even the most comprehensive plan cannot possibly incorporate all production and circulation activities. One of our major and inescapable tasks, therefore, is to create a more rational connection between farmers and the market. We must enable farmers to enter into the market, and allow supply and demand to help determine their allocation of resources with respect to production.

3. The relationship between farmers and organizations

One of the great feats of our Party was to unite several hundreds of millions of farmers through various levels of grassroots organizations [after 1949]. The 'construction' work of these grassroots organizations over the three decades since the founding of the country have taught us much, both in terms of the failures and the successes. In the most recent 10 years, with the broad implementation of the household contract system, the relationship between farmers and those original grassroots organizations has radically changed. Some of the changes have been beneficial to farmers, and some have not, in fact some have created a degree of mayhem among rural communities. It could be said that the relationship between farmers and organizations has currently reached a critical turning point.

Considering recent socioeconomic progress in rural areas, in point of fact there are two different categories of relationships. One category relates to the old community organizations at the grassroots level, and their relationship to farmers. The original grassroots community organizations incorporated in one entity the functions of both government and enterprise. When the people's communes were abolished, these grassroots community organizations were in a very anomalous position. Their role as 'new' organizations was not clarified in any explicit way, and they also were basically unfunded. As a result, their activities were what could be called irregular. The question has become how to deal with them. The issue is of critical importance to the economic development of rural communities today. Our view is that any answer to that question should first take into account the necessity for social and economic stability. Second, it should foster new rural cooperative economic organizations that are based on a commodity economy. Therefore, we should not be rash in forcefully demanding a complete separation between 'government' and 'enterprise' at the grassroots level. The reality in most of the countryside right now is that grassroots community organizations are able to provide considerably less in the way of technical and economic support to farming households than the governmental functions they provide. One of the most important governmental functions is procuring grain for the government at low cost. Since there is no real alternative to these organizations right now, particularly in that regard, any separation of 'governmental administration' and 'enterprise management' is going to have to be a gradual process.

A more pressing issue at the moment is that we need to make sure there is indeed someone minding affairs at the most basic level in the countryside. This is not just in the government's interests but in the interests of farmers. Without any 'organization,' there is the danger of having an utter vacuum when it comes to such things as procurement of grain, or family planning. There is the danger of not having anyone looking after public security, about which farmers are greatly concerned, or public endeavors that transcend the capacities of a single household such as public projects and agricultural infrastructure. Therefore, in the near or medium term, we must continue to pursue policies that stimulate socioeconomic development, and that stabilize community organizations and the ranks of cadres. At the same time, we must improve democratic procedures that oversee and regulate these organizations and cadres, in order to protect the interests of the community. We must ensure that more of the community revenue is used to provide various economic and technological services for farmers. We must find ways to make sure that community organizations and cadres do actually resolve farmers' pressing social problems. Only if we are successful in this will farmers begin to feel that there is any value in these community organizations.

A second category relates to 'new cooperative economic organizations' and their relationship with farmers. Right now, since more agricultural products are being traded on the market and nonagricultural sectors are also transaction driven, people are already forming new kinds of organizations in the countryside that transcend the boundaries of the former 'communities.' Farmers are voluntarily linking up with other [nonlocal] people in these organizations in the spheres of both production and circulation of goods. This is one of the important starting points for developing true rural cooperative economic organizations. However, existing laws, regulations, and policies do not really relate to them and so they are in a grey area in terms of their legal status. They also lack the preferential treatment that should be accorded to what could be called individual [*ge-ti*] and privately operated [*si-ying*] business. As a result, they have not yet emerged from the status of being loose coalitions under temporary arrangements. Laws need to be formulated as soon as possible with respect to these new rural economic cooperative organizations. They should state explicitly that so long as new economic organizations of farmers meet the following conditions they should be granted explicit status as 'cooperative economic organizations,' and they should enjoy all policy and economic advantages that the government normally accords to cooperative economic organizations. The conditions are: 1. People may join voluntarily or leave freely, as they wish. 2. Management is by democratic decision making, one member, one vote. 3. Dividends on shares should not be the primary way that profits are distributed. 4. Public assets of the organization should be made to grow over time and cannot be divided up [or split off]. These policies should help in building up assets in rural areas. They should also be a motivation to farmers to form cooperative economies [businesses], so as to improve their own economic standing.

In addressing the relationship between farmers and organizations, the focus must be on making sure such organizations provide services, support, and guarantees for farmers. So long as these organizations are not understood purely as entities that can 'manage and control' their members, farmers should not be reluctant to join them or alternatively glad to leave them.

4. The relationship between farmers and employment

By all rights, the term 'farmer' should be an occupation like any other, such as workers, teachers, or doctors. Instead, under the system that we currently employ in our country, the term has become a way to identify a person's social status under the law. A 'farmer' is not legally allowed to take up permanent residence in a city. A 'farmer' is not granted the right to enjoy lower, [government-subsidized] prices on a number of things, including grain, housing, and healthcare. In point of fact, however, many of those called 'farmers' are actually engaged in nonfarming work, indeed some 100 million of them are not 'farming' at all. The way in which 'farmer' came to embody such complexities is the reflection of an extremely complicated phenomenon in China's social and economic life. The causes of this phenomenon, and the many contradictions that it conceals, are too numerous to relate here. One element is well recognized by all, however, and that is that this phenomenon is intimately related to the problem of unemployment in the rural population.

The amount of our country's farmland has consistently been declining since 1957. The number of people living in rural areas has been constantly increasing. A comparison of figures in 1988 and 1961 shows that the rural population increased by 342.76 million in that period, or 62 percent. Per capita arable land decreased by 60 percent. The pressure to find jobs for people on the limited amount of farmland in our country can be deduced from these figures. Right now, our 'farming' population stands at 900 million (the exact number in 1988 was 895.323 million).

Dealing with the employment problems of such a massive number of people is an economic challenge of unique proportions on this globe.

In the 40 years since the founding of our country, both industry and cities have experienced tremendous growth. The new job opportunities that this has generated are not even enough, however, to accommodate the new, nonagricultural, component of so-called farmers, not to mention the increase in numbers of real 'farmers.' How are these people ever going to find jobs? With the amount of farmland decreasing by the day, and the labor force increasing by the moment, we are witnessing the formation of an extremely acute socioeconomic conflict.

The evidence shows that we have not even begun to address this conflict through our past economic development strategies or a whole series of socioeconomic measures. As a result, the problem has simply been growing in the countryside. It has been creating an ever-greater obstacle to realizing the needs of farmers and of rural development. From this perspective, the sudden appearance in recent years of a guerilla force of 'township-and village-enterprises,' and the appearance of millions, indeed tens of millions of farmers going to urban centers in what is described as a 'blind migration,' has profound socioeconomic causes. One cannot simply condemn farmers for not 'following their own proper occupation.' One cannot blame the nonagricultural activities of 'farmers' for competing against State-owned industries for raw materials, energy resources, and markets. These are in fact actions taken out of desperation given the intense pressure people are facing. The employment 'framework' that 1 billion *mu* of farmland can provide has long since been inadequate to a population that is relying on farmland as a source of employment, a population that has, in the meantime, doubled.

We must admit that the employment of farmers is something that was simply overlooked for a long time. Moreover, when the problem had reached a certain level, we must also admit that farmers themselves took it into their hands to find solutions in a very 'unplanned' manner, solutions that lay in the realm of nonagricultural business. At that point, when farmers began flowing into cities, we again did not undertake even the most basic economic and social preparations. In 1989, the number of farmers employed by township enterprises fell for the first time, and there was a great reverse migration of 'farmers' who were already in cities going back to rural areas. Although this was connected to the short-term effect of policies to 'restore order and rectify the situation,' this also indicated that the employment crisis among farmers had intensified. By now, the situation presents a very serious threat to the stability of our society. [Note: the literal translation would be: It presents an extremely unfavorable negative factor in terms of seeking social stability.]

It is important to note that agriculture per se is not what is going to be providing jobs in the future. New industries that rely on agriculture, service industries, the constantly evolving science and technology that derive from agricultural development, these are what are going to provide the jobs. Farmers are being highly rational, therefore, in seeking other forms of employment in recent years. They are also very much in alignment with the laws of socioeconomic development. Continuing to tackle 'farmers' employment' as though it were a 'farming' question will deprive us of enormous potential opportunities, not just for rural residents but for the country as a whole.

No fundamental resolution of the problem is possible in the short term, but if we are not truly aware of the magnitude of the problem, and if we don't begin to address it with an overall plan, we may find that we are too late even in the long run. In a certain sense, this problem of farmers' employment is the core issue in the relationship between the Party as it stands today and farmers. It is a core issue between the government and farmers. Resolving employment is the key issue in rural development. It has to be approached from the perspective of unifying our urban and rural socioeconomic development plans and industrial structures. It must be recognized that major adjustments will be necessary in our economic development strategy. If we do not undertake these, finding solutions to the employment problem is going to be hard.

Although employment is undeniably a huge issue, at the same time it can provide a strong impetus for economic growth if handled correctly. So long as we make the proper distinctions between 'farming' and 'farmers' and evaluate rural issues in the right light, and so long as we integrate those issues in organic fashion into our overall socioeconomic development plans, we should be able to move toward incremental solutions.

Ten years ago, when the Great Reform of our rural areas was just beginning in the course of China's economic restructuring [1978], a person who had long been responsible for ideological work in the Party noted the following.

'China has a population of one billion people. Among them, 800 million are farmers living in the countryside. If rural affairs are poorly handled, China's affairs cannot go well. If farmers are impoverished, China cannot become rich. If farming remains as it was in ancient times, there is no way China is going to become a modern nation.'

Spoken 10 years ago, this statement expressed recognition of the central importance of farmers and rural issues. It suggested that the very reason for the Great Reform of our rural areas was an understanding that proper treatment of farmers is crucial. Now one decade has passed and we are again experiencing a downturn in agriculture. Once again, the solutions lie in adjusting relations with farmers. As Mao Zedong himself said 28 years ago, 'This country of ours, China – you can forget about getting anything done if you don't include the farmers!

Notes

* This article was originally published in Li Guodu, ed., *Development Research Bulletin (1986–1989)*, Last Volume, Beijing Normal School Publishing House, 1990.
1 National Bureau of Statistics, *China Statistical Yearbook 1989,* China Statistics Publishing House, 1989, p. 719, pp. 709–710.
2 Household Division of the Rural Survey Team, National Bureau of Statistics, 'Initial Analysis of the Impact of Price Changes on Farmers' Income,' *Economic Research Journal,* Issue 9, 1989.
3 National Bureau of Statistics, *China Statistical Yearbook 1989,* China Statistics Publishing House, 1989, p. 721.

4 Ibid., p. 45.
5 Ibid., p. 101.
6 Ibid., p. 192.
7 Ibid., p. 721.
8 Ibid., p. 720.
9 Ibid., p. 721.
10 Ibid., p. 101.
11 Ibid., p. 87.
12 Ibid., p. 716.
13 Ibid., p. 706.
14 Ibid., p. 657.
15 Ibid., p. 113, p. 116.
16 Ibid., p. 657, p. 673.
17 'A Multitude of Subsidies in China,' *Wen Wei Po*, July 16, 1989, p. 4.
18 National Bureau of Statistics, *China Statistical Yearbook 1989*, China Statistics Publishing House, 1989, p. 683.
19 Ibid., p. 29.
20 Ibid., p. 657.
21 Ibid., p. 116, p. 487.
22 Household Division of the Rural Survey Team, National Bureau of Statistics, 'Initial Analysis of the Impact of Price Changes on Farmers' Income,' *Economic Research Journal*, Issue 9, 1989.
23 National Bureau of Statistics, *China Statistical Yearbook 1989*, China Statistics Publishing House, 1989, p. 657.
24 Wei Jie, 'Impact of Fast Growing Consumer Demands on Reform and Development,' *Economic Daily*, November 14, 1989.
25 'A Multitude of Subsidies in China,' *Wen Wei Po*, July 16, 1989, p. 4.
26 National Bureau of Statistics, *China Statistical Yearbook 1989*, China Statistics Publishing House, 1989, p. 669.
27 Ibid., p. 706.
28 Ibid., p. 47.
29 Ibid., p. 101.
30 Ibid., p. 87.
31 World Bank, *World Development Report 1989*, China Financial & Economic Publishing House, 1989.
32 National Statistics Bureau, *Progress in Four Decades*, China Statistics Publishing House, 1989, p. 350, p. 352.
33 National Bureau of Statistics, *China Statistical Yearbook 1989*, China Statistics Publishing House, 1989, p. 669.
34 *Pang Xianzhi, Mao Zedong and His Secretary Tian Jiaying, Central Party Literature Press, 1989.*
35 Ibid.
36 *Economic Encyclopedia: Agriculture*, Shanghai Lexicographical Publishing House and China Agriculture Press, 1983.
37 Pang Xianzhi, *Mao Zedong and His Secretary Tian Jiaying*, Central Party Literature Press, 1989.

3 New problems facing rural reform and development in the 1990s*

(1992)

'Rural reform and development' is facing issues in the 1990s that have broad rami-fications for our economy in general. The problems are therefore going to have to be approached in the context of the overall economic situation. Most will not find solutions in the short term, but we need to address them now, and with a very clear-minded appreciation for their importance. If we want to ensure smooth develop-ment of the rural economy for the rest of the 1990s and into the next century, we need to adopt policies now that are effective in resolving the issues incrementally. Four main aspects of the problems we face are summarized below.

I. The first aspect relates to how to maintain an ongoing increase in the income of farmers

Farmers' per capita net income has grown dramatically since reforms first began. Between 1979 and 1988, per capita net income of farmers in real terms (inflation-adjusted net income) increased at an annual average rate of 11.8 percent, which was quite high. In recent years, however, the situation has changed considerably, as shown most notably in the way agricultural production has gone up but farmers' incomes have either not continued to rise or have actually fallen. This anomaly has resulted in overall stagnation in the real income of farmers.

Over the last seven years, between 1985 and today, we can recognize two dis-tinct periods in terms of the relationship between increases in agricultural output and changes in farmers' income. In the four years between 1985 and 1988, agricul-ture underperformed, especially in terms of crop farming, yet farmers' net incomes rose in real terms year after year. This can be attributed to rapid restructuring of rural industrial production (43.4 million farm workers shifted into nonagricultural work, accounting for 65 percent of the shift in labor force for the entire period between 1979 and 1991), and it can be attributed as well to favorable conditions for trade in agricultural products.

The situation was precisely the opposite, however, in 1989 and 1990. In 1989, gross grain output hit a record high, up by 3.4 percent over the previous year, yet farmers' per capita real net income dropped by 1.6 percent, which represented the first drop since the start of reforms. The year 1990 saw bumper crops of grains, cotton, and edible oils. Sales of those products grew by 15.3 percent, 23.7 percent, and 23.5 percent, respectively, over the previous year. Yet farmers' per capita real net income increased by only 1.8 percent in 1990, out of all proportion to the rise in agricultural output. Moreover, the situation of farmers showed a sharp contrast with that of urban residents. Even as the economic situation declined in 1989 and 1990, with marked declines in results, the consumption component of urban incomes increased by 5.2 percent. In 1991, farmers' per capita real net income grew by only 2 percent, while per capita actual living expenses of urban residents increased by 7.7 percent. This sharp contrast shows that it has been farmers who have the paid the price of the economic consequences of our 'control and rectification' policies after 1989. It also tells us that the distribution of national income is not conducive to protecting the economic interests of agriculture and farmers. If we do not turn this around right away, it will undoubtedly have an impact on farmers' enthusiasm to produce agricultural products. Allowed to carry on, it will eventually have negative consequences for a balanced and steady development of the national economy.

The fact that improvement in farmers' income has come to a halt has the following consequences.

First, it directly holds down any improvement in the level of their consumption. In 1989, actual living expenses declined by 1.3 percent over the previous year and in 1990 they declined by 0.5 percent over 1989. This pulled the gap between farmer and urban incomes even wider. In 1979, the 'level of consumption ratio' of rural and urban inhabitants was 1 to 2.9 [urban residents consumed 2.9 times the amount that rural residents consumed]. This declined in the course of reforms, to 1 to 2.2 in 1985, but in 1989 and 1990, it went back up to 1 to 2.8. It should be said that this is not merely an economic issue. It has serious implications for social stability and is highly unfavorable for what we refer to as 'consolidating the alliance between workers and farmers.'

The second consequence is that it prevents farmers from investing more into production. Total retail sales of the agricultural 'means of production' increased by only 2.2 percent in 1990, as opposed to 13.5 percent in 1989. The growth of farmers' investment in production in 1990 was negligible, which is clearly going to impact agriculture over the next few years.

Third, it keeps farmers' purchasing power from growing, forcing a decline in the percentage of retail sales sold to rural areas and therefore leading to an overall contraction in the market. In 1989, retail sales to rural areas fell by 0.4 percent over 1988, and in 1990 they fell by 1.4 percent over 1989. They now hold only 55 percent of total retail sales, down 4.2 percent from a high in 1984. In 1990, total retail sales of 'social commodities' came to RMB 830 billion, so each percentage point represented RMB 8.3 billion. A decline of 1.8 percentage points in purchases therefore represented a decline of RMB 14.94 billion in the market. A drop of 4.2 percentage points represented a decline of RMB 34.86 billion. Given that, it is fair to say that the softness in the market for industrial products over the past two years, quite apart from issues of the kinds and quality of products, can mainly be attributed to a decline in farmers' purchasing power and the total sales volume in rural areas.

Seen from this perspective, the issue of farmers' income is not a stand-alone problem. It impacts the whole economy. The problem has been caused mainly by an irrational price relationship between agricultural and industrial products. It clearly has not come about because of any decline in the rural economy. In the way our economic system currently functions, the exchange of goods is not simply one of exchanging the goods themselves, but incorporates the [policy] functions of transferring and allocating income. In the past two years, the terms of trade for agricultural products deteriorated as farm prices fell dramatically. This was an outstanding reason for the halt in any increase in farmers' incomes. In 1989, the procurement price index for agricultural and sideline products was 3.8 percentage points lower than the rural retail price index in 1989. In 1990, the overall agricultural price index was negative over the previous year, and was lower than the rural retail price index by 5.8 percent. As a result, farmers' real income fell by RMB 28.2 billion in 1989 and by RMB 24.1 billion in 1990.

Farmers have long been in an unfavorable position with respect to their share of national income, but the problem has become more acute, given the situation over the past two years. In point of fact, what we have is a persistent problem that has never been adequately resolved. Between 1953 and 1990, urban incomes rose by an annual average of 3.6 percent. Over the same period, farmers' incomes rose on average 3.2 percent. Between 1985 and 1990, urban incomes rose an average of 5.5 percent per year, while farmers' income rose an average of 4.0 percent per year. That is not leading us in the direction of 'closing the gap,' as we like to think. Looking at the overall picture, in 1990, agricultural labor was 60.2 percent of the national total, but only created 34.7 percent of national income. Our rural population accounted for 78.4 percent of the total, but took in only 57.9 percent of allocated 'national income for consumption.' Realized purchasing power in rural areas came to only 55 percent of total retail sales of 'social commodities' (48.7 percent if one takes out the share held by the agricultural means of production). Naturally, low labor productivity in rural areas plays a role in this situation. At the end of the day, however, this unequal allocation of national income keeps farmers from accumulating funds for investment, it keeps down their incomes, and it keeps us from expanding our domestic market for industrial products.

We must adopt effective measures that change this unequal allocation of national income. We must adjust the relative prices for farm products and industrial goods, but at the same time we are constrained by certain factors. Those include national financial strength, the capacity of citizens and enterprises to absorb change, and also international commodity prices. As a result, we should not have unrealistic expectations. How are we ever to arrive at a rational pattern of income allocation? Clearly, it will not be enough just to make 'adjustments' to the already-formed pattern of income distribution. The important thing will be to focus on the means of production. As Marx said: 'distribution starts with distribution of the means of production.' The solution can only be to provide farmers with a diversified range of means of production, and to give them employment alternatives beyond just tilling the land. The number of work days that has to go into agricultural production is not in fact such a small figure, even for grain production which, relatively speaking, is less profitable. The problem is that the number of effective work days that farmers can invest in agriculture is constrained by available resources. Developing agriculture that is oriented toward quality and efficiency, in response to changing demand structures, will increasingly require capital-intensive and technology-intensive farming. That will require providing farmers with more factors of production. That will mean lowering the total number of agricultural jobs and enabling more people who are currently 'farmers' to shift over to newly created employment positions, in order to create new kinds of wealth. If we do not in fact undertake this process, we will find that it is hard to make the economic pie much bigger, and it will be hard to readjust income distribution in any meaningful way.

Three consecutive years of a lack of any growth in the income of farmers shows that the rural economy is standing at an inflection point. We have only two ways to break through the knot [and decide which way to go]: One is to develop highly efficient agriculture by adjusting the structure of types or 'qualities' of agricultural goods. The second is to increase farmers' employment opportunities through non-agricultural sectors. The prerequisite for both of these is to change how resources are allocated between rural and urban areas.

II. The second aspect relates to selecting the right model for rural economic development

Since reforms began, but particularly since 1984, the emergence of township enterprises [Town-and-Village Enterprises or TVE in development literature] has given people great hope for an overall improvement in the rural economy. Given that these enterprises are already playing a tremendously positive role, people have quite unconsciously begun to recognize their key role in rural economic development. Such people include cadres engaged in rural affairs, and farmers themselves. There is a general consensus that we must put all effort into developing these enterprises and we feel that this is all quite right and proper.

However, there is also another side to the problem. Township enterprises mainly engage in industrial production. In 1990, 'industrial output' accounted for 74 percent of the 'total output' of these enterprises, so developing township enterprises means developing industry. This involves changes in our industrial structure and its location throughout the country, which therefore relates to our long-term development model. One fact that should be noted is the incredibly fast rate at which output of these township enterprises is increasing relative to the country's total industrial output. In 1979, township enterprises accounted for 9.1 percent of the value of gross national industrial output. By 1984, that figure went to 16.3 percent, and then to 29.7 percent in 1990. At this rate, the share is expected to reach 50 percent by the end of this century. That is to say, by the end of this century, roughly half of all our industrial production will be deriving from production in rural areas.

This naturally has its positive aspects, but other aspects should not be overlooked in the process. The most prominent is that our industrial structure will move strongly in the direction of light industry.

An analysis of the 1990 output of township enterprises shows that 84.7 percent of the industrial output value of township enterprises was created by processing industries, and only 15.3 percent by mining and raw and semifinished-materials industries. Clearly, this structure is moving in the direction of light industry. In addition, due to limited investment, township enterprises tend to be relatively small scale and dispersed. A large country cannot, however, afford to be overly reliant on light industry in its industrial structure. The reason is that the primary market for goods in large countries tends to be domestic. Reliance on international trade is relatively lower in large countries [than it is in smaller countries]. If we move toward an excess of light industry in our industrial structure, we may be forced to rely excessively on the international market for energy and raw materials. First, that will make it hard for us to maintain equilibrium in our balance of payments. Second, it will expose us to the volatility and attendant risk of international commodity prices. Objectively speaking, it is rational for a large country like China to keep a more optimum ratio between light and heavy industry. We should also remember that if we do not in fact rely on international markets for raw materials, the bottlenecks in domestic supply of energy and raw materials to township enterprises will get worse by the day. That not only will affect efficient production but will constrain the growth of township enterprises altogether.

A second issue is the whole relationship between industrialization and urbanization. In essence, the impetus for our industrialization has involved a process by which land rents are transformed into industrial capital. In this process, the capital accumulates where it can be maximized, hence leading to urbanization. The development of township enterprises is also a process whereby land rents are turned into industrial capital with the difference being that the accumulation of such capital stays in place and is therefore dispersed. Other than in a few places, the process does not lead to urbanization. As a result, the development of township industries has undeniably stimulated our country's further industrialization but it has also exacerbated the contradiction in our unique situation of having urbanization lag behind industrialization. As this contradiction grows even larger, it will lead to a loss of the economies of scale that generally accompany concentration of industries. It will, in particular, hold back the growth of tertiary industries, and with them the increase in employment opportunities.

The prerequisite for growing tertiary industries is that there be a customer base for the services that is sufficiently concentrated. Instead, employment has been declining in our township enterprises, from a high in 1988 of 95.455 million, to ongoing declines in 1989 and 1990. Naturally, this is related to the overall context of our policies regarding 'control and rectification,' but it also indicates that focusing solely on industrialization and not a concurrent growth in services will not lead to higher employment. In fact, that capacity to absorb employment will gradually decline.

Division of labor and operations, and a shift of labor away from agriculture, is necessary for any kind of rural development. The fact that farmers want to create township enterprises is not the direct and sole cause of our problems of industrial structure or inadequate urbanization. But neither can we imagine that we have found the panacea to rural development in the development of township enterprises. We should think again if we believe that township enterprises are going to solve farmers' employment and income problems in any ultimate way.

The most important goal of township enterprises is to provide employment for and increase income of farmers. In order to achieve this, however, is it absolutely necessary for factories to be located in rural areas? Only 32.3 percent of the output value of township enterprises comes from agricultural raw materials, so why are factories located in the countryside? The most important reason, among many, relates to the 'status' or the legal standing of a person defined as a 'farmer.' This is an increasingly problematic constraint.

By all rights, the term 'farmer' should be an occupation like any other, such as 'worker,' 'teacher,' or 'doctor.' Instead, under the system that we currently employ in our country, the term has become a way to identify a person's social status or legal 'identity' under the law. A 'farmer' is not legally allowed to take up permanent residence in a city. Right now, there are roughly 100 million laborers working in nonagricultural jobs in township enterprises. There is also a very large number of 'farmers' employed in jobs that have nothing to do with farming in cities. Despite this, these people are still referred to as 'farmers' and treated as having 'farmer' identities under our regulations; clearly, their jobs can change but not their 'status.' This system of managing a rural population may once have been necessary in the course of our nation's history. No matter what one might say in defense of it, however, by now it has deprived our rural population of far too many opportunities. In addition, our inadequate level of urbanization is also closely related to this system of managing people through managing their legal 'identities.'

As the disadvantages of being overly dispersed have long since been apparent, many township enterprises have spontaneously begun to develop industrial parks and 'development zones' in towns and villages. Many 'cities' are springing up that are made up of people with 'farmer' status. We believe that all these efforts will be ever more successful as reform of our urban welfare system proceeds.

Do the urbanization of township enterprises and the broadening of our policy to ask industry to help subsidize agriculture absolutely have to be gradual? Whether they are or not, they are in line with objective reality and social progress. Our reform measures should 'go with the flow.' Only then will we be able to use our very limited resources to greater effect.

III. The change in rural property relationships and the status of the household contract system

The system that contracts production to the household level and links remuneration to output has changed the entire way the rural system operates. In addition, it has led to a change in the relationship between assets and people living in rural areas.

We generally give three reasons for saying that this 'household contract system' is still 'socialist' in nature. They are first, that the land that is being farmed by households still belongs to the public as represented by the collective. Second, that the principle of distribution according to labor is still thoroughly respected, and if you work more, you get more. Third, that the whole concept of household operations is an 'operating level' within the scope of the economy of the collective.

If you look into the realities behind the above three considerations, however, you soon find that the situation is not at all that simple. At least two issues of 'theory' call for further study.

The first is that although the household contract system has not in theory changed the underlying ownership of the land, the method of 'occupancy' or 'possession' of the land has changed. This brings with it a new complication. That is, collective 'ownership' of the land conflicts with what is mostly private product coming off the land, under a dispersed or decentralized system of operations. This means that the 'means of production' is increasingly being held by private households even if the land is ostensibly held by the collective.

Under the household contract system, although the nature of 'ownership rights' to land has not changed, the 'possession' rights and 'operating' [or usage] rights to land have indeed changed in substance. By taking on contracts, farmers individually operate and 'possess' publicly held land as owned by the collective. Although the contracts can be adjusted from time to time, farmers have individually gained the right to possess and operate collectively owned land in an independent way. The formation of this right not only leads to changes in the internal economic system of the collective, but to a degree it leads to changes in the relationship of assets to people. The reasons are as follows.

1   Although rural households do not 'own' the land they are contracting, they own most of the products that are produced from the land. Once certain quotas are deducted from total production for both the State and the collective, the rest is owned by the household. This is precisely the purpose of the system: to provide incentives by allowing people to gain more of the results of their own labor.

2   Once 'farmers' have submitted the required amounts to both the State and the collective, they are allowed to keep the rest and that excess amount is obviously not going to be all for their own personal consumption. They use it to build up their own private 'means of production,' since farmers are both consumers but also producers. Therefore, they are using what is a publicly owned asset to create privately owned products. In the course of that process, some of the means of production become privately owned. Under the household contract system, it is inevitable that 'public' ownership of the means of production gradually evolves into 'private' ownership of the means of production, and it is also inevitable that the privately owned component gradually increases as production goes on. The works of Marx and Engels describe this process in terms of the agricultural communities in ancient times, when private property gradually grew out of publicly owned land.

According to a random-sample survey conducted by the rural investigation team of the National Bureau of Statistics on a sample of 67,000 households, at the end of 1990, each household 'owned' fixed assets used in production that were valued at an average of RMB 1258.06. At the end of 1990, our country had a total of 222.372

million rural households nationwide. Based on the survey figure for average fixed assets per household, total privately owned fixed assets in the country came to a value of RMB 297.957 billion. Compared to five years earlier, this represented an increase of 58.74 percent, or an annual average increase of 9.68 percent, that is, in 'fixed assets used in production per rural household.' The gross value of fixed assets altogether, owned privately by households, grew by 85.04 percent in five years, at an annual rate of 13.10 percent.

These figures demonstrate the very considerable degree to which rural households have been able to amass assets over the past 10 or so years under the system of household contracts. The underlying land continues to be owned by the public as represented by collectives, but privately owned fixed assets are quite substantial, whether in terms of the aggregate amount or the rate of increase. A system of independent 'possession' and 'operating' of land that is publicly owned is allowing that public asset to become the 'wellsprings' of private assets. Moreover, as soon as any producer has earned himself private assets, these will be put to work earning profits through various means. It stands to reason that the yield should be no less than what can be derived from putting earnings in the bank at a long-term deposit rate. The result is that the vaunted principle of 'distribution according to labor' has to give way, to the extent that further returns are actually made off capital.

This first contradiction in our theory leads directly to a second contradiction that can be described by posing the question: 'Are rural households operating solely as units within the collective economy, or have they actually become relatively independent economic entities unto themselves?' Clearly, any analysis has to take the collective into account and not just the individual household. It has to evaluate changes in how collectives themselves conduct 'unified operations.'

It is relatively easier to recognize the changes in terms of rural households. When the former system of 'contracting production to the household' [*bao chan dao hu*] was replaced with the new system of 'contracting all decisions to the household' [*bao gan dao hu*], this was definitely not simply a matter of changing the method of contracting. The essence of the matter was that it altered the accounting unit. Under the former system, the household was to carry out production *according to the collective's plans.* Although the household might be entitled to additional investment and differential land rent, the collective organization was still the economic accounting unit for agricultural production of the entity as a whole. Although the rural household performed certain accounting functions (e.g., accounting for additional investment and any economic results that exceeded the mandated quota), it did not constitute a complete and independent accounting unit. In contrast, under the latter system, 'contracting all decisions to the household,' all product that resulted from a household's labor off contracted land belonged to it personally, after the necessary deductions had been made for the State and the collective. Economically, such 'production results' included what paid for the household's living expenses, its costs for engaging in direct production but also any funds reserved for secondary production. After this change, the collective no longer bore responsibility for allocating consumer goods to the household. Moreover, both operating costs and funding additional fixed assets for further production now became economic functions the household was to cover. From this perspective, one could well say that, at least in the sphere of crop farming, the collective was no longer the economic accounting unit, while the rural household had become a relatively independent and self-contained operating and accounting unit. As a result, a rural household family could no longer be thought of merely as an 'operating level' within the collective as primary entity, but instead had grown into a full-blown 'economic entity' itself. At this point, the concept of a 'rural-household economy' had taken real shape.

The above analysis addresses how property relationships changed in rural areas once the system of 'contracting production to the household' was changed to 'contracting all decisions to the household.' It notes how this change led to a transformation in the economic status of rural households. Obviously, the key to understanding this change is in recognizing that 'ownership rights' to most product derived from land now belonged to the household. We must therefore take this objective reality into full consideration in attempting to improve our policies for rural economic development.

IV. Toward a more correct understanding of the relationships among rural-household economies, cooperative economies, and collective economies

Our purpose is to strengthen and develop the 'socialist collective economy' in rural areas. This is the direction of our rural economic reform and one from which we will not deviate. Given the realities of rural economies, however, how precisely are we to achieve that purpose? How are we to strengthen the 'collective economy'? In addition to being a question with respect to 'theory,' it is a very practical matter. At the very least, we are confronted with two very real issues. One is how to deal with the newly acquired and constantly increasing 'means of production' that is privately held by people in rural areas, specifically, how to do that in a way that does not cut their motivation to produce yet still is beneficial to the strength of the collective's economy. The second relates to the fact that there is very little left in the 'collective economy' in many places once production is contracted to households. The collective is therefore no longer able to transfer resources on the basis of 'leveling things out without discrimination' [so-called *ping diao*]. Nor can it rely any more on uncompensated assistance from the State. Under such a situation, how is the collective going to produce any new collectively owned assets?

Underlying these two practical issues is a profound theoretical issue, namely, the nature of the relationship among the rural household economy, the cooperative economy, and the collective economy. This theoretical issue can be approached from two different angles. One is how cooperative economies and collective economies are to be distinguished from one another and how they are related to one another. The second is the route or process by which rural household economies can ultimately be absorbed into collective economies. Each of these is discussed below.

First, with regard to differentiating 'cooperative' and 'collective' economies, and understanding how they are related.

The longstanding mainstream point of view among economic theorists in our country has been that cooperative economies are themselves collective economies under a socialist system. I believe that this is not entirely in accord with the original intent of the authors of Marxist classics.

As we all know, cooperative economies were already in existence before the creation of Marxist-Leninist theory. They had come about as a competitive response to large-scale capital, as smaller dispersed operations organized into cooperatives or 'joint operations' so as to avoid the exploitation of middlemen and the difficulty of competing directly with large-scale capital. As commodity economies developed under capitalist systems, such cooperative economies formed to protect their own interests. Therefore, the prerequisite for the formation of cooperative economies was a commodity economy.

Cooperative-economy systems vary around the world, with each country having its own particular characteristics, but the underlying basic principles of cooperation are broadly recognized as being the same. The most important among these are the following. First, entry and exit from the cooperative is voluntary. Second, a democratic management system is applied that features one person, one vote. Third, the primary means of distribution is not via dividends on shares. Fourth, in the course of joint operations, the gradual accumulation of results is indivisible and becomes commonly held property of the entire body.

Obviously, these principles embody some features of a private ownership system. For example, they allow for private ownership of assets by those who enter into the cooperative, and they allow for a certain degree of authority to distribute assets. Nonetheless, the reason Marx and Engels espoused a cooperative system as the path for reforming small-time agriculture was not that they had not discerned the private-economy aspects of the system. It was not even that they felt that elements intrinsic to cooperative systems could directly transform into socialism (such as the democratic management, the restrictions on dividend distribution, the collective ownership of accumulated assets, and so on). Rather, it was that they felt that this kind of economic structure was helpful in changing the psychology and traditional ways of small-time producers and enabling them to adapt to more socialized large-scale production. It allowed them gradually to accept a socialist mode of production. This is why Engels noted, 'in the transition towards a completely communist economy, we must broadly adopt cooperative production as an intermediary link. Marx and I have never had any doubt about this.' Obviously, Marx and Engels did not believe that cooperative economies were intrinsically already completely socialist in nature. Otherwise, they would never have called them an 'intermediary link,' and instead would have described them as the final achievement in transforming small-scale farming. Cooperative economies cannot, therefore, be equated to collective economies that feature public ownership of the means of production. Mao Zedong was explicit about this himself in the work called *Get Organized.* He said, 'The only route to achieving collectivization, as according to Engels, is through cooperatives.' It is obvious that cooperative economies are merely a necessary step along the way to collective economies.

In terms of actual practice as well, cooperative and collective economies truly are distinguishable.

First, the cooperative allows members to enjoy private ownership of the shares representing assets and to a certain degree allows them the right to gain distribution [or income] from those privately owned assets. If this were not the case, it would be hard to attract farmers and get them to join voluntarily and it would certainly not be possible to allow them to withdraw voluntarily. In contrast, collective economies intrinsically do not allow for privately owned assets or the right to have distributions based on participation. Second, the cooperative economy, as an 'intermediate link' in transforming small-time farming, takes the elimination of private ownership by farmers as its ultimate goal. In contrast, both in the Soviet Union and in our own country's practical experience over these years, eliminating private ownership among farmers was the starting point for the collective economy. From this distinction alone, we can see that a collective economy will result from the ongoing development of collective economies under socialist conditions. Cooperative and collective economies clearly are not at the same stage of development and they are quite different in their 'nature.'

Confusing the two, and treating them indiscriminately both in terms of our policies and our theory, is harmful to our 'guidance' when it comes to actual practice.

The Party's Sixth Plenary Session of the 11th [Central Committee] [December 18–22, 1978] passed the *Resolution* called 'On The Resolution of Various Historic Issues to Do with the Party Since the Establishment of the Country.' This stated:

> 'After the summer of 1955, the "cooperativization" of agriculture was too rushed, as well as the demand that we transform industry and individual commerce [*ge-ti*]. The work was done too crudely, the change was too fast. Forms that the work took were too simplified and indiscriminate, without allowing for diverse situations. That left us with a long-standing legacy of problems.'

In my opinion, one of the extremely important causes of this deviation was that we soon turned the 'cooperativization' of agriculture into the 'collectivization' of agriculture.

Second, with regard to the question of how to grow a strong collective economy without damaging the interests of farmers. It should be noted that it will be easier to address the principles of this issue once we clarify the differences as well as the links between collective and cooperative economies. That is, with respect to private ownership of farmers, we cannot adopt any 'forms' that are exploitative. Instead, we can only adopt methods that are cooperative and that promote joint operations. On this basis, we can gradually accumulate public assets that belong to the collective and are indivisible.

Cooperative economies play a transformative role in helping small-time farmers in two respects, both of which are incremental processes. First is the jointly operated nature of the economies, which can help farmers gradually move away from the old traditional psychology [of independent operations] and allow them to adapt gradually to large-scale socialized production. Second, in the course of joint operations, indivisible public property can be accumulated and, as the strength of the collective economy expands, private factors will gradually diminish. Naturally, this whole process will take a very considerable length of time, but there is no better alternative.

When we speak of 'using cooperative systems,' in essence what we mean is a twofold proposition: allowing farming households to enter into cooperatives in which their own property is still regarded as 'private,' and allowing farming households to enter into cooperatives in which they enjoy a certain right to distribution of assets [i.e., to earn returns from the cooperative's assets]. The aim is to guide farmers in the direction of transition to a collective economy; it is absolutely not to enable consolidation of small-time private ownership. If we do not adopt this approach, and indeed if there is no cooperative economy at all, we will be even further from ever realizing a collective economy.

With a system of contracting production to the household and linking remuneration to output, farming households once again have the opportunity to increase the 'means of production' that they themselves own personally. At the end of the day, this system is required by the objective conditions of our country, that is, our current stage of productive forces, but it also in fact is very helpful in developing our rural economy. Therefore, our attitude toward this system must be consistent with the objective law that the relations of production must be in accord with the development of productive forces. The amount of damage to our rural productive forces will be hard to imagine if we fail to deal properly with the relationship between farmers' private property and the growth of the collective economy.

A group of collective economies in our country's rural areas has indeed developed very well and serve as model examples. Around 7,000 'production brigades' are still operating in the original mold, according to surveys, a number that represents 0.94 percent of the total number of 'units' at the village level of government. It should be said that rural people in these areas are highly supportive of these collective economies. However, two considerations should be taken into account. One is that these areas are also generally highly developed in terms of 'township enterprises,' and therefore enjoy the gains of industry as a way of supplementing agricultural production. This comes from the relatively strong financial support of the various collectives, which is put either into township enterprises or such things as resource development in mining, forestry, or water-grown products. Second, given the advanced state of their enterprises, many of these places have to import labor from elsewhere, and in terms of income distribution are in fact not able to compensate on an equal basis. The economic surplus of these places is therefore partially drawn from external labor as a way to 'supplement agriculture with industrial development.' As we evaluate the current viability of collective economies, we have to wonder just how many places can be similarly successful in adopting this model. Naturally, we should support and encourage those collective economies that are doing well. At the same time, in approaching the larger issue of rural economic development, we must recognize that 1 percent of areas may be doing well but we must deal also with the other 99 percent. We must put greater efforts into assuring that the great majority of rural areas develops and strengthens the collective economy.

Only by focusing on the larger issues can we assure that our basic policies with respect to rural areas are in accord with the interests and the hopes of 900 million rural inhabitants.

Note

* The article was published in the fifth issue of *Chinese Rural Economy* in 1992.

4 Bringing about a gradual modernization of agriculture through management that is based on the household-contracting system*

(1998)

One of the greatest achievements of our rural reform has been the elimination of the system of people's communes that focused on both 'size,' and the greatest degree of 'public ownership,' as epitomized by the phrase 'first: big, second: public.' That achievement helped rid agriculture of a highly centralized form of management. Based on the widespread adoption of the household-contracting system, we now have a two-tiered management system that combines the 'dispersed' [or decentralized] and the 'centralized.' The results over the past 20 years of this new system have been apparent to all. The Central Committee of the Party has long since explicitly declared that the new structure represents a 'basic system' that will be maintained for a long time to come as an organizational form in our country's township-and-village collective economies. The Party has made it clear that there should be no doubt in anyone's mind about its being changed.

Everyone has long since come to recognize the necessity of implementing the household-contracting system of management, given our existing level of productive forces in agriculture. However, people continue to hold different opinions on the extent to which our agriculture can be modernized under the system of household contracting. Whether or not agriculture can modernize under such a system should, by all rights, not be in question. Essentially all countries that have modernized their agriculture have employed a system by which households manage agriculture – there is virtually no exception. The reason some of our cadres have doubts about whether or not we can follow in the same path is that our country has such a huge population on such a small amount of land, which necessarily results in extremely small-scale farming.

These doubts are not so unreasonable. Nonetheless, we should recognize that the small scale of agriculture in our country is not due to agriculture itself but rather to the underdeveloped state of our secondary and tertiary industries and to the fact that we are not highly urbanized. This means that a great deal of surplus labor has not been able to move off the land. Without moving that labor into alternative employment, we will have the same tiny per capita amount of land even if we consolidate it and manage it collectively. With the same logic, if we are able to move agricultural labor into other employment, per capita amounts of land being farmed under a household contracting system will increase – this fact is not disputed. We therefore return to the starting point of the issue: Can agriculture modernize under our household-contracting system? Will we in fact be able to maintain a stable and unchanging policy over a long period of time, that is, continue to have a two-layered structure with both dispersed operations and unified management?

To answer these questions accurately, we must first clarify the issue of why household operations must remain the basis for agriculture. Generally speaking, given our current stage of development in agriculture, we are at a low level of productivity with backward means of production, and recognizing this is simply in accord with reality. Breaking out of the constraints of the commune system gave incentives to farmers to be more proactive in production methods and to raise productivity. This was yet another demonstration of the universal principle that the relations of production must be in alignment with the means of production.

However, believing that we should carry out household operations merely because of this universal principle would be a mistake, since other factors are also at work. After all, highly modernized agriculture in developed countries is also generally carried on through household operations. We should not regard our own household operations as a unique feature of the results of our own economic reforms. A glance at agriculture through history, both here and abroad, shows that in fact household operations have been a kind of pervasive global phenomenon. It is not hard to see that in fact the way in which agriculture is conducted relates to the particular nature of the industry.

With regard to that particular nature, the classical works of Marxist writings focus on two main points. First, agriculture is a process that combines economic production with nature's production. Second, the timeframe in which farming is carried out differs from the normal timeframe of normal 'labor.' This dictates the unique forms and management processes required for agriculture. First, decision makers in agriculture are also those directly engaged in production. Unlike in other industries, agricultural decision makers must conform not only to economic laws but also to the laws of nature. These are manifested in two different ways, first through changes in sunlight, temperature, water, and climatic conditions, and second through the growth requirements of the plants and animals themselves, as the 'objects' of labor. Agriculture needs to accommodate changes in these two aspects at all times, in order to make timely and accurate decisions about production. Obviously, it would be hard for someone not present at the site of production, and not directly involved in agricultural production, to have a good grasp of all the considerations.

A second 'unique form and management process required by agriculture' is the fact that agricultural producers need to manage the entire process of production, the entire cycle. Producing animals or plants for food is an ongoing continuous process, and only when it is in its final stage can all the intermediate steps be evaluated for their effectiveness. Only then can the 'labor' inputs into each link in the process be realized. This means that agricultural producers must be responsible for the entire production cycle if their labor is to be linked to the final product.

Third, agricultural producers should have the ability to organize their own 'surplus labor time' on their own. Since the timeframes for agricultural production and normal 'labor' are different, with agricultural production being quite extended and continuous, while normal labor is brief and intermittent in comparison, at each stage in the agricultural process, farmers have a certain amount of surplus time. Only when they themselves manage this time effectively for their own purposes can both agricultural and 'sideline industries' develop in tandem. Among our existing forms of operation and organization, household-based operations are most suited to the specific nature of agricultural production. And since household operations are really determined by the intrinsic nature and laws of agriculture itself, if the laws of agricultural production do not change there is no reason to change a system of household production of agriculture. This fact appears to have been borne out in many different countries and situations, irrespective of social systems and level of productive forces. The unique aspect of our own situation is that the underlying land is owned by the collective. As a result, our system involves households contracting collectively owned land for agricultural production.

Such a household contracting system is a realistic base for gradual agricultural modernization in our country. If we depart from this base, not only will we fail to move toward modernization but we will negate the basic 'two-tiered' system of management in rural areas and move yet again along the old path of 'first: big, second: public.' It is imperative that we maintain the household contracting system, with the understanding that the policy is long-term and stable. Some of our cadres regard the system as something supplementary and 'small-scale,' as though it were incompatible with modernization and with our current situation of developing a market economy. This needs to be discussed. Given our national conditions, it is quite true that our limited amount of land makes household operations quite small, but this should not be equated to 'small-time production.' The term is generally thought of as referring to 'self-sufficiency' in a 'natural economy.' Under a commodity economy, it simply means that production is not 'socialized' or mass-produced in the sense of division of labor. It cannot be denied that both kinds of 'small-time production' coexist in some areas that have uneven development. Nonetheless, simply consolidating land and undertaking so-called unified operations may look better superficially but does not change the fundamental nature of our farming methods.

Getting rid of the household contracting system and moving toward larger 'unified' operations is not the answer. Until we change the economic and social structure that surrounds our agricultural production, we will not fundamentally change our mode of agricultural production. And indeed, in many parts of our country, such changes are occurring as the economy develops and industrial structure changes. Many excellent reforms are underway, such as greater circulation of factors of production, greater division of labor, and economic cooperation and combinations among various forms [of ownership]. These undeniably show that our rural areas are progressing from a 'closed' to a more 'open' situation. In fact, under the impact of competition and the great wave of a 'market economy' that is now upon us, a 'small-time' mode of production will find it hard to exist and household operations are going to have to adopt more large-scale mass production methods. In recent years, many things are indicating that farmers want to adopt such methods, including the fact that they are setting up socialized service systems and developing industrialized management structures that integrate trade, industry, and agriculture. We are already seeing our farming household operations move gradually toward modernization in such ways as producing for a market, and using division-of-labor cooperative modes of mass production. Therefore, to reiterate my point, in modernizing our agriculture, we should not abandon 'household operations' but rather should change the socioeconomic environment surrounding our agriculture.

Building a socialized service system of agriculture and developing 'industrialized' management structures that feature an integration of trade, industry, and agriculture are all measures to improve the general environment and conditions for household operations. Given these things, it is entirely possible for our existing household management system to begin to adopt modern technology, expand operations, begin to produce for a market. It is entirely possible to modernize our agriculture. In fact, the kind of 'modernized agriculture' that we see in advanced countries involves a whole network of coordinated aspects involving marketing, value-added processing, advanced product production. It involves what I am calling 'socialized service systems' and not solely the modernization of household production operations. Certain parts of our country are already showing the possibilities, with the strengthening of that kind of network and the improved management of agriculture as an industry.

We firmly believe, therefore, that our agriculture will indeed modernize if we adhere to the orientation set forth by the Third Plenary Session of the Party's 15th Central Committee and the 15th Party Congress. That is to say, we must not diverge from keeping household-contracting the basis for our agricultural production.

Note

* This article was originally published in the twentieth issue of *Qiu Shi* in 1998.

5 A recommendation to suspend taxes on agriculture for one year, specifically the agricultural tax, the tax on special agricultural products, the tax on pig slaughtering, and the rural levies for education*

(1999)

This year, 'Central' set forth two main objectives for our work in rural areas. One was raising farmers' incomes, and the second was preserving rural stability. These were highly attuned to the realities in rural areas and have been commended and supported on all sides. However, given the realities of rural economies and agriculture at the moment, it is going to be hard to realize the goal of 'raising farmers' income.' The fact is that sales of farm products remain sluggish and prices are depressed, with dramatic declines in pork prices in particular. The result is that first-quarter cash incomes of farmers are actually showing a negative rate over the previous year's first quarter, with an average decline of RMB 4.8 or some 1.5 percent. People engaged in raising livestock are showing a decline in income of RMB 12.38 on average, or 12.8 percent.

At the same time, the larger economic context for farming includes our policies aimed at restructuring the economy. These are leading to lower growth rates among township-and-village enterprises, fewer opportunities for local employment, and also fewer opportunities for rural people to be hired for labor outside of their home base. Meanwhile, the policy that was recently released with respect to adjusting prices of grain and cotton, and our means of acquiring and selling these products, will eventually result in a better agricultural structure. The policy will lift product quality and raise farmers' income in the long run, but in the short run it lowers farmers' income.

Given that factors that serve to lower farmers' income outweigh those that increase income right now, it is particularly important that we come up with effective means to lessen the very real burden on farmers. We recommend that the government suspend taxes on farmers for one year, specifically in the areas of the agricultural tax, the tax on special farm products, the pig slaughtering tax, and the rural levies for education. We propose that the resulting shortfall in the budget be made up for by issuing local bonds. Our specific reasoning is as follows.

1   The lessons of history prove that farmers bear a disproportionate [tax] burden when their incomes fail to rise. Moreover, when incomes fail to rise and that burden is also not lessened [through central policies], the direct result is increased rural instability. This has frequently been the backdrop for 'mass incidents' [*jitixing shijian*] in our history, and 'malignant occurrences' [*exing anjian*]. Suspending the three kinds of tax noted above, as well as levies for rural education, not only will show farmers that the government is concerned, but will ensure that the benefit of the measures reaches farmers directly, goes into their hands rather than the hands of others. Moreover, it will be immeasurably helpful in consolidating rural support for the Party and the government, in terms of national policies. It will contribute to the very major consideration of the need to preserve rural stability.

2   The short-term result of our adjustments of grain and cotton prices and our policies that modify procurement and sale practices will be negative for farmers. They will face a certain loss of income. Replacing price supports with decreased taxes, or exemption from taxes, will not only provide farmers with appropriate subsidies, but will help stimulate structural changes in agricultural production. It will provide very real benefits directly to farmers and it will be a signal that guides them in the direction of less grain production for the immediate term. This will ameliorate our situation of having an oversupply of grain. In 1997, the total amount of agricultural tax that was levied amounted to 24.66 billion *jin* [12.33 billion kg] in flour and rice in terms of actual product. That came to 2.5 percent of total grain production. Right now, our grain inventories are tremendous, supply exceeds demand, and it is hard to make sales. Stopping the requisition of grain as agricultural tax for one year can only help us – there is little downside. Second, our current tax system incorporates all kinds of sideline products under the rubric of the 'agricultural tax,' in addition to the primary tax on grain, cotton, and edible oils. In the majority of places, methods of levying the tax on these sideline products is highly irregular, which serves as a negative incentive to farmers to produce these things. The tax is therefore an obstacle to restructuring our agricultural production. Third, since the beginning of this year, the prices of both live pigs and piglets have dropped precipitously to the extent that most people who are raising pigs right now are facing a loss. Suspending the pig-slaughtering tax for one year is a necessary protection if we want to encourage people to keep on raising pigs.

3   Irregular tax collection methods in rural areas, especially taxes on special agricultural products and pig slaughtering, are now raising an outcry among farmers in quite a few places. The amount of tax on these two items is figured in terms of the budgetary needs of the county in many places. It is set by calculating the county's expenditures and then levying the tax. In many areas, a fixed tax rate is not applied to the actual amount produced. Instead, farmers are taxed according to 'tax quotas.' The tax on special agricultural products is a head-count tax, or is figured on the amount of land that is contracted. Often the agricultural tax and the tax on 'special agricultural products' duplicate each other, so the farmer pays twice. Figuring the pig-slaughtering tax is done

by head-count, so that, as the farmers say, the 'pig-head tax is counted by people-heads.' These practices are widespread. Suspending the tax on special agricultural products and on pig slaughtering not only will bring direct benefit to farmers but should help 'freeze out' the disorderly way in which the taxes are collected. It should also set up a favorable environment for carrying on with reform of rural taxation.

4   Taxes levied by local authorities for education fall outside the scope of the 5 percent of their net income 'tax burden' on farmers. These levies are primarily spent on improving and rebuilding school buildings and dormitories. Right now, however, not only do farmers have little prospect of additional income but they also face the legacy of accumulated 'complex problems' from the past that relate simply to getting along. For example, in 1997 there was an unmitigated stream of disasters including drought, flooding, and pests. In some places, farmers simply need to regroup and rebuild their basic farming operations. As another example, the campaign to clean up what are known as 'rural cooperative fund associations' [illegal lending groups] is underway, and is being put into all-round implementation. A certain number of farmers will be negatively impacted by this, in that they will lose a certain amount of their savings. Cadres in a number of counties and townships are quite concerned about the consequences in terms of social unrest. This round of educational levies has already been going on for five years; suspending it for one year is not only feasible but necessary, given the situation in the countryside.

5   This year we are celebrating the fiftieth anniversary of the founding of our country. Throughout our history, momentous events have been commemorated by the gesture of reducing or exempting taxes, so as to enable all to join in the celebration. Suspending the three agricultural taxes and the education levies will therefore have a special political significance this year, both in terms of stabilizing the situation in the countryside and in terms of making farmers feel that the Party and the government are concerned about them. Moreover, pegging the reduction in taxes to the fiftieth anniversary will reinforce the understanding that this is a one-year event, not a long-term policy. It will be easier for farmers to understand and accept the change when we need to reintroduce taxes.

In 1997, total taxes on agriculture and animal husbandry came to RMB 20.587 billion. Taxes on special agricultural products came to RMB 16.973 billion, and on pig slaughtering to RMB 2 billion. These figures are such as can be ascertained by the relevant departments. (They estimate that the pig-slaughter tax figure is an actual RMB 4 billion, but only half the figures are in yet.) Educational levies came to RMB 6.5 billion. The total for 'the three taxes and the one levy' came to RMB 48 billion. The educational levies were mainly used on building schools and dormitories, so suspending them for one year will not pose a major problem. The actual grain that was to be taxed through the agricultural tax will not be easily sold for the time being, so there will be a storage issue that just requires an increase in fees for managing inventories. The only real impact on our budget will come from the tax on special agricultural products and on pig slaughtering, the total of which is around RMB 21 billion. In order to make up for the shortfall in local budgets that will be caused by suspending these taxes, we recommend issuing local bonds.

Our country has never issued local bonds before, and we should not undertake this move lightly. It might be considered appropriate, however, under special circumstances and very well-defined conditions, and after examination and approval by Central authorities. We recommend that the figure used for the bond issuance be the average of actual total amounts levied over the previous three years of the three different types of taxes. (Further research should be done on whether or not to include the agricultural tax.) The term of the bonds should be three years. Provincial governments should be in charge of issuing them, with applications made to Central for examination and approval. They should be issued through banks. From date of issue, financial authorities at each level of government will be responsible for repayment of interest and principal.

Wanton levying of taxes has become a pervasive problem in our country's rural areas. We should therefore take this opportunity of a one-year suspension of taxes to accelerate rural tax reform – to formulate and implement a program. In early 1997, when the *Law on Land Management* was revised, Central first announced that it would be freezing approvals on any further applications that turned farmland into land for other uses and that made 'county' administrations into 'municipal' administrations. In addition, while revising the *Criminal Law,* Central increased various provisions to do with penalties on land-use crimes. This was helpful in putting an effective stop to misconduct during the period that the *Law on Land Management* was being formulated, and it facilitated the transformation of management systems and mechanisms after the law was promulgated. Reform of our rural tax system can adopt the same effective practice. We should first put a one-year freeze on collecting the 'three taxes,' then formulate a program for rural tax reform that sets forth regulations for a rural tax system. In the interim period, before the new tax regime is in place, farmers will have a reprieve and feel a breath of fresh air. They will feel governed in a way that is more transparent, upright, and enlightened.

Note

* This article was the No. 1 chosen document specially sent to the Development Research Center of the State Council in 1999.

6 Recommendations on improving our reform of the grain 'circulation' system*

(April 1999)

In 1997, the State Council set forth the *Decision on Going a Step Further in Reforming the Grain Circulation System.* In the three years since that time, we have done a tremendous amount of work, put great effort into realizing policies that centered around what were called the 'three policies and one reform' with respect to grain, and we have achieved a considerable measure of success. This whole reform emanated from a desire to maintain steady production of grain. In the context of plentiful supply, it was intended to protect our capacity for grain production, to maintain incentives for farmers, and to avoid volatility in grain output after successive seasons of bumper harvests. Experience has proven that the policy decision was correct, in that it played an irreplaceable role in preventing great fluctuations in grain production. If we had not implemented a policy of buying surplus grain at subsidized prices ['protective prices'], grain production would be nothing like as promising as it is today.

I. Problems facing reform of our grain circulation system

As our country's agriculture enters a new stage of development, and as our rural economy develops as well, we now have the underlying conditions to apply more market mechanisms to the conduct of our agriculture. Indeed, it is becoming necessary for us to use market mechanisms to adjust the quantities and types of agricultural products that we produce, as a way of furthering our strategic restructuring of the rural economy. A series of good harvests and abundant stocks of grain at this moment will greatly help us actually realize policies to reform grain-circulation systems that have not in fact been put into effect in any fundamental way. We currently have both the means and the need to further such policies in order to address the very heavy public-finance burden of grain subsidies. Right now, the main problems facing our grain-circulation system are the following.

1 *It is increasing difficult to implement subsidized-grain purchasing policies as they were formulated.* For the previous two years, due to plentiful stocks of grain and also solid funding, subsidized-pricing policies were implemented

in most places. From last year, however, inventories have been going up while local-government budgets are not able to cover, creating a gap in funding. State-owned grain companies are feeling the pressure as their ability to purchase the stocks declines. In order to stay in business, many purchasing enterprises in many places are adopting methods that not only try to lower prices but that try to buy lesser-quality grades of grain. The result is that the actual price of grain has consistently declined, to the extent that last year prices for both wheat and rice had broken through the RMB 0.4 level. Subsidized or 'protected prices' exist only in name. Some grassroots cadres are commenting, in a caustic way, that 'buying farmers' surplus grain at subsidized prices' [as per the policy] is all a big lie.

2   ***Inventories of grain in State-owned grain enterprises are increasing dramatically.*** For five years now, harvests have been excellent, even as the government agrees to 'purchase without limit,' so that high-priced quantities of grain bought at both the 'order price' [*ding-gou jia*] and the 'subsidized price' [*bao-hu jia*] are piling in. Right now, grain stocks stand at more than 500 billion *jin* [250 billion kg], far surpassing our normal need for such inventories (which should generally be some 20 percent of annual production). In order to ensure profits from their operations, grain enterprises put grain that they have bought at low prices into the market, while they put grain that they have bought at fixed 'order' prices into their grain elevators. Grain circulating in the market is therefore generally from the same year's harvest, while grain bought at the higher subsidized price on fixed contracts goes into storage, which continues to pile up there. The risk involved in this process is considerable: Not only does it continue to 'occupy' or hold down funds, but the State must continue to pay out for maintaining the inventories and for the interest on the invested capital. As time goes on, losses are incurred as quality deteriorates and grain is lost through damage and waste.

3   ***Subsidies to State-owned grain enterprises continue to increase for overstocks of grain.*** The amount involved has reached RMB 70 billion per year, given the RMB 40 billion subsidies coupled with losses of the Agricultural Development Bank. Yet farmers themselves have received no benefit from this sum, since procurement prices from them have been forced down.

4   ***Hidden or 'implicit' losses are increasing.*** Market prices are going down and costs of storage are going up, which means that the overall operating costs of State-owned grain enterprises are increasing. The actions of the enterprises are contributing to that trend, in fact, as they push down the quality-grade of grain being purchased as well as the price. The result is that the price of stored grain is increasingly diverging from the price of grain on the market. Stored grain is increasingly hard to sell at market prices and losses of State-owned grain companies simply mount up.

What is the reason for these problems? We feel that the most fundamental reason is that supply exceeds demand. There is inadequate regulation over the total amount of grain being produced even as quality enhancement is low, which makes it hard to increase the size of the market. Selling at market prices [prices that comply with the market] is even harder. Moreover, at present there are two very important 'weak links' in our grain distribution system that must be addressed.

First, we are trying to 'protect' [or subsidize] an overly broad swath of people, and to subsidize an overly large amount of product. This leads to two problems. First, farmers lack any sense of urgency about reconfiguring the amount of grain they produce. No matter what they plant, or how much, the government will guarantee purchase. Recently, some grains have been withdrawn from the system of guaranteed purchase, but not many. The amount is not enough to influence the overall total. Southern early rice varieties [indica] and spring wheat in the northeast, as well as substandard maize, only constitute 10 percent of our country's total, moreover they are still being produced. The remaining 90 percent has not been affected. The quantity is still excessive, elevators continue to bulge. What's more, we still have not resolved the whole issue of how grains that have been withdrawn from the subsidy system are to be 'circulated.' Second, the amount of grain held in storage by industrial users, consumers, and farmers themselves has decreased dramatically. The cost of storing grain that, by all rights, should be borne by society at large, is now being covered by the State. So long as the State is buying and storing, why should users be obliged to cover that cost? Whenever grain is needed, it can be purchased. This greatly reduces cash flow requirements. Urban residents don't worry about volatility in prices. Grain is increasingly cheap, and they have no need to hoard it. The result is that everyone regards State-owned grain companies as their own cost-free grain elevator.

Second, reform of grain enterprises is on hold, and the old practice of 'combining government influence with commercial interests' has not diminished to any fundamental degree. In terms of the external environment, reform of the grain system, the so-called three reforms, will depend on the relationship of supply and demand. In terms of internal operations, it will depend on one specific reform, namely, reform of State-owned grain enterprises. That includes a separation of governmental and commercial interests, reduction in personnel, and an increase in efficiency. Only when we truly separate out governmental functions from commercial interests or 'market functions,' and create a highly professional rank of people to staff the companies, a team that is responsible for its own profits and losses, will we force these enterprises to engage in market competition, purchase proactively at market prices, and sell at market-driven prices as well.

Over the past three years, experience has shown us that, among the reforms [i.e., the 'three policies and one reform'], the one related to State-owned grain enterprises has been least effective. People are saying that these enterprises are the greatest 'pot of rice' remaining in the entire country. Although reforms have indeed accomplished great things in these past few years, the response of these companies to the needs of the State and of farmers is far from adequate.

First, government functions are still not separated out from enterprise management. Despite the assertion that [governmental] grain bureaus did set up separate 'grain operating companies,' what they actually did was to allocate some of their cadres to operate these concerns, while the heads of the bureaus themselves continue to be the general managers of the companies.

Second, the process of 'separately allocating staff' [hiving off government staff to companies] has been incomplete in that many places not only have *not* made the resulting employment a separate category but they have simply turned seasonal government workers into long-term or permanent workers [and kept them on government rolls]. As the staffing multiplies, the costs [to local governments] only increase to the extent that participating in any kind of normal market competition is out of the question. The only solution is to beg for more government subsidies to pay the costs. Public funding is what helps swell the ranks, while such dependency on public funding only increases further dependency. There is little incentive to go forth and be proactive in consciously implementing government policies of buying surplus grain at subsidized prices.

As widely reported by grassroots-level personnel, private traders appear fully able to travel the countryside, buying grain and making a living, while State-owned grain enterprises sit back and act official. Even grain sent 'up' to them by farmers is refused or bought in limited amounts, and the reason is that these enterprises can 'eat off' government subsidies instead of really doing any business.

Third, there has in fact been no separation between the business operations of State-owned grain enterprises and the policy-oriented purchasing and storage of grain for the government. Value-added processing, circulation [sales], and so on remain mixed in together with governmental business. State-owned grain enterprises concentrate government functions and commercial behavior in one entity, and when grain is plentiful they engage in price-cutting and purchasing lesser grades, while when grain is scarce they snap up supplies. This not only intensifies market disruptions but renders meaningless any signals the government is trying to impart to the market in order to exercise controls. As such, the enterprises fail to stimulate market circulation, as intended, nor do they contribute to structural change in what is being produced.

Fourth, State-owned grain companies are in the position of being monopolies and yet they do not implement State policies with regard to protective [or subsidized] prices. The State's purpose in extending the authority to purchase grain to State-Owned Enterprises [on behalf of the State] was originally to control the grain market and prevent private commerce from either running up or forcing down prices. It was to stabilize market supply and to stabilize grain prices. In reality, these companies do not carry out governmental policies in purchasing at subsidized prices. Farmers, in the meanwhile, have no alternative but to go through them for sales. This gives the enterprises full power to manipulate pricing at will, forcing it down and obtaining low-cost grain. This has at least two negative consequences. One is that farmers' interests are severely damaged. The second is that operating costs all the way down the line are affected, since these enterprises buy in grain at low prices, sell it at high prices, and force feedstock companies, processing industries, and other non-State-owned users of grain to add to their costs as well. These non-State-Owned Enterprises, unable to survive in normal fashion, are then either forced to shut down or to engage in fraudulent practices by colluding with State-Owned Enterprises. In reality what happens is that certain capable private traders 'borrow a shingle' from State-Owned Enterprises. They pose as State-owned, behind the front of a State-owned license. They then carry on in private business for the benefit of those involved.

II. Two recommendations for improving reform of our grain circulation system

The overall concept is to make the system more responsive to current supply and demand considerations and less dependent on such human factors as the initiative and self-constraint of purchasing teams. It is to transform the system into something that relies more on the force of systems and mechanisms and thereby protects our productive capacity while allowing market mechanisms to begin to regulate total grain supply.

1. Further reduce the coverage of protection [i.e., the coverage of subsidized prices and guaranteed purchase]

All levels of government have an unshirkable duty to protect the initiative and enthusiasm of farmers to produce grain. This policy orientation cannot change in any time or place. However, in our current situation of supply exceeding demand, the scope of our protection cannot be too broad as that will prevent farmers from voluntarily adjusting what they produce, both in terms of quantity and better-quality varieties. Certain varieties have already been withdrawn from the 'protection' system, but several issues remain. The first is that the types and quantities of withdrawn items are not enough to impact overall production. The second is that whether or not some grain will be withdrawn depends on the grade or class of grain, but the differential between grades is very small while the price differential is large, and lower-grade products are easier to sell. Higher-grade varieties that are less easy to sell are those that are still under protective guidelines. Moreover, the decision about what grain to buy, and what kinds of grain have been withdrawn, is made at each buying station with technical methods that are hard for higher authorities or farmers themselves to control. The result is that considerable fraudulent activity goes on. Buyers force down both prices and grade levels. Third, it is very hard to control what happens at purchasing stations. The costs of monitoring are extremely high. It is hard to check up on whether or not stations are actually buying grain outside the scope of allowed grades, or buying grain that is inside the allowed scope but no longer meant to be purchased under protected guidelines.

Our aim is to make the protected-price system [subsidized prices] stimulate farmers' initiative and thereby guarantee a secure supply of grain, while also encouraging faster adjustment in the structure of what is being raised so as to meet the demand for greater diversity and higher quality as dictated by our growing national economy. We therefore should make greater adjustments to the extent of our protective coverage.

First, the overall objective in doing this is to distinguish between edible grains and both feedstock grains and grain grown for seeds, to ensure the purchase and supply of edible grains but allow the other two to be 'opened' [i.e., released from controls and allowed to operate under market supply and demand conditions].

Second, we would switch from a quality-grade-type determination of what is to be protected to a determination based on type of grain and location of production. For example, all corn from the northeast would be withdrawn from protection. The only wheat that would continue to be protected would be that from the Yellow Sea and Huaihai area, while the entire Yangtze River basin would be withdrawn from protection.

Third, grain varieties that are withdrawn from protection would be fully open to purchase and sale on the market; grain enterprises would be allowed to engage freely in market operations. Grain units [enterprises] would be allowed to enter the market to purchase grains that are still under protected pricing.

2. Further reform State-owned grain enterprises

This reform would stand on a very solid footing in that the governmental functions of grain enterprises would be totally separated out from the market functions of these companies. Some would become truly governmental in nature, holding grain stocks as the government and independently buying and selling grain as governmental agencies. They would serve the function of regulating the amount of surplus grain and stabilizing grain prices. Others would become market-oriented and compete on an equal basis with other companies. In specific terms, grain enterprises would be divided into the following two categories.

The first would be national granaries, mainly newly established entities set up directly under the aegis of the Central government, the number to depend on the actual storage requirements of the country. These would take on the mission of being the grain repositories of the nation, they would not undertake any operating role and would not engage in any trade, purchasing would be solely at the command of the government, as well as storage and transportation. All costs, including employee salaries, would be borne in full by the State.

Remaining granaries would fall into the second category. These would not have any governmental functions but would instead be market-oriented and competitive. If the government needed for them to reserve grain or purchase grain under protected pricing conditions, it could pay them storage charges and associated costs. The county-level grain bureaus would allocate the grain out using a tender system or other form of distributing the responsibility, and expenses associated with this portion of grain would be borne by the government. The grain would not be a part of the operations of the enterprise. Authority over allocation of this grain would rest with the government; the enterprise would merely store it and not be allowed to sell it. As for grain bought at subsidized prices, the enterprise could voluntarily sell this and the margin between purchase and sales price would accrue to the enterprise. Any portion that was not sold could be sold to the State.

III. On the problem of existing inventories

We currently have stocks of more than 500 billion *jin* of grain [250 billion kg]. Of this, some 300 billion *jin* [150 billion kg] exceed current demand, that is, are 'overstocked.' Prospects for selling this at market prices are very slim, given our current supply and demand situation.

First, there is very little margin for grain prices to go higher. Even though prices right now are overly low, from a long-term perspective, especially in terms of joining the World Trade Organization, we cannot have grain prices that are set too high. When agricultural prices experience a tremendous increase, especially food prices, this often leads to wholesale inflation of all commodity prices. If prices were at a sufficiently high level to sell out existing stocks at appropriate prices, the impact on commodity prices might be excessive.

Second, we do not see any great reduction in our grain production figures in the course of a normal year. The greatest reduction over the past 20 years came in 1985, when grain production declined by 60 billion *jin* [30 billion kg]. Even if we had a similar decline now, that would not greatly impact our existing stocks of 500 billion *jin* [250 billion kg].

What are we to do with our tremendous inventory of grain? We might consider the following option. It would help ease the transition of State-owned grain enterprises as they cease to undertake governmental functions and move entirely toward market operations. It would also prevent them from carrying out a price war in dumping grain on the market and destroying stable market conditions. We would allow them to purchase grain from overstocked granaries, at a preferential price that is slightly below the market price. The State would bear the loss. Since the price was slightly less than market, the granaries [now disassociated from State operations] would expect to make a small profit on it. The amount would serve as a kind of 'start-up' funding of enterprises that are now meant to be market-oriented and severed from governmental functions. It would help as they become fully responsible for their own profits and losses. Whether or not operations went well from that point onward would depend on each employee's realization that he was working for his own interests and should perform. As a result, the grain would not simply be dumped at low prices on the market which would preserve market order. Another result in handling things this way would be that the portion of stockpiled grain [formerly] held at a loss would be brought into the light of day. With profits to be made off it, and with the risk of not having guaranteed stocks to sell, enterprises would shift their *modus operandi*. They would become proactive, rather than sitting back and letting the business come to them. They would begin to think of all ways and means to sell their product, search out processing industries, try to increase the amount of value-added on grain in order to expand their own markets.

IV. Possible side effects of limiting the scope of subsidies and of separating out the functions of 'government' and 'enterprise' in the grain circulation system

1. Some State-owned grain enterprises will not be able to adapt to stiff market competition

They will simply be washed out of the business, some will close shop while others will be acquired, and as a result a certain number of employees will lose their jobs. This is the cost of undertaking enterprise reform.

2. With intense market competition, the number of entities involved in buying and selling grain will increase greatly as well as the quantity of grain that is circulating in the market

This will undoubtedly bring with it a degree of market volatility and it will increase people's expectations of a price increase. Both enterprises and urban consumers may start to store up more grain, which actually will be beneficial in reducing the government's overfull granaries.

3. Since large areas will be withdrawn from the protective price system for corn and wheat, and since some areas have a higher cost structure that cannot withstand this, certain farmers will see a decline in income if they have no alternative way to make a living

At the same time, the supply of grain in the market will decline. This will help ameliorate the pressure of overstocked granaries and will also stimulate a restructuring of production. From a long-term perspective, total grain production may be a little less, which will also help improve the relative efficiencies in raising grain.

4. Certain areas may see larger fluctuations in grain prices

Some enterprises with extremely poor operations, whose managers have little confidence in the future, may engage in the short-term behavior of underselling or 'flinging' grain out on the market. Overall, however, most enterprises will operate in a rational manner. If the lower limit on prices sold to enterprises is designed at a proper level, irrational behavior should not be the rule. Improving our administrative oversight of industry and commerce should also help control market volatility.

Note

* This is an advisory that the author provided on April 23, 1999, to the State Council leaders.

7 The turning point in our supply and demand situation for grain, and regulating the structure of agricultural production*

(2000)

Grain yields have increased considerably since the start of 'reform.' This can be attributed to correct rural policies and to constant increase in inputs as well as improvements in farming technology. The overall judgment of the Party's Third Plenary Session of the 15th Central Committee [1998] with respect to supply and demand was that, 'we are generally in balance in terms of total quantity and we have a surplus in good years.' In the five years since 1995, grain output has enjoyed bumper harvests and we have been accumulating surpluses both in government stocks and in farmers' own stocks. State grain department inventories of grain reached 550 billion *jin* over these five years, while farmers' inventories came to some 132.4 *jin* per capita at the end of 1998. Subtracting out grain for personal needs and self-supplied production [of livestock], the amount still comes to around 500 *jin* per capita. Based on this estimate, the total inventory in farmers' hands is over 450 billion *jin*. Not counting this fall's production, from 1999, at present we have a total supply of surplus grain of around 1 trillion *jin,* more or less. This figure is roughly equal to one year's total production. It now behooves us to put serious thought into our supply and demand situation, and what our next steps should be in adjusting rural economic policies and agricultural policies in particular.

I. Since the mid-1990s, our grain production capacity has undeniably reached a whole new level

Upon entering the 1990s, but particularly since Central strengthened macroeconomic adjustments in 1993, our grain production has improved but more important, our overall capacity for grain production has reached a whole new level. The fact that we have enjoyed five consecutive years of bumper harvests since 1995 can be attributed to three main factors.

First, Central has adopted correct agricultural policies. Most important, these include extending the contracting periods for the 'household contracting system,' and stabilizing the relationships involved. In 1994 and 1996, purchasing prices for grain were lifted very considerably, increasing the overall price at which the government procured grain by 102 percent. Policies were implemented guaranteeing subsidized prices for all governmental grain purchases of farmers' surplus grain. These very effectively motivated farmers to produce, as shown by three relevant statistics. One: The land area devoted to grain was increased. Between 1992 and 1994, an average of 1.653 billion *mu* was planted in grain every year, while between 1995 and 1998, this amount increased to 1.685 billion *mu* every year. Every year, an additional 32 million *mu* was put into grain. Two: The area of irrigated land increased. Between 1992 and 1998, it increased by 55.6 million *mu,* or an increase in irrigated land of 7.63 percent. Three: The use of fertilizers increased. Between 1992 and 1994, an average of 31.333 million tons of fertilizer was applied per year (this refers to the net amount, which applies to figures below as well), while between 1995 and 1998, that amount had increased by 23.6 percent to an average per year of 38.72 million tons.

Second, scientific advances have been tremendously important in stimulating better yields. In these years, the unified or centrally directed supply of better seed varieties, the use of [plastic] sheeting on the ground, intercropping and interplanting [of different kinds of crops], water-conservation methods, dry-land farming methods, 'facility' farming, and greater mechanization have all advanced, leading to marked improvements in yield per unit of area. In 1998, the per *mu* yield of cereal crops reached 660.4 *jin* [330.2 kg], 14 percent more than the 579 *jin* [289.5 kg] in 1992. The gross grain yield in 1998 was 15.7 percent more than that in 1992, which was mainly because of increased yields per unit of area.

Third, we must be frank in admitting that one of the reasons for these figures is that there have been no natural disasters over these years, influencing grain production. Although we did have flooding in 1998 in the river basins of the Yangtze, the Songhua, and the Nenjiang, the greater threat to our country's agriculture has always been drought. Over these years, we had limited areas of drought in the north China plain, affecting fall harvests in 1997 and 1999 in particular. In 1997, production of one variety of corn was reduced by drought, to the extent of 46.32 billion *jin,* and in 1999, the fall harvest will be reduced by almost 20 billion *jin.* This shows that we are still quite vulnerable to drought. Nonetheless, over these years we fortunately have been in a cycle of fairly abundant precipitation. That has put pressure on the ability of our rivers to withstand flooding, but it has been quite beneficial to grain production. From the record of the past five years, our grain production capacity can be said to approach 1 trillion *jin* per annum (it was 9,888 billion *jin* per annum on average in the four years from 1995–1998). This figure precludes the effect of any major, widespread, persistent natural disasters. It therefore should not be taken as an absolutely firm indicator of our productive capacity.

II. Demand for grain has also demonstrated marked changes

Even as the supply of grain has increased markedly, the demand for grain has been changing, influenced by the overall economic environment, both domestically and abroad. This is mainly reflected in the following two ways.

The first relates to changes in consumption behavior of our citizens but especially urban residents. Since the growth in our national economy has entered a whole new stage, stage-specific changes in consumption patterns are emerging. Our economy experienced fast growth in the first half of the 1990s. Between 1991 and 1995, GDP grew at an average annual rate of 11.98 percent. That changed after the mid-1990s, however, given changes in the global as well as domestic economic environment. Between 1996 and 1998, GDP grew at a lower average annual rate of 8.72 percent. In 1998, the rate was 7.8 percent. This was already 6.4 percentage points lower than in 1992, and the rate went down further to 7.1 percent in 1999. The softening in economic growth naturally influenced the rate at which people's incomes increased. Between 1996 and 1998, disposable income for urban residents increased at an average annual rate of 4.35 percent, which was 3.6 percentage points lower than it had been during 1991 to 1995. As disposable income growth rates declined, people's expectations about future earnings also changed and they began to save more. In the three years between 1996 and 1998, savings increased by RMB 2.37452 trillion. This exceeded the total increase in savings during the earlier five-year period, which was RMB 2.25425 trillion for the years 1991 to 1995. Average annual savings in the latter three-year period increased over the earlier five-year period by 75.56 percent. Given this data, it is clear that consumption of our citizens, but particularly our urban residents, will grow at a slower rate. This is reflected particularly sharply in expenditures on food. In 1998, the absolute amount spent on food declined over the previous year by 0.81 percentage points. Expenditures on grain declined by 4.75 percentage points. Expenditures on meat and poultry and byproducts of those foods declined by 6.16 percentage points.

Expenditures on vegetables dropped by 3.37 percent and those on fruit dropped by 4.96 percent. During this period, the price index also declined, which means that not all of this directly correlated to a drop in consumption of these items. Nonetheless, as compared to a dramatically increasing supply of agricultural products, there was a notably weaker increase in demand for those products.

Second, urban residents have now entered into a period that is regarded as 'moderately prosperous,' which means that their demand has shifted from simply wanting greater 'quantity' to wanting better 'quality.' Our country's Engel's coefficient has already dropped to 44.48 percent, close to 10 percentage points lower than the 54.24 percent it was in 1990. In 1998, the grain ration of urban residents was 173.44 *jin* [86.72 kg], which had decreased by 33.7 percent from the 261.44 *jin* [130.72 kg] that it was in 1990. Per capita consumption of meat in 1998, including pork, beef, and mutton, was 38.44 *jin* [19.22 kg], among which pork alone accounted for 31.76 *jin* [15.88 kg]. These figures were down by 11.6 percent and 14 percent, respectively, over 1990. However, during this same period the urban demand for poultry, eggs, and aquatic products has been continuing to increase. This indicates that more feedstock grains will be going toward production of these foods in the future and less toward meat. Since they have a higher 'transformation rate' of grains, the indirect consumption of feedstock grains by urban residents will in the future be increasing at a slower rate.

The above two aspects show that the current slow growth in grain consumption is unique and stage-specific. The reason we currently have a fairly large surplus of grain is that supply is increasing faster than demand.

III. Our current surplus of grain should be seen in the context of low consumption rates, and is regional, structural, and temporary due to being 'stage-specific'

A surplus of grain due to being 'stage-specific' refers to two main aspects. One is that the consumption patterns of urban residents are at a critical turning point in terms of the makeup of overall expenditures. Certain long-term expenditures are increasing markedly, such as those on housing, automobiles, children's education, and old-age insurance. Relatively speaking, expenditures on food have slowed down. Second, the money spent on food by rural inhabitants has still not started to increase markedly. Rural people still eat only 60 percent the amount of meat that urban residents eat, only 26.4 *jin* of such things as beef, pork, and mutton. Per capita rural consumption of poultry is only 50 percent what it is in cities, while per capita consumption of eggs and aquatic products is only 40 percent what it is in cities. It is not hard to see that our country's demand for feedstock grains will increase by some 60 percent once rural inhabitants have the same diet as urban dwellers. This figure doesn't even take into account the natural increase in population. The current surplus in grain is therefore stage-specific and unique to the current situation.

The 'structural surplus' that we are experiencing refers to the way the structure of our grain production is out of sync with the structure of consumption in terms of types and qualities of grain. For a variety of reasons, we continue to produce a large quantity of grains that are hard to sell in the marketplace. One example is indica rice, production of which comes to some 80 to 90 billion *jin* every year [40–45 billion kg]. Another example is the corn grown in the three northeastern provinces and the eastern part of Inner Mongolia, which has a relatively high moisture content – every year we produce a similar 80 to 90 billion *jin* [40–45 billion kg]. Additionally, we produce 20 to 30 billion *jin* every year [40–60 billion kg] of spring wheat grown in the northeast and winter wheat grown in the south. These all constitute some 20 percent of our total grain production, they are low-grade types of grain, and they constitute the bulk of our overstocked inventories. It is likely that we will move into a transitional stage in the future in which the quality of our grains improves, while the quantity may actually show a slight decline. This will be due to structural adjustments in what farmers are producing, as well as scientific advances and the response of farmers to policy incentives.

The 'regional nature' of our surplus refers to grain grown in eight or nine specific provinces, among which the most important are the corn-growing regions in the northeastern provinces and Mongolia and the indica rice-growing regions in the south. If one visits entities that utilize grain in these areas, one soon discovers that they are not storing the grain themselves but are relying on State-owned granaries to store it for them. Grain-processing plants, feedstock plants, and even urban residents maintain far less grain on hand than they need in a normal year. The plentiful stocks on hand in State-owned grain enterprises mean that these units either hold less grain themselves or indeed none at all, which in fact intensifies the surpluses carried in producing regions. At the same time, we should not overlook the disparities among regions and the lack of adequate grain in some areas. Every year, due to natural disasters, some areas face grain shortages. Moreover, the country still has over 40 million farmers in poverty-stricken areas who have inadequate food and clothing.

'Surpluses in the context of low consumption rates' refers mainly to the way our country's inhabitants, both rural and urban, are still consuming fairly unprocessed foods due to their generally low level of income and standard of consumption. This puts a constraint on the growth of our processing industries and on transforming food processing to a higher level. At present, our food-processing industries have a total output value that is roughly 80 percent the output value of agricultural production as a whole. In advanced countries, the figure is generally three to four times the value of agricultural production. Consequently, as incomes in our country rise and processing industries develop, we will see a major increase in the demand for grain and primary agricultural products in general.

In addition, our consumption is still influenced by certain traditional eating habits, such as not consuming very much milk. Last year, our country's total production of milk was 6.62 tons, a quantity that was only one-fourth the amount of alcohol produced. As incomes rise, and traditional concepts change, we should see a tremendous increase in consumption of food items that 'transform' grain, such as milk.

Therefore, while we should recognize that we do indeed have a surplus of grain at the moment, we should also understand that this is stage-specific to our current situation. It is structural, regional, and has arisen in the context of a fairly low rate of grain consumption. Given the very real fact of our limited land and large population, this has to be seen as a temporary phenomenon. It cannot and will not continue for long.

IV. We must implement policies with regard to agriculture and rural economies that aim at strategic restructuring

The Central Rural Work Conference held at the end of 1998 analyzed the supply and demand situation of our main agricultural products. The Conference noted that both agriculture and rural economies are entering a new stage in development and that, given the fact of fairly large surpluses of grain stocks, our core task now should be to make structural adjustments in agriculture and the rural economy in general. Looking at the actual situation in 1999, we have made some progress in terms of restructuring agricultural production. The area devoted to grain production decreased over the previous year by 12 million *mu;* that devoted to cotton decreased by 10 million *mu,* and to sugar by over 4 million *mu.* At the same time, the area devoted to oilseed crops increased by 12.6 million *mu* and that to vegetables by 15 million *mu.* In addition to adjustments in the acreage planted to these crops, we have also seen change in the structural composition of grains. For rice, we have reduced the amount of early rice and increased higher-quality strains; for wheat, we have improved the regional distribution of planting and increased production of special-use varieties. Our emphasis in corn production has been to control cross-regional planting in the northeast.

Nonetheless, in light of our stage-specific surplus, these adjustments are not enough. In the near term, we must go further in changing the structure of what is being produced. As a result, the 2000 Central Rural Work Conference that has just concluded explicitly set forth the idea that strategic structural adjustments should be our core task for the 'new stage' of agriculture as well as for our rural work. In terms of grain production, we need to set limits on the total amount produced, and to implement measures that improve quality. Otherwise, we will not be able to absorb [use up] the current overstocks, farmers' new grain will not be saleable or not saleable at good prices, and it will be hard to bring back up the real price of grain. These are all detrimental both to the State and to farmers. The whole issue of grain does not stand alone, however, but is closely linked to agriculture in general and the rural economy in general. Therefore, any policies to do with grain must be integrated with strategic restructuring of those things as well. This term 'strategic restructuring' means we cannot merely recommend planting more or less of this or that, but need to set our sights on the overall situation, in agriculture and indeed in the national economy as a whole. We need also to look to long-term growth. Second, it means that we should take advantage of the current opportune moment, given our surpluses, and undertake major actions that we wanted to do in the past but were unable to accomplish. It is time now to enable our agriculture and rural areas to enter into a whole new stage that focuses on efficiency and on quality. In the immediate future, this means putting our efforts into restructuring the following.

1. Improve the overall quality of agricultural products

One of the main indicators that agriculture is entering a new stage is that sheer quantity becomes less important than quality and type of product. To take grain as an example: Of our annual production of 500 million tons, around 100 million tons are of relatively inferior varieties. Once produced, these are hard to sell and end up as tremendous amounts of overstocked inventory with no effective outlet. If we did not in fact produce these varieties, however, we would have problems with unemployment among farmers and inadequate incomes which necessarily would then lead to inadequate supplies of grain. The realistic solution is to transition to using higher-grade varieties. We have an extremely valuable opportunity at this particular time of grain surpluses, and should begin the process of improving both grain varieties and quality in general.

At this particular stage, in overall terms it is better for us to produce a little less, when it comes to agricultural products, but produce higher quality. This holds for crop production and also for the raising of livestock. As we develop new varieties and more mature technologies with respect to both of these industries, our gross production of agricultural products will continue to increase.

2. Put major effort into promoting the 'transformation' or processing of primary agricultural products

Due to the low elasticity of income expenditures on agricultural products, once people have basically enough to eat and to wear, any expansion of primary agricultural products, in terms of the direct-consumption market, faces considerable constraints. Therefore, any attempt to expand the market for agricultural products must involve the transforming of and value-added processing of primary products. 'Transforming' refers mainly to animal husbandry and aquatic product industries. The developmental level of animal husbandry is one of the indicators of the level of a country's overall agriculture, and the level of consumption of meat products is an indicator of a nation's quality of life. In 1998, the gross value of our country's animal-husbandry output was only 28.6 percent of our overall agricultural output. When aquatic products were added in, the percentage only came to 38.4 percent. Clearly, our level of 'transformation' is quite low. Nonetheless, it should be recognized that grain supply was inadequate in the past, which limited the raising of animals and aquatic products to a considerable degree. Now that the supply and demand situation is far more relaxed, conditions are ripe for extensive development of these two industries. Transforming primary agricultural products into more meat, eggs, and poultry, as well as aquatic products, is not only necessary in raising people's standard of living but is an objective requirement if we want to continue to expand agricultural markets. At present, our country's market for animal husbandry products also appears to be saturated but, if one analyzes more closely, it still has tremendous potential.

The first opportunity lies in improving quality of varieties, for example, hogs bred for leaner meat, free-range chickens, and so on. For these, demand greatly exceeds supply. Optimizing varieties and quality in animal husbandry is as important as it is in crop production in expanding market size.

The second opportunity lies in producing milk products. Both production and consumption of these are still quite low. Milk is one of the most nourishing foods humans can eat, in terms of animal products, and as both incomes and awareness of health increase, milk products become one of the new key items in people's food consumption.

A third opportunity lies in providing rural residents with animal protein. Rural consumption of animal foods is still quite low, but as incomes increase, the rural market is sure to become a tremendous consumer market for such foods.

A fourth opportunity lies in the international market. Our crop products and livestock products still enjoy an advantage overseas. Right now, our exports of both live animals and animal byproducts maintain a consistent value of around

USD 4 billion, but once we resolve both policy and technical considerations, there is considerably more potential to be developed. Once agricultural products are processed, not only can they serve as more diversified and higher-quality consumables, but they can become the raw materials for industry. Developing the value-added processing of our agricultural products is undoubtedly a key route to expanding markets. Right now, our processing industries stand at a low level, but with newer and higher technologies that apply processing to primary products, there should be a broad margin in the market that enables our agricultural products to sustain further growth.

3. Give full play to regional comparative advantages by optimizing the distribution of the productive forces of agriculture

When a situation prevails in which supply does not meet demand, localities have no alternative but to pursue their own self-supply. Our supply and demand situation is more forgiving right now, allowing for the very real possibility of optimizing comparative advantages of different regions in terms of their agricultural production. In trying to do this, we will have to address four main levels of issues, as follows.

First, the economically developed southeastern coastal areas, and the outskirts of large and medium-sized cities will not have to pursue self-sufficiency in grain so long as conditions are conducive to planting other more highly valued economic crops. If these areas can be sure to raise their overall productive capacity, and to protect the surrounding environment as they do so, they should be able to 'stride out' in restructuring their agricultural production. The moment the market changes, they should be able to adjust depending on need.

Second, in places where ecosystems were destroyed due to the pressures of immediate survival, where forests, grasslands, and lakes were 'blindly' turned into fields, we should take planned-out, incremental steps to restore these places. We should rehabilitate the forests, the grasslands, and the lakes, and we should gradually withdraw all farming from substandard land. While attempting to restore a balance between supply and demand in the short term, for agricultural products, we should also have an eye to the future, which means strengthening environmental work, and making sure that farming and all of our economic activity in general is sustainable.

Third, as they are improving diversity and quality of products, our primary producing areas should go further in raising their overall productive capacity. They will need to make up for the lower agricultural production in economically developed areas and areas with marginal land. At the same time, they need to improve the situation in which they supply mainly primary products. They must raise their own economic efficiencies as they begin to 'transform' primary products through value-added processing.

Fourth, each region should give full play to its own comparative advantages, its unique location and natural resources. Each should vigorously develop those products that are unique to itself, make its products and brands competitive in the market, and make every effort to stabilize and expand its own market share.

An organic integration of the above four aspects should stimulate all parts of our country to arrive at a situation in which various parts complement each other and the whole is greater than the parts.

4. Further develop township enterprises and actively promote healthy development of small cities

In a country such as ours, with such a huge rural population, the fundamental issue when it comes to making 'farmers' more prosperous is reducing the number of 'farmers.' Only when surplus labor in agriculture is shifted to secondary and tertiary industries, and when rural residents gradually become urban dwellers, will agriculture be able to accomplish economies of scale, become more capital- and technology-intensive, lower production costs, raise economic efficiencies, and improve farmers' incomes. Since reform began, township enterprises have been a highly successful route for transferring surplus labor off the land; they have been created by the great masses of rural people under the leadership of the Party. The sudden rise of this vanguard has not only already shifted countless millions of surplus laborers away from agriculture, but has made a tremendous contribution in supporting higher technologies in agriculture and social development in rural areas. Township enterprises have long since become a central pillar supporting rural economies, as well as an important 'vital new force' in our overall national economy. Right now, these enterprises are at a critical moment. They are restructuring, as our economy reconfigures its overall structure. As a result, all levels of government should adopt policies and measures that provide an environment for their ongoing sustainable growth. Our country will not be able to rely exclusively on township enterprises for shifting the massive weight of surplus labor in rural areas out of agriculture and into other occupations. Moreover, the highly dispersed nature of township enterprise operations is not advantageous to their own sustainable development. For this reason, the Party's Third Plenary Session of the 15th [Central Committee, in 1998] brought forth the very important strategic policy of developing 'small' cities.

Developing small cities will stimulate transfer of surplus labor on a far larger scale away from agriculture, and will also enable township enterprises to become more concentrated, thereby allowing more people to enjoy the fruits of modern urban civilization. The policy will have major repercussions in expanding our domestic demand as well, helping to increase domestic investment and optimize our economic structure. We should regard it as a substantive part of the effort to restructure agricultural production and the rural economy in general. In developing small cities, however, we must be sure to have adequate planning in advance. Only a well-defined urban planning system can avoid the kind of pell-mell rush to implement a policy in blind fashion. We must give adequate weight to the key points in urban planning, and enable those places with superior conditions and potential to move ahead first. We must understand the radial influence that a city has on its surrounding areas. Second, we should formulate a series of specific policies and measures that promote not just the growth of cities but the healthy growth of cities. These will include policies to do with land use for urban construction, policies to do with how to manage household registration or *hukou,* policies to do with basic infrastructure and public works, social security systems for rural inhabitants, and management systems that are in alignment with a socialist market economy as well as the needs of small urban centers. Third, our starting point with respect to developing small cities should always emanate from the desire to create viable economies, for only if economic activity accompanies the creation of small cities will they be able to grow in any kind of sustainable and healthy manner.

Right now, it is an objective fact that we have a surplus in grain. The surplus is 'stage-specific,' but nevertheless it is necessary for us to control grain production within certain limits over the short run. As we do this, we must make sure to integrate other considerations, such as national food security, accommodating structural changes in people's food consumption behavior, raising the overall efficiencies and competitiveness of our agriculture, implementing policies that are sustainable, and so on. We must integrate short-term and long-term strategic considerations. Only then can we assure that this round of structural adjustments is in line with strategic goals.

V. Over the long run, we must ensure that we maintain adequate capacity in grain production, by emphasizing the maintenance of current capacity and ongoing increases in capacity

The major trends underway in our country are not going to change over the next two to three decades. First, our overall population is going to continue to increase. Although the rate of increase is slowing, the base is getting ever larger and hence the absolute number of people being added to the population every year is still tremendous. Second, our people's standard of living will consistently improve. As we move into the next century, our rural population in particular will see a qualitative change in their lives. Third, the pace of industrialization and urbanization will pick up, which means that there will continue to be a gradual loss of farmland. The intersection of these three major trends, namely 'more people, less land, and high living standards,' will create two pairs of correlated factors over the next 20 to 30 years.

One links the increase in population to the decrease in farmland. The other notes that as food consumption changes, perhaps decreases in total quantity but greatly improves in quality, the amount of grain used to produce more 'transformed' and processed food will increase. The conclusion to be made is that, despite our current surplus in grain, over the medium term and long term, we must be highly aware of the need to maintain adequate grain production capacity.

That capacity must be secured by a sufficient amount of farmland. Japan currently has a population of 130 million people and something approaching 74 million *mu* of arable land. That comes to less than six-tenths of one *mu* per person. Japan itself supplies only 28 percent of its cereals, however. In terms of caloric self-sufficiency, the country is producing 41 percent of its own needs. Given the amount of agricultural products that the country needs to import, Japan is 'occupying' or using up some 180 million *mu* of foreign farmland. In terms of its total consumption of agricultural products, therefore, the country in fact needs a supply of 254 million *mu* of land, or 2 *mu* per person.

We here in China have around 1.56 *mu* per person of farmland. That figure is calculated using what may be the unrealistic figure of 195.1 million *mu* of total arable land. Therefore, any statement that we have 'too much farmland,' or that over the medium and long term we have an excess capacity in grain production, is simply not in line with reality. Only if we maintain a baseline amount of arable land, and put a basic amount of improvement into the land, will we be able to maintain control over making structural adjustments. When there is too much grain, we can always plant other crops, when the market changes and demand increases, we always have the ability to change back. Therefore, we should never relax a very firm hold over two basic tenets: protecting farmland, and maintaining adequate inputs into the land.

For a very considerable time to come, our country is going to continue to be a 'developing nation.' For that reason, we must maintain a certain rate of growth in the national economy. This then determines the fact that, while preventing deflation is the immediate focus of our macroeconomic adjustments, over the medium and long term, avoiding inflation is going to be a recurring task.

From the last few bouts of inflation, we should recognize that they are often driven by a rapid increase in agricultural prices and especially food prices. These often take the lead [serve as the 'dragon-head'] in across-the-board price rises. The reason is that food still constitutes a large percentage of the average family's budget. In 1998, it made up 44.48 percent of an urban resident's living expenses and 53.43 percent of a farmer's living expenses. Keeping agricultural prices and especially food prices fundamentally steady is of ultimate importance in our country, whether that is with respect to people's lives or to overall economic stability. No matter what, we cannot allow great volatility in agriculture, and the corollary is that we must consistently maintain sufficient grain production capacity. Production amounts can always be adjusted from year to year by both market and government forces, but the underlying capacity has to be both stable and gradually increasing. This is simply a fact that is dictated by our national conditions.

Note

* This article was originally published in No. 9 Survey Report of the Development Research Center of the State Council in 2000.

8 Agriculture, the rural economy, and farmers*

Issues for the next stage

(2001)

In October 1998, the Third Plenary Session of the 15th Central Committee of the Party adopted a *Decision on Several Major Agricultural and Rural Issues*. This *Decision* made an important determination with respect to defining our current stage of agriculture in the country. It noted that we had passed from a longstanding period of insufficient supply to one in which 'total supply is in balance [with demand] overall, and in good years we have a surplus.' This statement indicated a fundamental shift in our situation, an easing of tight supply, and an understanding that we would now be modifying the previous fundamental goal of seeking to increase the quantity of basic agricultural products such as grain. With this determination, our country's agriculture has entered into a whole new stage of development.

I. The real essence of agricultural and rural issues in the new stage relates to increasing farmers' income

Generations of Chinese people have always dreamed of growing enough grain for the country. Actually accomplishing that feat these days is of historic significance in our country's socialist economic development. It is simply of inestimable importance. However, even as people are still applauding these words, 'in good years we have a surplus,' they are discovering that rural areas, so long championed as the first victory in the course of our reform, are now exploding with all kinds of highly disturbing problems.

In recent years, when discussing our country's various economic problems, the focus turns to one topic: farmers. Their 'incomes are not increasing yet their [tax] burden is not going down.' This shows that our focal point has shifted from balancing supply and demand of agricultural products to a concern about farmers themselves.

From all angles, socioeconomic analysis is indicating that the barriers to any increase in farmers' income are also barriers to improving our national economy as a whole. They are a serious constraint on creating any kind of 'virtuous cycle' in the economy. Has resolving the problem of supply and demand of agricultural products actually been a 'bitter medicine' for farmers? The common-sense answer is that any product that enjoys an excess of supply over demand will not make its producers much money. The producer will either see a reduction in income or even go out of business altogether. Farmers were not 'singing a happy tune,' however, even when our supply could not meet demand. When that was the case, farmers saw the results of their economic surplus get raked off and sent to cities, and to investment in industry, through the unified system of centralized purchasing and selling. When supply exceeded demand, the government maintained a protected [subsidized] price for agricultural goods, but the economic results 'flowed out' in considerable measure into the hands of the monopoly departments who served as government buyers.

It is obvious that the ones to be hurt in the end will always be farmers, whether or not there are grain surpluses, until we break completely away from the planned-economy system. Right now, we are in a transitional period in which the market-economy system is incomplete and the planned-economy system carries on in its usual way – the difficulties that farmers are facing are, therefore, to a large extent, caused by systemic constraints.

During the ninth Five-Year Plan period, the rate of increase in incomes of farmers went down year by year in a stair-stepped fashion: in 1996, per capita net income of farmers rose on an average of 9.0 percent. In 1997, the rate of increase declined to 4.6 percent; in 1998 it declined further to 4.3 percent, in 1999, it was 3.8 percent. In 2000, farmers' income grew by a mere 2.1 percent. For the three ensuing years, income grew on average by 3.4 percent, less than half of what rural inhabitants enjoyed in the same period, 7.2 percent. The discrepancy in incomes (i.e., disposable income of urban dwellers to net income of farmers) went from 2.47 to 1 in 1997, and from 2.79 to 1 in the year 2000. We should note that this is the average ratio for all people nationwide. Given that there are radical differences in degree of 'socialist economic development' in our country, such averaged figures often cover over a multitude of problems and contradictions. (Average per capita income in Shanghai in the year 2000 was RMB 5,596.09, but it was only RMB 1,374.16 in the province of Guizhou.) To understand just how severe the situation is with respect to farmers' incomes, therefore, we need to delve into the analysis more deeply.

1. The outstanding problem underlying sluggish growth in farmers' income is diminished income from agriculture

The slowdown in growth of farmers' income in recent years is only a superficial indicator of farmers' income problems. The actual severity of the problem can be seen far more clearly in the fact that farming incomes over successive years have been going down. Table 8.1 shows net per capita farming income over the past four years, its composition, and its changes.

It is obvious that although farmers' net income per capita from total production in 2000 was RMB 142.27 more than it was in 1997, farmers' net income per capita from agriculture during the same period decreased by RMB 131.61, or 10.4 percent down compared to 1997. Between 1998 and 2000, farmers' net income per capita from agriculture decreased year on year, by RMB 30.25 from 1997 to 1998,

Table 8.1 Sources of farmers' net income per capita, 1997–2000

Year	Net income from all production (RMB)	Net income from primary industries (RMB)	Net income from secondary industries (RMB)	Net income from tertiary industries (RMB)
1997	1,987.28	1,267.68	437.78	281.81
1998	2,039.58	1,237.44	498.92	303.22
1999	2,078.62	1,180.02	564.30	334.30
2000	2,129.27	1,136.08	598.27	395.20
2000 vs. 1997	+142.27	−131.61	+160.49	+113.39

RMB 57.42 from 1998 to 1999, and RMB 43.94 from 1999 to 2000. According to the agricultural census, only 59.3 percent of all rural households in the country are 'pure agricultural households,' or households engaged solely or mainly in agriculture. An additional 18.2 percent are 'agricultural households engaging also in other occupations' (with more family members engaged in agriculture than those in other economic sectors). Together, these two categories account for 77.5 percent of the total number of rural households. Since agricultural income has been decreasing for three successive years, it is not hard to see that the majority of households whose income comes primarily from agriculture has in fact also seen negative growth rates in net income.

It is against this backdrop that net per capita income of a number of farmers has dropped precipitously in major agricultural provinces, as well as poorer regions in the west that are less developed. In 1999 and 2000, farmers in six provinces and regions in the country had declining net per capita incomes over the previous year among farmers. Details are as shown in Table 8.2.

Liaoning, Jilin, and Heilongjiang provinces have seen two consecutive two years of declining net income per capita among farmers. The combined two-year decrease in farmers' net income per capita in Jilin totaled RMB 361.10, with net income per capita in 2000 over 1998 down by 15.2 percent.

The fundamental reason for this decline in agricultural income can be attributed to changes in the market for agricultural products. Since reform, the main sources of agricultural income have seen two major changes. Between 1979 and 1984, our country's agricultural products, of all kinds, were in short supply. The household

Table 8.2 Decreases in the farmers' net income per capita in some provinces in 1999 and 2000

Per Capita Income Decrease in 1999 (RMB)	Shanxi	Liaoning	Jilin	Heilongjiang	Gansu	Xinjiang
	85.98	78.75	123.01	87.17	35.77	126.98
Per Capita Income Decrease in 2000 (RMB)	Guangxi	Liaoning	Jilin	Heilongjiang	Shaanxi	Ningxia
	183.82	145.46	238.09	17.71	12.00	29.85

contracting system then stimulated farmers to produce and the total quantity of goods rose ferociously in the short space of five to six years. An increase in farmers' incomes came primarily from an increase in the quantity of production of these goods. Starting in 1984, the phenomenon of shortage of agricultural goods was largely mitigated and instead such things as grain and cotton went through two short periods of surplus, of being 'hard to sell.' As a result, farmers were not going to be able to increase incomes by simply relying on increased quantity of production. From the mid-1980s onward, increases in farming income came primarily from an increase in prices of farm goods. In 1996, farmers' net per capita income rose by 9 percent, and the reason was that in that year the State procurement price of grain was lifted by 42 percent. From the mid-1990s, however, the supply of most agricultural products in our country exceeded demand, yet at the same time prices were mostly above international market levels. This meant that there was very little margin left in which to increase prices as well as to increase production. This then led to a sustained drop in net farming income for farmers. Clearly, methods that worked earlier during the course of our reform are no longer effective in raising farmers' incomes. In our current market environment for farm goods, we need to chart a new course if we want to realize an increase in farmer's incomes as well as in agriculture in general. The solution must address structural adjustments in the overall national economy.

2. Underemployment is the underlying cause for the difficulties in raising farmers' incomes

In 2000, the total number of 'rural laborers' had already reached 479.62 million. Among these, some 68.4 percent, or 327.975 million, were engaged in agriculture, forestry, animal husbandry, and fisheries. That figure of nearly 328 million accounted for 46.1 percent of our country's total number of employees. In that same year, however, agriculture's share in the gross value of all domestic production came to only 15.9 percent. The discrepancy in the two figures indicates that the productivity per person of agriculture was only around one-third of what it was in the country in general. Herein lies the crux of the problem as farmers try to keep increasing their income by relying on agriculture alone.

While there are many reasons for the low productivity of labor employed in farming, one of the most persistent and most important is that there is too much 'labor' working too little arable land. This is the fundamental reason for low productivity as well as for the inability to increase incomes off farming. Starting in the mid-1980s, the 'vanguard' of township enterprises began to absorb surplus labor into secondary and tertiary industries in the countryside, in a major way. It was only in 1992, however, that the absolute number of laborers engaged in farming, forestry, animal husbandry, and fisheries showed a decline. In recent years, given the changes in the surrounding economic environment for township enterprises, they themselves are at a turning point in terms of structural adjustments and systemic innovations. Rather than continuing to absorb new labor into their ranks, therefore, in 1997 and 1998 they actually reduced their ranks by about 10 million jobs. From 1997, the total number of people engaged in agriculture rebounded as a result and continued along an increasing trend for the next three years. By 1999, the total number of people employed in agriculture had already surpassed the figure of 1996 by 6.514 million people. Although the number of people employed in agriculture in 2000 was slightly less, it was still 5.371 million more than it had been in 1996. During the eighth Five-Year Plan period [1991–1995], not only did the number of laborers employed in agriculture not decrease, but it went up by another 4.63 million people, making an already severe excess of labor even more extreme. The underemployment situation among farmers is now going from bad to worse.

During the ninth Five-Year Plan period [1996–2000], our country's total rural labor force increased by 29.2 million people. The average annual increase was 5.84 million people. Given our experience of the past few years, the underemployed labor force in agriculture will again be entering a period of rapid increase if we do not find an alternative channel into which to shift these excess workers. If we rely merely on rural areas themselves to absorb the employment, and on township enterprises, it is going to be extremely difficult to increase farmers' income and to try to maintain rural stability. In fact, the only reason overall farm incomes were able to maintain at least a minor increase over three consecutive years of decreasing income from agriculture alone was the supplementary income provided by workers who 'went out' to work for hire, the so-called rural migrant workers. In 1997, agriculture-derived income constituted 63.8 percent of farmers' net per capita income. By 2000, this figure had dropped to 53.3 percent, or a decline of 10.5 percentage points over three years. Naturally, this kind of change also relates to relatively low efficiencies in agriculture, but it also acutely points to the fact that we must work very hard to stimulate adequate employment for the rural labor force if we want to maintain a normal increase in farmers' incomes.

Only by decreasing the number of farmers will we be able to make farmers more prosperous. This is the common experience worldwide in development programs for agriculture and for rural areas. In our country, the greatest problems lie in shifting labor to secondary and tertiary industries and to urban areas. The disconnect in our country between industrialization and urbanization, and the disconnect between the declining share of agriculture in our GDP and the increasing numbers of 'farm labor' in our rural areas provide the greatest obstacles to realizing any hope of rural people for higher incomes. In recent years, the slow pace at which we have been urbanizing is directly related to the difficulties farmers face in improving their incomes. Between 1979 and 1995, the percentage of 'urban dwellers' in our country increased from 17.92 percent to 29.04 percent. On average, the 'urbanization rate' went up every year by 0.654 percentage points. In contrast, between 1996 and 1999, urban populations only increased by 1.85 percent, with an average annual rate of only 0.463 percentage points. 'Imposing ramparts' have stood to block farmers from shifting their place of residence to cities for more than 40 years. A quota administered by relevant departments strictly has controlled the number of 'rural' people who could 'shift from rural to nonrural' every year. This quota was set at 0.15 percent of the level of the urban population in any given place. The fifth population census, conducted in the year 2000, showed an urban population of 458.44 million people. Based on past regulations as noted above, the number allowed to 'shift from rural to nonrural' would in 2000 have come to fewer than 685,000 people. This is not even 12 percent of our country's natural increase in the rural population every year. Our former regulations preventing movement of rural people to urban areas obviously have been directly counter to our goal of needing to 'decrease the number of farmers.'

Against a very unforgiving backdrop of too many people and too little land, combined with 'imposing ramparts' that kept people out of cities, two remarkable movements began in the countryside as a very practical response to the need to find employment. One was the 'vanguard' force of township enterprises which capitalized on the times. The other was the surging force of migrant labor that 'left family and the old well behind' and 'flooded out' to find any opportunity for work. Both of these have to be regarded as an instinctive native ability to survive within the context of the existing economic system, an expression of the desire of the great mass of farmers to grow and develop. Right now, the contradiction between this desire and the system in which farmers are operating has reached a point of incompatibility. It has reached that stage at which 'fire and water find they cannot merge.' Clearly, if we truly want to increase farmers' income, we must expand farmers' opportunities for employment. Otherwise, not only will we hold back any increase in farmers' income but we will keep agricultural productivity at a low level, the cost of agricultural products will continue to rise, and our agriculture as a whole will gradually lose any competitive advantage.

3. The situation of poor growth in farmers' income in recent years is severely impacting any expansion of domestic demand

Given the overall context of poor growth in rural incomes, since 1998 average household expenditures in rural areas have either been declining or simply holding steady and not increasing. Table 8.3 gives details.

Table 8.3 Per capita household operating costs and expenditures on normal consumption from 1997 to 2000

Year	Total expenditures (RMB)	Household operating costs (RMB)	Expenditures for normal living consumption (RMB)	Food (RMB)	Clothing (RMB)
1997	2,536.79	706.27	1,617.15	890.28	109.41
1998	1,457.17	652.48	1,590.33	849.64	98.06
1999	2,390.37	599.77	1,577.42	829.02	92.04
2000	2,652.38	654.26	1,970.11	820.51	95.95

Expenditures on rural household operating costs per capita declined in 1998 and yet again in 1999, with the figure in 1999 already 15.1 percent lower than it had been in 1997 (a reduction of RMB 106.5). Spending on operating costs increased in 2000, but this was partially 'restorative' or getting back to normal, and partially compelled by necessary increases on antidrought measures and increased fuel prices.

Changes in the farmers' living expenses per capita show a similar pattern. Spending decreased in the years 1998 and 1999, with 1999 expenditures 2.5 percent less than they had been in 1997 (or RMB 39.73 less). Amounts went up in 2000 by RMB 92.69, but this also was of a compulsory nature. First, spending on food continued to decrease and spending on clothing stayed lower than 1997 and 1998 levels, despite a modest increase over 1999. The main thing compelling higher spending was such service-industry costs as healthcare, which increased by 35.5 percent (RMB 24.4), and education (the category includes entertainment and cultural activities), which increased by 10.9 percent (RMB 18.38). In sum, spending on compulsory items as noted above increased by RMB 60.33 RMB, which accounted for 65.1 percent of the total increase in living expenses per capita in the year 2000. Therefore, although farmers' living expenses per capita in 2000 increased, a very modest part of their spending contributed to any improvement in living standards.

The above data on per capita production and living expenses of farmers simply gives average figures, and the reality is that most rural households who rely on agriculture as their main source of income are spending far less than they were before. Their situation is markedly different from the average. This is the main reason 'rural' consumption has declined as a percentage of consumption overall in the country. (See Table 8.4.)

It can be seen from the above data that the contraction of farmers' spending is in fact impacting our stated desire to expand domestic consumption. Once the Asian financial crisis 'exploded' on the scene, the Central Committee of the Party and the State Council took timely and appropriate action to increase domestic demand, which is already showing some results. However, we must not forget the fact that 63.8 percent of our population is in rural areas, as according to the fifth population census taken in the year 2000. (The figure is 73.3 percent for

Table 8.4 Share of all retail sales of consumer goods that are being sold at the county level or below the county level [i.e., in the countryside], from 1996 to 2000

Year	Market share of consumer goods at county level and below (%)
1996	39.65
1997	39.01
1998	38.86
1999	38.68
2000	38.18

the 'agricultural population' when using household registration statistics, or *hukou*.) If we find it difficult to lift the purchasing power of the majority of our population, then our huge domestic market is going to stay 'potential' rather than realized.

Consequently, specific measures to increase domestic demand are going to have to focus effectively on increasing employment for rural people and increasing sales of agricultural products. Otherwise, farmers will not see improved incomes and will not enjoy any enhanced spending capacity in order to lift domestic demand. Measures that have in fact been taken to increase domestic demand are not aimed at this problem. The most notable among them include huge infrastructure projects and increasing the income of urban workers. These are indeed stimulating domestic demand but they are having no noticeable effect on raising farmers' income. Large-scale infrastructure projects have very little impact on farmers' job opportunities or on sale of goods being produced by township enterprises. Meanwhile, increasing incomes of urban workers is mainly affecting such newly emerging consumer sectors as housing, automobiles, education, and travel, as well as increasing savings. Given that the total number of urban residents is limited, the measures are having a very limited impact in terms of increasing sale of agricultural goods.

Statistics show that the per capita disposable income of urban residents increased by RMB 1,441.1 between 1996 and 2000, but during these four years per capita spending on food only increased by RMB 53.6. The income elasticity coefficient for food was less than 0.04. This means that for each additional RMB of disposable income in this period, only 0.04 of 1 RMB was spent on food and this amount also included spending on eating outside the home. The key to realizing any effective increase in domestic demand is going to have to involve measures to increase farmers' income and their own consumption. It is going to have to be aimed in the direction of rural areas, not urban, and specifically toward farmers.

In what we are calling the 'new stage' of rural economic development and agricultural development, clearly we have a less fraught situation with respect to supply and demand. Given this situation, we now should focus our attention less on increasing supply of agricultural products and more on increasing incomes of farmers. China is not going to have any kind of real 'modernization' without improving the prosperity of 800 to 900 million farmers, and without providing the fruits of civilization to them as well. Forty years ago, in the midst of intense economic hardship in our country, Mao Zedong said to high-ranking cadres in the Party, 'China has 500 million farmers. If you do not unite with them, no matter how strong your industry is, how big your Anshan Iron and Steel Company is, *you will be overturned.*' He also concluded that it was pointless to even think of doing anything in the country if the government distanced itself from farmers. Today, China has a far larger number of farmers than it did when Mao Zedong said these words in 1961. We therefore need an even more acute understanding of the importance of this subject. Compared to 40 years ago, we need to have a much more profound awareness of the overall significance to our country of increasing farmers' incomes and purchasing power.

II. The basic approach to rural economic development during the tenth Five-Year-Plan period

1. *Objectives for agriculture and rural economic development during the tenth Five-Year-Plan period*

The approach of the Central Committee of the Party with respect to the 'new stage' of agriculture and rural economic development is very clear in terms of analyzing and addressing the issues and improving rural economic conditions. The Central Committee has determined that we are indeed in a 'new stage' with respect to advancing agriculture, and that the core mission in this new stage is strategic restructuring. It has defined the fundamental objective in this process to be increasing farmers' income. The outline of the tenth Five-Year Plan now has to set forth specific targets of a 'guiding nature' that are in line with the Central Committee's determination, its analysis, and its requirements. Those should address the following four aspects of agricultural and rural concerns.

The first is the share of agricultural output in our total GDP. The aim is to decrease that share to below 13 percent within the next five years, which means lowering the current share of agriculture in GDP by 3 percent. This is fully in line with the normal progression of industrialization and urbanization. Pointing it out explicitly is being done to enable us to make the simultaneous point that agriculture retains its central and fundamental position in our national economy. From all angles, we must reinforce and consolidate the understanding that a decline in agriculture's share of GDP does not mean a decline in the fundamental importance of agriculture to our economy.

The second is the share of animal husbandry output in our total GDP. The aim is to increase that share to over 35 percent over the course of the tenth Five-Year Plan. It was 29.8 percent at the end of the ninth Five-Year Plan, which means increasing it by 5 percent. Realizing this target corresponds to the 'new stage' of agriculture, in which we put our efforts into 'transforming' primary agricultural products. To a great extent, the level of a country's animal byproducts industry is a measure of its quality of life. Focusing on improving that industry therefore contributes not only to agricultural development itself but also to an improved standard of living for our people.

The third is shifting surplus labor out of the agricultural sphere. The goal is to transfer 40 million laborers out of agriculture within the next five years, which is a massive and highly complex task. If we do not speed up our attempts in this regard, however, we clearly are not going to be able to extricate our rural areas from a very difficult situation, nor are we going to be able to raise farmers' income.

The fourth is to increase per capita income of farmers. The goal is to increase it by an average 5 percentage points per year over the next five years, which is 1 percentage point more than the goal set forth in the ninth Five-Year Plan. Since the rate of increase in incomes declined over the ninth Five-Year Plan, and by the year 2000 the overall increase had come to only 2.1 percent, accomplishing this goal is not going to be easy. Nonetheless, if we do not achieve this target, it will be difficult to move our entire economy into a 'virtuous cycle.'

2. 'Strategic restructuring' as the main theme in agriculture and rural economic development during the tenth Five-Year-Plan period

As our agriculture and rural economy enter a 'new stage,' we are going to be confronted by new challenges that require a whole series of conceptual changes, changes in our approach, and changes in our policies. The process is going to require strategic restructuring of our entire rural and agricultural economy. It includes the following considerations.

1   Optimizing the kinds of agricultural products that are being produced, improving quality, and shifting the focus of agricultural development to 'higher quality' and 'greater efficiency' as the core concerns. In the early 1990s, we espoused a similar approach when we called for increasing production, improving quality, and achieving greater efficiency, but our real focus remained increasing the *quantity* of production. Given our current favorable situation with respect to supply and demand, while maintaining a secure capacity to produce basic agricultural products, we should begin to move in the direction of better-quality products and more efficient production methods. We should accelerate the establishment of market information systems, and the establishment of food safety standards and quality control standards. We must set up inspection procedures and systems that enable us to meet both domestic and international market requirements if we expect to be internationally competitive with high-quality, safe, agricultural products.

2   Optimizing the location of agricultural production so that each area can capitalize on its comparative advantages. In the past, each locality attempted to be self-sufficient in basic agricultural commodities, which was in fact necessitated by the defects of the planned-economy system. By now, we have a 'basic balance in overall quantity and a surplus in good years.' The recent determination by the State Council regarding systemic reform of our distribution system ['circulation system'] for cotton and grain now has created better underlying conditions for moving this process forward. We can restructure the 'deployment' of agricultural production, in terms of where crops are grown, and enable each area to use its comparative advantages. Earlier this year [2001], Zhejiang Province was the first to cancel its mandatory grain purchasing contracts. Farmers can voluntarily sign contracts as they wish with State grain-purchase-and-sale enterprises, on terms that match market prices. This has stimulated a tremendous restructuring of agricultural production. The deficit in Zhejiang's grain production is made up for by contracting for grain from grain-producing regions, including Heilongjiang, Jilin, Hubei, Jiangxi, and Anhui. The contracts 'guarantee a fixed quantity but at "released" prices.' This whole process has attracted a large number of grain merchants into Zhejiang Province, revitalizing the whole grain trade among provinces, along market-driven practices. This has contributed greatly to restructuring Zhejiang's agricultural production but it has also served to expand agricultural exports, to increase farmers' income, and to create markets for grain-producing regions.

Since they can take advantage of their own unique conditions, farmers in these grain-producing regions too are reaping the benefits.

3   Increasing the degree to which primary products are 'transformed' and processed. Two inevitable trends accompany economic development, once people's standard of living reaches a certain level. One is that the Engel's coefficient with respect to spending on living expenses declines, and the other is that income elasticity with respect to food purchases declines. This poses a formidable challenge to agricultural development. Relying on growth in production of primary products becomes increasingly difficult. It becomes necessary to 'transform' agricultural products [such as transforming grain into animal protein], and to engage in processing in order to increase the 'value' of farm products. It becomes necessary to use modern technology to create a diversified range of products to attract consumers and open up new farm-product markets. As agriculture 'industrializes,' the resulting operating modes not only spur greater sales but help to further a reorganization of rural economies in general. They enable farmers to receive current market information, they promote modern applied technologies, they lower market-entry risks. The process provides a realistic way for our country's agriculture to modernize while still being grounded in a system that features contracting by households.

4   Promoting urbanization in a proactive but very deliberate way. In 1998, the Third Plenary Session of the 15th Central Committee of the Party put forth a highly strategic way to advance rural economies and social progress in general, namely, the establishment of 'small cities.' The Tenth Five-Year Plan then specified a plan of action for this form of urbanization. A tremendous debate still continues among our theoretical circles as to exactly how our country should pursue what people are calling 'large-townification' [*cheng-zhen-hua*]. Some cadres feel that this term is not adequately 'scientific,' and that we should simply call it 'urbanization' [*cheng-shi-hua*]. Other cadres feel that we should focus on developing large- and medium-sized cities, so as to achieve economies of scale and to enable large cities to take full advantage of their 'radial influence.' The proposals put forth in the Tenth Five-Year Plan set forth a path of coordinated development of cities of all sizes, large, medium, and small, in addition to 'small towns.' It argued for a path of 'townification' that carried specifically Chinese attributes. It also set out specific requirements in this process. Developing large- and medium-sized cities naturally does indeed provide economic efficiencies and certain economies of scale, but from the perspective of shifting agricultural labor into other occupations, 'small towns' are a more realistic option. Large- and medium-sized cities provide employment opportunities for rural laborers when they 'move' into cities, but living standards and social security standards are such that it is very hard for farmers to take up permanent residence in these places in a short period of time. The more common situation is that laborers enter cities, work for a while, build up a little savings, and then return to their original place of residence, say a county seat or a 'statutory town,' where they turn into a 'nonagricultural' population. Specific mention, therefore, of

developing 'small towns' in the Tenth Five-Year Plan is not meant to restrict the growth of larger cities, but rather to meet the very real needs of these people by accelerating the process of finding them alternative employment. In point of fact, only if we have coordinated development of all sizes of urban centers will we be able to provide alternative employment for our great amount of surplus labor.

In terms of smaller-sized cities, the focal point should be county seats and those 'statutory towns' that can meet the necessary conditions and have the right potential. Our country has more than 2,000 'county seats,' which includes what are defined as both 'county-level cities' and 'prefectures.' It has more than 19,000 'statutory towns,' that is, those that are authorized with a 'town jurisdiction' [*jian-zhi-zhen*]. We need to focus on these and not simply allow rampant building to begin everywhere, for that would entail a calamitous waste of resources and man-power. If we can select a small group of the best candidates from among the 19,000 statutory towns, and then include in the 2,000 county seats, and apply excellent urban planning and systems as they develop, in 10 to 20 years we should have some 4,000 to 5,000 'small cities.' These should play an extremely positive role in shifting rural populations [out of agriculture]. They should help improve our country's overall industrial structure, the distribution patterns of enterprises and populations in general [i.e., where they are located], and the employment structure of the labor force.

III. Two fundamental policies with regard to rural areas that we should focus on in particular

1. Reduce the tax burden on farmers

Reducing the tax burden on farmers is something that the Central Committee of the Party and the State Council have consistently regarded as high priority in terms of fundamental rural policies. Over the years, a number of measures have been adopted that try to curtail the trend of an increasing tax load on farmers. In point of fact, however, taxes on farmers continue to increase. According to Ministry of Agriculture statistics, in the year 2000, the total sum of taxes and levies directly imposed on farmers nationwide came to RMB 177.89 billion. This means that the average farmer is paying RMB 199.8 per year in taxes. Included in this figure are, first, straight 'taxes' of various kinds amounting to RMB 92.6. Second are levies commonly known as the 'three reserves and five levies' [*san-ti-wu-tong*], which amount to RMB 66.2 per farmer. (The three reserves are for public reserve funds, public welfare funds, and management fees, and the five levies are charges for rural education, family planning, militia training, rural road construction, and subsidies to entitled groups.) Third are payments required of farmers to offset what are known as the 'two labor services,' namely, 'the rural voluntary labor service and the labor accumulation service,' which come to RMB 6.31 per farmer. Finally there are various 'social taxes' such as 'fund raising fees' that come to an average of RMB 34.68 per farmer. Clearly, the attempt to lower farmers' taxes cannot rely solely on governmental policy regulations and 'restrictions.' Instead of treating symptoms, we have to research a more permanent cure if we truly want to accomplish this stated goal.

After widespread study of the issue and after soliciting opinions from all sides, in 2000 the Central Committee of the Party drew up a plan for 'reform of taxes and fees' [or 'levies'], and began a pilot project to test it out in Anhui Province. Results have indicated that the reform is clearly effective. Provincewide, the average farmer paid RMB 30 less in taxes and fees, a reduction of more than 30 percent. The pilot project also exposed certain problems in the reform plan itself, however. The main problem was that the calculation of tax was quite complex, and the result was that different rural households were taxed on an unequal basis. Under the way in which we currently handle agricultural production, it is not easy for either farmers or our grassroots-level cadres to really understand how to calculate taxes. Calculations involve such things as the extent of business that should be taxed, the pricing of products on which taxes are applied, the output in a given year, and so on. The reason for the rise of unequal taxation has mainly been changes in the entity being taxed. In the past, the greatest portion of tax was charged per capita. If there were a lot of people and little land among them, then each paid a disproportionate amount. After reform, taxes and levies were incorporated into the 'agricultural tax,' which was a unified or standard amount. The tax went along with the land, so if there was a lot of land and few people farming, each paid more. To resolve these things, we will need to collect experience from our pilot sites and carry out adjustments as necessary to improve the system.

Quite apart from improving our program with respect to taxes and levies, however, we clearly need to tackle more profound issues if we really want to lighten the load on farmers. If we do not tackle these issues, three key aspects will be very hard to resolve in the future, namely, furthering various social undertakings in rural areas, ensuring that grassroots governmental bodies can function properly, and reducing the tax burden on farmers. If we fail in all three, the problems will reappear sooner or later, even if we are able to lighten the tax burden temporarily.

At the very least, we have to address the following four issues.

1   *The issue of public finance in rural areas.* The crux of the problem here is that administrative functions are not aligned with financial authority of governmental bodies at the grassroots level. Actual operations at the lowest level of government show that the main budgetary spending goes for education. Such spending at the township level is generally over 60 percent of the entire budget, while in some places it is over 80 percent. Farmers therefore have a saying, 'the [tax] burden revolves around education.' This is not to say that education is unimportant or that the spending of townships on education is too great. It is to point out that the financial capacity of the lowest level of government is inconsistent with that level's responsibility with respect to education. Starting in 2001, salaries of teachers have been paid directly by counties, in a standard and centralized way, but the source of the funds still

comes from towns. This means that the problem has not fundamentally been resolved. A second issue is that while a large percentage of townships can keep up payments for teachers' salaries, they cannot fund the operating costs of schools. The result is that they are 'supporting soldiers but unable to fight any kind of war.' Farmers are naturally upset, since their local governments provide little in the way of services. From the perspective of aligning financial responsibility with necessary functions, reform of the public finance systems of counties and towns is going to be necessary.

2   *The issue of setting up and defining the proper position and function of governmental departments in local areas.* Having redundant personnel in higher levels of government is perhaps mainly a matter of mere inefficiencies. At the lower levels of government, in rural areas, it becomes an urgent budgetary issue. Statistics from the year 2000 indicate that 69.7 percent of all governmental staffing costs in the country were born by governments at the county and township level. (This figure does not include army personnel or armed police.) For the same period, however, the public revenues of counties and townships accounted for a mere 20.7 percent of all public revenues in the country. If localities want to maintain salaries for people, and also cover operating costs, it is clear that the tax burden on farmers in most places is necessarily high. Organizational reform, restructuring governmental functions, reduction in forces – all of these are a prerequisite for lowering farmers' taxes.

3   *Economic development and well-being at the county level as well as lower levels of government.* Any improvement in the budgets of county-level governments is going to have to rely on improvements in the local economy. One of the notable features of both county and township economies is the lack of State-owned business, particularly large- and medium-sized State-Owned Enterprises. As a result, counties and townships have been able to get very little in the way of necessary funding support, especially since both fiscal and financial resources were directed toward large- and medium-sized State-Owned Enterprises for a long period of time. Meanwhile, in the central and western parts of the country, such State-Owned Enterprises as there were are now facing extremely hard times for various reasons, while 'people-operated' enterprises [*min-ying*] are also finding it hard to grow, given the lack of adequate funding. Local county and township economies in these areas are unable to come up with new 'growth points,' hence local governments have no new sources of tax revenue, and again the burden comes down on farmers. The number of people with residence permits or *hukou* that are registered in county-level governments or below in our country approaches 1.1 million. Among these, 920 million people are officially an 'agricultural' population, while an additional 170 million people are registered in county seats and in 'statutory towns.' Were the economies of these places to dry up completely for any reason, and were tax revenues to cease, there would be massive consequences. It behooves us to think about this now and to adopt measures to address this looming problem as soon as possible.

4   ***Ideological and work attitudes of a portion of rural cadres who are at the county and township level.*** Even though the fundamental problem of overly heavy tax burdens on farmers is a systemic issue, and not caused by local cadres, the attitudes and work ethics of certain cadres is adding fuel to the fire in many places. They are not helping to resolve the issue of overly heavy taxes on farmers. Some rural cadres initiate projects that are not based on any realistic calculations and that greatly exceed the economic means of their tax base. Other cadres are brazenly corrupt and working in their own interests, to the extent that they are profligate and irresponsible with farmers' hard-earned money. Still others treat farmers as though they were ignorant simpletons, with no understanding of the hardships some people have been through. Other than improving the ideological training of cadres, any fundamental resolution of these issues is going to have to include an expansion of democratic participation at the grassroots level in rural areas. It is going to have to include strengthening self-governance systems of rural people, and improving the mechanisms for selecting and supervising cadres.

From the above, it should be apparent that any reform of rural taxes actually involves a large amount of systems engineering. It involves coordinated reforms in many different areas. At this immediate stage, therefore, rolling out reform of rural taxes and levies should be tightly integrated with strict administrative procedures. We have to treat both the symptom and the underlying disease at the same time. Only if we hold down the overall level of taxes that farmers are paying in this transitional period will we be able to ensure ongoing growth of agriculture, improvement of farmers' lives, and social stability in our rural areas.

2. Stabilize rural land-contracting relationships and establish a foundation for the legal transfer of land-use rights

New developments are currently appearing in land-use rights for farmland, in terms of transferability and concentrating larger parcels. This is happening even as we are in the midst of plans for restructuring agriculture. According to statistics of the Ministry of Agriculture, transferable land-use rights constitute some 5 percent to 6 percent of all land under contracted cultivation. Most of this is happening along the coast, in more developed provinces and urban areas. Around 8 percent to 10 percent of land under contract in these developed areas is 'transferable' – in some areas the amount can be as much as 20 percent to 30 percent. In more inland areas, the amount is more like 1 percent to 2 percent of contracted land. In overall terms, the amount of farmland that is being 'transferred' or 'concentrated' is not all that great. The attention it has drawn from the media, and from theoretical circles, is out of proportion to the reality but still has made the subject a 'hot topic' in rural issues.

In addition to the propensity of the media to fasten on any new and sensitive subject, the reason for the divergence between reality and public opinion is that there are different views on such major policies as modernization of agriculture and the whole contracting system for land. Given that our contracting system is the cornerstone of the 'basic operating system' in rural areas, and that it was formed after reform began, we must adopt a very rational and respectful attitude in handling the issues, and base our approach to 'transferability' and 'concentration' on the great majority of rural areas. We do not want to stir up any doubts about the basic operating system currently in place in rural areas.

We are currently seeing an increase in the method of contracting land known as 'leasing back and "flip" contracting.' The village or township pays a certain sum to the farming household and consolidates its contracted land with that of others; it then rents the land out either to companies from 'outside' the locality or to larger households who are capable of larger-scale operations. Alternatively, it puts a certain amount of investment into the land and then re-rents it to other farming households in the village. This kind of 'flip' contracting increases the price and presents the opportunity for a certain profit. Whichever method is used, the 'collective' receives a higher rent than it would have by contracting land directly to farmers. The end result is that cadres of the town or village earn more money, which is why the practice has spread so rapidly.

It should be noted that 'leasing back and flip contracting' comes in many varieties. Some places have acted properly in ensuring that farmers' rights are respected, by implementing land-contracting policies in accordance with the rules. At the same time, they have been able to improve production efficiencies, and to increase farmers' income. Quite a few places, on the other hand, have distorted the rules and even gone against policy guidelines. These transgressions have occurred mainly in the following three ways. First, [officials] have not respected the wishes of farmers. When leasing back farmland, villages attach all kinds of extraneous and unrealistic provisions. If a farmer refuses, the village superficially agrees and does not force the issue, but in allocating different land to the farmer, it cheats him by choosing inferior and more remote parcels. The farmer ends up realizing he has lost more than he has gained and yet also realizing he has no alternative. Second, [officials] have intentionally mixed up the concepts of land-use rights and land-contracting rights, to the detriment of farmers. In some places, after a farmer rents out his 'land-use rights,' [the village, or officials] simply cancel the 'contracting-rights' that the farmer has to that land. A more widespread situation is that once a farmer rents out land-use rights, although in name he retains his 'contracting rights,' in reality he has lost the fundamental authority over operating contracting rights on that land. The whole concept of 'contracting rights' evolves into a mere pittance of rental money for leasing the land. Third, 'officials' ostensibly 'rent back' the land, but in reality 'flips' contracting rights to it, in a way that is non-transparent with respect to who earns the resulting income. All the farmer knows is the final sum of money he receives from the village for 'renting' his contracted land. He has no idea of the price at which it was re-rented or 'flipped' to others. The amount of money that the village derives through such means frequently exceeds the amount any farmer receives for 'transferring' his 'land-use rights.' The sums received by the 'village organization' are therefore not rightful income that should indeed go to an intermediary as a kind of 'service fee,' but instead are equivalent to what could be called payment for 'second-hand land renting.'

Household contracting of farmland, and what we call a 'double-layered system' that integrates a unified [or centralized] and a dispersed [or decentralized] method of managing land, has provided farmers with two major systemic results: It has enabled them to contract for collectively owned land, and it has given them authority over operating that land themselves. Once the above practices began, that is, such things as 'leasing back and flip contracting,' farmers have maintained the right to earn a modicum of rent off contracted land, but they have lost all autonomous authority over managing that land. In reality, village organizations are now 'buying out' the land contracting rights of farmers.

Given this kind of 'buying out,' farmers are yet again losing their status as 'operating entities' on land. It is unclear just how this kind of deep-seated modification is going to influence systemic practices in rural areas. It is unclear whether or not our entire socioeconomic system is prepared for the consequences. The whole subject truly requires extensive research and analysis.

Supply and demand of agricultural products have entered a 'new stage' in our country, and for that reason we are confronting unprecedented situations and completely new issues. It is perhaps due to this situation that certain areas are welcoming these 'leasing back and flip contracting' practices. Transferability and concentration of land-use rights are perhaps seen as a solution to new problems. The term being used is 'shifting' or 'moving' land [*dong-di*], meaning changing usage rights to land. We now need to think very seriously about whether or not these practices will lead to even more complex problems.

We should conduct in-depth analysis on the following three considerations in particular.

1   *Cyclical fluctuations in supply and demand of agricultural products, and how these relate to our land-use system for farmland.* We currently are experiencing an excess of supply over demand, and the comparative results of investment in agriculture are at a low ebb. This has dis-incentivized farmers to produce. Some leave farmland uncultivated; others feel it is a better deal for them to rent their land out and collect payments. Supply and demand in agriculture tends to be cyclical, however. When the market is basically in balance, or supply lags demand a little, prices rise and farmers again are motivated to produce. At that point, they may demand a return of their land-use rights – such a thing has happened many times in the past. The more critical issue and one we need to be aware of is that fluctuations in prices are a short-term phenomenon, while 'land systems' create a fundamental socioeconomic structure. Changing a fundamental structure in order to accommodate short-term problems frequently results in more loss than gain.

2   *How the instability of rural migrant labor employment relates to our system of agricultural land use.* The number of rural migrant workers has indeed been increasing in recent years, but the thing to note is that those who are able to take up permanent residence somewhere else, and not have to return to the countryside, are few and far between. For some time to come, the great majority of farmers must rely on their own contracted patch of land for security.

This is ultimately the place to which they can return if they need to, simply in order to eat. We therefore must maintain a stable land-contracting system, to enable these people to carry on 'two-way mobility' in finding jobs and to assure stability in rural areas, not to mention our entire society. The reason some developing countries spawn slums around major cities is that bankrupt farmers have lost their land and have no alternative but to make a one-way journey into cities, despite not having any employment there. This creates an element of social instability. Until there are other means of assuring basic security for farmers' livelihood as a substitute for relying on land, we must maintain the stability of our original land-contracting system for rural migrant workers.

3   *How the entry of corporations into the sphere of agriculture is affecting farmers' employment and an evolving rural social structure.* Household operations in farming are not just a mode of operations but a mode of living. As a result, countries around the world are highly cautious about allowing the entry of corporate activities into farming. They commonly allow corporations to engage only in preproduction and postproduction processing and have stringent controls over participating in agricultural production per se. Japan instituted land reform after World War II, and for the next 15 years the country not only had strict legal prohibitions about corporate entities directly engaging in agricultural production but forbade nonagricultural producers from owning farmland. The country ruled that farming households were not allowed to own more than three hectares of land apiece and could not rent out more than one hectare. Mandatory purchase by the government was required for any amount over those limits. The rationale behind these restrictions was to prevent large-scale capital from squeezing out farmers and consolidating land, until a sufficient number of the rural population had been able to shift to alternative employment. By the time the laws were amended, in 1961, the number of people involved in farming in Japan had dropped from 50 percent in 1946 to 27 percent in 1961. Even after being amended, Japan's laws still provide for a whole series of supplementary conditions on corporate entry into direct agricultural production.

The United States also maintains restrictions to this day in nine of the Midwestern states noted for the large size of farms. It forbids 'nonhousehold-type companies from possessing farmland.' The pursuit of efficiencies in farming, and the displacement of small-time farmers through use of large amounts of capital, must be preceded by socioeconomic restructuring if it is not to create serious social problems. Limitations imposed by the United States and Japan have emanated from a number of considerations, among which are the following. First, they have intended to give job security to farmers. Wholesale 'wrapping up' of land must unavoidably lead to a certain amount of unemployment among the rural population. Second, they have intended to enable farmers' 'status' to evolve. When large corporate operations squeeze out small farmers who have not yet transitioned to other occupations, and they become employees as opposed to 'farmers' themselves, the process profoundly influences the entire social structure of a rural area, and affects the psychology and the behavior of the population. Third, limitations imposed by Japan and the United States have meant to influence the way land is used. When generations of farmers work the land, and pass it on to their children, they regard it as 'wealth' to be preserved, an asset that needs to be cared for. When companies or enterprises 'rent' land for a given period, it becomes simply a factor of production. Long-term problems such as damage to the overall ecosystem can easily be the result.

It behooves us to give serious thought to whether or not allowing corporate operations to enter into direct farming operations without any restrictions will affect the long-term basic interests of farmers. We therefore have to be alert to such things as 'leasing back and flip contracting,' and having companies or enterprises directly engage in agricultural production. On the one hand, we should encourage and support the entry of industrial and commercial enterprises into agriculture, but primarily into preproduction and postproduction phases. They should be encouraged to invest in developing industries and services that support farming, but not to occupy farmers' land and undertake direct agricultural production themselves.

Some cadres feel that sticking to 30-year contract terms for household contracting of land serves as a barrier to the transferability and greater concentration of land parcels. This in fact is a misunderstanding. Three main documents present the land policy of the Central Committee of the Party with respect to this issue. They all emphasize that land-use rights should be transferable, based on the foundation of stable household-contracting relationships. The first of these is the *Document No. 1* issued in 1984 which prescribes a 15-year term for 'contracts' in which such contracts may not change, but the document explicitly encourages 'able cultivators' to consolidate 'land-use rights.' The second of these is Central's *Document No. 11,* issued in 1993. This sets forth a 30-year term for contracts in which such contracts may not change, and it is even more explicit about allowing farmers, on a voluntary basis, to transfer 'land-use rights' for compensation as according to specific laws. The third of these is called *Notice Regarding Stabilizing Land-Contracting Relationships,* which was issued in 1997. This provides various specific regulations with respect to the transfer of land. In terms of the legal framework for transferring land, the Land Management Law also provides specific regulations.

Given the above [explicit references in documents of the Central Committee], there is no contradiction between extending the terms for contracted land and allowing the transferability of land-use rights. What Central [the Central Committee of the Party] is trying to encourage is both stability in land-contract relationships of farming households and the ability of those households to transfer land-use rights on a voluntary basis within the term of their contracts. We undeniably have a problem of overly small plots of land in our agricultural operations, but this is caused by the inescapable fact that we have a very large rural population on a small amount of land. The necessary underlying conditions for resolving this problem include accelerating the process of industrialization and urbanization. By doing that, we enable a large-scale shift in our labor force away from agriculture. Diverging from these underlying conditions, and merely allowing larger operations on more consolidated land, is not going to affect the underlying issues. It simply merges land-holdings through artificial annexation, and turns self-employed farmers into employees. By maintaining the stability of contracting relationships, we enable farmers to continue to make their own decisions and be masters of their own operations. This has to be the foundation on which we allow transfer of land-use rights during the term of household contracts.

Note

* This article was published in No. 171 Survey Report of the Development Research Center of the State Council in 2001.

9 Promoting the building up of a 'new socialist countryside'*

(2005)

Our goal is to build a 'moderately prosperous society in an all-round way,' that is, in a way that extends to all parts of our society, and the most difficult challenge in that process is assuring that rural areas participate. It was in the context of this very real fact about our country's situation that the Central Committee of the Party deliberated on and passed a *Recommendation* at the Fifth Plenary Session of the 16th Central Committee [October 2005]. Called the *Recommendation on Formulating the Eleventh Five-Year Plan for Developing Our Economy and Society,* this deals with rural development from the standpoint of overall socialist modernization. It calls for continuing to place the 'three agricultural issues' at the forefront of Party work, for having industry repay or 're-nurture' agriculture, and for municipalities to support urban areas in order to satisfy the need to build up what the *Recommendation* calls a 'new socialist countryside.'

I. Promoting a 'new socialist countryside' is imperative at this 'New Stage' in our country's socioeconomic development

The goal of setting up such a 'new socialist countryside' had been mentioned in numerous Party documents in the past. The fact that it reappeared in the *Recommendation* of the Fifth Plenary Session of the '16th' relates to distinct characteristics of this particular era.

1. The hardest task in building a 'moderately prosperous society in an all-round way' is going to be changing a decidedly backward state of affairs in our rural areas

We have picked up the pace of industrialization and urbanization in recent years, and our national economy has enjoyed sustained and fairly rapid growth. Urban-rural disparities continue to widen, however, leading to a number of new problems in what is a whole new backdrop for economic growth. The most obvious among these problems are declining grain production and the inability to raise farmers' income. The gap between urban and rural incomes continues to grow.

To address this situation, the Central Committee of the Party and the State Council have issued a whole series of forceful policy measures. They have set forth explicit guidelines with respect to 'invigorating' agriculture, the rural economy, and farmers themselves, by 'giving more and taking less' [i.e., having the State give more and take less]. In 2004, Central [the Central Committee of the Party] issued *Document No. 1,* in order to implement a policy of what was called the 'two reductions and three subsidies.' This reduced the load of or exempted farmers altogether from the agricultural tax, it stopped levies on special agricultural products with the exception of tobacco, and it provided direct subsidies for planting grain, for purchase of better seed varieties, and for purchase of large farm equipment. The direct benefit to farmers from these actions came to RMB 45.1 billion. In 2005, another *Document No. 1* from Central continued to strengthen the provisions of the 'two reductions and three subsidies,' resulting in an additional RMB 25.14 billion in direct benefits to farmers. Under the powerful impetus of these policies, as well as a rebound in market prices for grain and relatively favorable weather, the situation with respect to agriculture and the rural economy in general has shown marked improvement. In 2004, total grain production reached 938.9 billion *jin* [469.45 kg], an increase of 77.5 billion *jin* [38.75 kg] over the previous year. This was the largest recorded increase in grain harvests in our history. Farmers' per capita income increased by RMB 314 over the previous year, reaching a per capita average for the year of RMB 2,936. The increase of 6.8 percent in per capita income of farmers was the highest since 1997. Both grain production and increasing incomes continue to show improvement in 2005.

Nonetheless, we should recognize that the pronounced stagnation in rural socioeconomic development has developed over a long period of time, and we are going to have to devote considerable effort over a similarly long period in order to turn it around. As Central's *Document No. 1* in 2005 pointed out,

> 'We must recognize very clearly that agriculture is still the weak link in our national economy. Investment is inadequate and agriculture still moves forward on the basis of a very weak foundation. We have not yet established long-lasting mechanisms for increasing grain production and improving farmers' incomes. Deep-seated issues that constrain the development of both agriculture and the rural economy persist, and there are no real prospects for any change in the very obvious stagnation of socioeconomic development in rural areas. Rural reform and development are still in the midst of an arduous upward struggle, and even maintaining positive momentum is difficult.'

The Eleventh Five-Year Plan period is important as a transition between all we have done and all that remains to be done in the future. The grand goal is to realize a 'moderately prosperous' society within the first two decades of this century. To accomplish that, we must promote the establishment of systems that incrementally change our 'dual-economy' structure, that quicken the pace of improving agriculture, rural economies, and farmers' incomes, and that spur the overall advance of rural socioeconomic conditions.

2. In overall terms, our country has already reached a stage in which 'industry spurs the advance of agriculture, and cities "bring along" the countryside'

This period in which we are experiencing a dual urban-rural economy is a developmental stage that many other developing countries have found it difficult to avoid. Our country started essentially with nothing, 'poor and blank' as the saying went, and began to try to industrialize based purely on self-reliance. At the beginning, the only way to accumulate capital for investment in industry was to rely on agriculture, which meant that agriculture and farmers made a massive contribution to the country's development. At the same time, however, this exacerbated the problem of an increasingly bipolar economic structure. By now, the backwardness of rural areas stands in marked contrast to our rapidly developing urban areas.

Rural people constitute the great majority of our population, so the unbalanced nature of urban and rural development not only holds back any improvement in rural quality of life and rural productivity, but also puts clear constraints on full expansion of our domestic market. Retail sales of consumer items at the county level and below hold only the following percentages: in 1993, 42 percent of the total for the country, in 1996, 39.6 percent of the total, in 2001, 37.4 percent of the total, and in 2004, only 34.1 percent of the total. Just this one facet of the situation shows how 'slow rural development' and 'slow increase in farmers' income' are serving as a bottleneck to rapid and sustained economic growth.

Aimed at redressing this outstanding disparity between urban and rural development, the 16th National Congress of the Communist Party of China set forth a requirement to 'coordinate socioeconomic development of rural and urban areas.' The Third Plenary Session of the '16th' [Central Committee of the Party] went further in explicitly reiterating this demand. At the Fourth Plenary Session of the 16th, comrade Hu Yaobang put forth the important 'theoretical point' [*lun-duan*] of what he called the 'two tendencies.' He said,

> 'In surveying the course of development in certain advanced countries, we see that the widespread tendency has been for agriculture to support industry in the initial phase of industrialization. Agriculture has provided the initial capital for the process. We also see, however, that at a certain point, the equally widespread tendency is for industry to "pay back" agriculture, or to "re-nurture" it, so that urban areas begin to support rural areas and both industry and agriculture, urban and rural, develop together.'

Our country has already basically arrived at a point at which industry needs to support agriculture and urban areas need to 'bring along' rural areas. Not only should we 'go with the flow' in aligning ourselves with this tendency, but we should very consciously facilitate it. We should adjust the distribution of our national income, and more actively support the development of the 'three agricultures' [*san-nong,* i.e., agriculture, rural development, and farmers]. From the two *No. 1 Documents* issued by Central in 2004 and 2005, it should be apparent to people that the policy to 're-nurture' agriculture is already being implemented and that we are intensifying measures to address the 'three agricultures.'

Given our rapidly growing economy and resulting national strength, we are constantly building up the prerequisite conditions for changing our dual-economy structure. Our GDP per capita in 2004 was 327.2 percent of what it had been in 1989, using comparable prices. Public revenues reached RMB 2.635588 trillion in 2004. During this same period, the share of primary industries in our economy fell from 25 percent to 15.2 percent. The percentage of our population that lives in rural areas fell from 73.79 percent to 58.24 percent. Promoting the building up of a 'new socialist countryside' and coordinating development of urban and rural areas has not only become an 'objective requirement' at our current stage of economic and social development, but is an urgent imperative.

II. Adhere to a policy of 'Coordinated Development' of urban and rural areas in order to build up the 'New Socialist Countryside'

A whole new feature of the process of building up a 'new socialist countryside' that the *Recommendation* puts forth is the coordinated development of urban-rural development, which means implementing the policy guideline of having industry 're-nurture' agriculture and having cities support rural areas. The *Recommendation* specifies certain measures:

> 'Adhere to the policy of "invigorating the countryside by giving more and taking less," increase investment at all levels of government into agricul-ture and rural affairs, expand the coverage of public-finance spending in rural areas, strengthen the government's public services in rural areas, set up longstanding mechanisms that enable industry to stimulate agriculture and that enable cities to "bring along" rural areas.'

Two policy guidelines must therefore be implemented in full, namely, one that incentivizes farmers and one that requires inputs from industry and urban areas into the countryside. Only by integrating these two forces will we be able to meet the demands of our current situation and further what we are calling the 'building up of a new countryside.'

Consequently, we must make reasonable adjustments in how we distribute our national income in order to create longstanding mechanisms for coordinated development of urban and rural areas. One of the main reasons for the slow devel-opment of rural areas has been the lack of or inadequacy of funding sources in those areas. That includes funding both from public-finance sources and from normal investment channels. In 2004, fixed-asset investment in rural areas was only 16.34 percent of total fixed-asset investment in our country. Public spending at all levels of government in rural areas was 5.89 percent of total public spending in the country. These percentages are clearly way out of line with the percentage of our population living in rural areas, as well as with the contribution of agriculture and rural economies to our total GDP. The *Recommendation* specifically calls for

> 'adjusting the structure of public-finance spending and accelerating the establishment of public finance systems in rural areas, improving transfer-payment mechanisms between the Central government and provincial-level governments, straightening out and organizing financial management systems at below-provincial-level governments, and, when called for, implementing management systems whereby the provincial level directly manages the county level.'

It calls for, 'deepening reform of financing capacities in rural areas, developing financing organizations that are appropriate to rural areas and that are standardized, exploring and then developing agricultural insurance, improving financial services in rural areas.' Implementing these requirements will be important prerequisites to 'building up a new socialist countryside' as we move into the 'new stage.'

We must accelerate the establishment of a market system or structure that enhances the development of agriculture and rural areas in general and that contributes to an increase in farmers' incomes. Setting up such a market system, that unifies countryside and urban areas, includes various considerations. As the *Recommendation* points out, the one most urgently needed by people living in rural areas is, 'the creation of a labor market and an employment system that provides for fair competition [between urban and rural inhabitants], and that provides legal guarantees for the rights and interests of laborers who travel into cities to work.' Given our limited amount of land and enormous rural population, shifting surplus labor in rural areas toward nonagricultural employment and toward cities is a path we must take in trying to increase rural incomes.

Changes in employment structure and changing sources of income are increasingly important to improved income status for what we call 'farmers.' In 1990, 75.56 percent of per capita net income of farmers came from 'household operations,' that is, farming, while 20.22 percent came from wage-type income. In 2004, those percentages had changed to 59.45 percent from household operations and 34.0 percent from wages. In the course of urbanization, therefore, we clearly must provide greater employment opportunities for 'farmers,' and opportunities that are also convenient and based on fairness or equal employment principles.

We must accelerate the formation of mechanisms that enable public undertakings in rural areas, which include such things as health, education, and welfare ['culture']. Lack of these things is the most pronounced indication of lagging development in rural areas. Due to financial constraints, for a long time the government has provided insufficient public services to rural areas, which has meant that such things as health, education, and welfare have had to be paid for by the 'collectives' [collective-economy organizations], or by farmers themselves. The situation has begun to change in recent years. In 2003, Central [the Central Committee of the Party] put forth the following requirement: 'From this year onward, the State must increase expenditures every year on education, health, and "culture" [welfare], with spending to go mainly to rural areas.' In *Document No. 1* of 2005, more explicit regulations were added in this regard. Starting in 2005, measures were taken in

592 'key county sites' for State-funded poverty relief work including exemptions of education fees and fees for textbooks during the compulsory education stage of children in impoverished households. Students required to live in dormitories away from home were given subsidized living expenses. The *Recommendation* went further in stating that, during the period of the eleventh Five-Year Plan, coverage of the 'two exemptions and one subsidy policy' was to be extended to all children of impoverished families who were of school age, and that all children irrespective of their family's situation were to receive education without having to pay fees.

In October 2002, the Central Committee of the Party and the State Council issued a *Decision* called *Decision on Further Strengthening Our Work in Health and Hygiene in Rural Areas.* This made more explicit and strengthened such publicly funded tasks as improving public health in general, furthering the establishment of health services systems, setting up and improving 'cooperative medical treatment systems' in 'new-type villages,' improving emergency medical care systems, and so on. These contributed to a certain improvement in health and medical care in rural areas. By the end of June 2005, among the 225 million people covered by 641 pilot 'cooperative medical treatment centers' in 641 counties [including municipalities and districts], 76 percent of people were voluntarily participating in the system. The *Recommendation* reiterated and reemphasized the need to 'strengthen the process of setting up public healthcare and basic medical treatment systems in rural areas, to the extent that a basic rural medical system is in place.' Starting in 2006, the State Council will go further in strengthening support for this effort by mandating both Central and local fiscal support for cooperative medical treatment systems in 'new-style villages,' so that by 2008 a basic system will provide coverage to rural areas nationwide. The *Recommendation* also points out that 'poverty-relief projects incorporating incentives for families that practice birth control should be implemented, as well as a program called "fewer births leads to quicker wealth."' This is to be based on experience gained from the pilot programs.

The *Recommendation* explicitly requires that public spending be increased on basic infrastructure in rural areas, that the building of such things as roads, electricity grids, information networks, and so on be accelerated, and that drinking-water problems and security issues in villages gradually be addressed. It recommends that clean-energy sources appropriate to rural conditions be developed, such as methane gas.

In addition, the *Recommendation* states,

> 'The most stringent methods must be used to assure the protection of farmland. We must speed up reform of the system of requisitioning land, and set up comprehensive mechanisms that guarantee reasonable compensation to farmers whose land has been requisitioned.'

This shows a high degree of concern for those farmers who lose all means of livelihood when their land is taken. Going further in improving existing rural social security measures that join the forces of State, collectives, and individual households, the *Recommendation* states, 'in those places where appropriate, based on the experience in pilot sites, we should adopt proactive measures that set up a system of guaranteed allowances for minimum living standards.'

III. In order to stimulate socioeconomic development in rural areas, promote policies that build up a 'new socialist countryside'

To advance the building up of a new socialist countryside, we must deepen rural reform in an all-round manner, stimulate the vitality inherent in the countryside itself, and with the nurturing and support of government policies, enhance rural productivity, improve overall conditions for rural life and production, and stimulate overall progress in the socioeconomic situation. Therefore, as per guidelines set forth in the *Recommendation* with respect to 'developing production, broadening people's horizons, creating a "civilized countryside," cleaning up the appearance of the countryside, and implementing democratic management,' we need to address all manner of tasks to enable the building up of a 'new countryside.'

We should maintain and improve the basic operating system in rural areas. We should continue to regard economic development as our central task and thereby stimulate productivity in rural areas, we should support sustained improvement in farmers' incomes. The principal task of building a new socialist countryside involves modernizing our agriculture. The *Recommendation* provides general requirements for that process: 'accelerating scientific and technical advances, improving facilities, changing the structure of what is produced, changing mode of increased production [from "more" to "higher quality,"], and raising overall productive capacity.' The key to carrying out this task lies in providing incentives to farmers to produce, it lies in protecting their interests and motivating them to grow their economies. Under the leadership of the Party, hundreds of millions of farmers have created a two-tiered operating system that is based on the household contracting procedure. This tremendous creation undertaken in the midst of reform is the 'basic rural operating system' as specifically stated in our country's constitution. It has tremendous vitality in that it is both adaptive and scalable. The *Recommendation* specifically states that we should

> 'stabilize and improve the household contracting system, as the base, with integrated two-tiered management of unified [centralized] and dispersed [decentralized] activities. It states that in certain areas with appropriate circumstances, transfer of the "contracted operating rights" to land can be done on a trial basis, and that different sizes of operations can be developed.'

Our country's agriculture has consistently borne the weight of two different responsibilities. One is assuring that the country has a secure source of grain, and the other is assuring that farmers' incomes increase. This is why we must continue to focus on economic development as the 'core' mission, to promote the modernization of agriculture, to raise grain production capacity, to stimulate sustained increase in farmers' incomes. These must be both our starting point and the fundamental goal of building up a new countryside.

The *Recommendation* stipulates that we must gradually establish a system of supporting agriculture in a way that meets our country's specific requirements. That includes stabilizing and improving the basic operating system in the countryside, improving dissemination of agricultural technologies, setting up systems of marketing agricultural products, setting up systems that monitor safety standards and product quality, setting up systems for control of pests and animal and plant diseases, and so on. On the basis of already existing agricultural-subsidy policies, the process involves setting up new protective systems. While strengthening the functions of village-level collective organizations, we must encourage and provide guidance to farmers to set up all different kinds of specialized cooperative organizations, and in general increase the organizational sophistication of our agriculture.

We must consolidate our existing achievements in rural tax reform, and take the reform further in various ways, so as to provide institutional guarantees for 'building up a new socialist countryside.' A series of systemic innovations must be orchestrated, among which one central task, one comprehensive nationwide reform, is to consolidate the accomplishments in reform of taxes and levies. The agricultural tax will be exempted nationwide in the first year of the eleventh Five-Year Plan period, marking an end to a 2,000-year-old practice of making farmers hand over a 'grain tax' to the State. This represents a significant adjustment in the interests of three parties, the State, local collectives, and farmers themselves. As such, it will necessarily stimulate far more wide-reaching, fundamental, multifaceted reform in rural areas in general.

The positive aspects of this move are easy to see, but it also brings other contradictions into sharp focus and will lead to new circumstances and also new problems. Only if we firmly resolve to carry on with reform, and carry out systemic innovation, can we consolidate the results that come from this tax exemption. Only then can we assure the stable advance of socioeconomic development in rural areas and a smooth implementation of the policy to build up a new countryside. Therefore, as the *Recommendation* points out, during the period of the eleventh Five-Year Plan, we must fundamentally complete reform of township institutions, rural compulsory education measures, and measures regarding the county and township fiscal management system. These reforms will impact all aspects of the rural economy and rural society. Their key purpose is to build a streamlined and efficient rural grassroots administrative management system and a public-finance system that incorporates all rural as well as urban areas. Comprehensive rural reform should be based on local conditions in every respect and should be based on lessons learned from pilot programs. It should be carried out in an active but stable way, so as to provide solid institutional guarantees for building up a new socialist countryside.

We must improve the planning process that is applied to rural construction and thereby gradually improve the appearance of the countryside. Always making sure that we are protecting the personal interests of farmers and resolving issues of direct concern to them, in both their work and their living conditions, we must reinforce the planning process. Countryside construction and management must conform to the requirements of a new socialist countryside. Implementing plans is a long-term task and we must focus not only on improving how construction takes place but also on the specific circumstances of different areas.

We have to respect the wishes and the intent of farmers. We have to take the limits of their resilient capacity into account. We must adhere to basic principles of conserving land and using it more intensively, but also take local aspects of livelihood into account. Levels of development differ widely among different regions, so that the work of 'improving the aspect of the countryside' will have different starting points, rates at which the process proceeds, and standards that should be followed, but we must never get too far from actual circumstances in any given place. We must not disregard the views of local people, or indiscriminately compare our actions with what has been done elsewhere. The people are the core part of the process, the 'main body' involved, as we go about setting up a new countryside. The process should be based on reality, specific to local situations, staged in a gradual progression, and carried out in stable manner.

Therefore, the *Recommendation* sets forth two main principles that we must grasp firmly throughout the process: 'use the specifics of any locality as the starting point and respect the farmers' wishes and intent,' and 'proceed by using the support and nurturing of State policies as well as the conscientious hard work of farmers.' Only if we adhere to these principles can we make sure that the 'setting up of a new countryside' is in fact what farmers want, make sure it really does bring benefit to farmers, that it really will be supported by farmers. Only then can we move forward on a firm basis.

We must also focus on nurturing and creating what could be called a 'new style' of farmer. That includes the formation of a positive social setting, with improved mechanisms for the self-governance of local people. 'Building up a *new countryside*' will depend on *new farmers.* The *Recommendation* therefore asks that we 'cultivate a new form of person with the ability to undertake operations, to understand technology, to behave in a cultured manner, a person whose overall caliber is improved.' The intent here is to turn the great pressure of surplus population in the countryside into an advantage in the form of human resources. It is to deepen the wellsprings of the force that will in fact build up and sustain our new socialist countryside. Measures should be taken to form a sound and healthy social atmosphere in rural areas for this 'new type of farmer,' such as developing rural education, holding healthy cultural and sports activities, strengthening the building up of 'spiritual civilization,' and improving vocational training systems.

In the course of transforming the functions of township governments, we must strengthen alternative grassroots-level organizations. We should carry out activities that sustain a Communist-party membership that is of a 'modern' or advanced nature, and we should strengthen the cohesiveness of local Party organizations, as well as their 'fighting capacity' and their creativity.

We should develop [encourage] grassroots-level democracy and through such things as the 'open village' system [full disclosure of village affairs], and the 'one case one decision' system [case-by-case mechanisms for determining judgments], we should ensure that farmers democratic rights and interests are protected as according to law. We should set up and improve upon vigorously active village self-governing mechanisms that are under the leadership of the village Party organization, so as to establish institutional guarantees for 'building up a new socialist countryside.'

Note

* This article was originally published in the *People's Daily* on November 4, 2005.

10 The current situation with respect to agriculture, rural areas, and farmers in our country*

(2006)

The Party and the State have consistently regarded the issues of agriculture, rural areas, and farmers, as being highly important. In the more than two decades since 'reform and opening up' began, our country's work with respect to the 'three agricultures' [*san-nong*] has accomplished remarkable things. In the most recent few years, Central has increased the intensity of efforts in this regard, by bringing forth a series of important policy guidelines. These have included 'coordinating urban and rural development,' 'giving priority to key issues,' 'giving more, taking less, and invigorating the countryside,' 'the two trends,' and 'industry should re-nurture agriculture, cities should support the countryside.'

Measures in support of the 'three agricultures' have accompanied these policy directions. For example, in 2004, Central issued a *Document No. 1* known as the 'two exemptions and three subsidies,' which increased spending over the base amount in 2004 of RMB 25.14 billion. Under the impetus of these powerful measures, things have begun to turn around in the last two years with respect to agriculture and the rural economy. The clearest indication of this is that grain production reached a total of 938.9 billion *jin* in 2004, up 75.5 billion *jin* from 2003, an increase that was the highest in history. Net income of farmers has also increased, by a per capita amount of 314 RMB in 2004 over 2003, to a total average annual income of RMB 2936, or up 6.8 percent. This is the largest increase in farmers' incomes since the year 1997. In 2005, both grain production and farmers' incomes continued this positive trend. Total grain production is projected to reach 968 billion *jin,* or 29.1 billion *jin* over 2004, and farmers' average per capita incomes are expected to increase by 314 over 2004, to a total of 3,250 for the year. After accounting for inflation and other factors, the real increase will be around 6 percent.

Nonetheless, our country still faces acute problems in the sphere of agriculture, rural areas, and farmers. Five main areas that will remain challenging over the long run are described below.

I. Money: The issue of improving farmers' income

1   The slow pace at which farmers' incomes are increasing is a major social issue and should not be regarded as merely an economic problem.

In the years between 1997 and 2003, farmers' incomes nationwide have increased at a rate that is roughly half that of urban residents. Over seven consecutive years, the rate of increase has remained below 5 percent. The average has been 4 percent, with the highest rate of increase in any one year 4.8 percent and the lowest 2.1 percent. In 2004, the situation improved under the impact of preferential policies toward farmers, but also due to favorable weather and a rebound in grain prices. The rate of increase rose to 6.8 percent. It looks as though it will be hard to maintain the favorable effect of those policies, however, from what we are seeing in 2005. Overall, in a normal year, for farmers' income to increase by 5 percent can be considered pretty good. What this means, however, is that the disparity between farmers' incomes and urban incomes continues to grow.

In 1978, the average per capita net income of farmers was RMB 133.6, as opposed to that of urban residents who had a disposable income of RMB 343.4. The ratio between the two was 1:2.57. By 2004, the per capita net income of farmers had increased to RMB 2,936.4, while that of urban residents had increased to 9,421.6, and the ratio between the two had widened to 1:3.21. That ratio has continued to widen in recent years.

Between 1998 and 2004, farmers' net per capita income increased by RMB 846.1, or an average annual rate of 4.3 percent, while urban per capita disposable incomes increased by RMB 4,261.3, or an average annual rate of 8.6 percent. The increase in farmers' incomes in 2004 was the best in eight years, with an increase of RMB 314.2, but urban disposable incomes increased that year by RMB 949.4. Clearly, we have not yet found a way to reduce the disparity between rural and urban incomes, or to keep that disparity from growing. The severity of this problem is highlighted by a context in which our overall economy is growing at a very fast pace. The fact that two major social groups are growing ever further apart in terms of income should give rise to great concern about what is a looming social problem.

2   The reason it is hard to raise farmers' incomes is that the decline in the number of people engaged in farming is markedly less than the decline in agriculture's contribution to GDP. Too many people continue to be engaged in farming.

In 2004, the gross value of primary-industry production contributed 15.2 percent of our total GDP. In that year, however, 46.9 percent of our total population was engaged in primary production. Our rural population constituted 72.5 percent of the total (942.54 million people, as calculated by *hukou* figures, that is, people registered as rural under the 'household registration' system). Apart from anything else, this overall structure of the economy has been a determining factor – farmers' income had to increase at a rate below that of urban residents.

From the perspective of farmers themselves, the 'farming' component of their income is not easy to increase to any great extent. In 1997, net income derived from actual farming totaled RMB 976 per capita, or just 46.7 percent of average rural per capita income. By 2004, that figure had merely increased to RMB 1,056, up RMB 80 over seven years, and income from actual farming on average constituted just 36 percent of average rural per capita income. Clearly, relying solely on farming has not been a way to increase income, which has led to the 'enormous surge' in rural migrant workers in recent years. At the same time, however, farmers' 'wage-type' earnings have been increasing rapidly. In 1997, per capita average wage-type earnings came to RMB 514, or 24.6 percent of the average person's net income for the year. In 2004, the figure was RMB 998, which constituted 34 percent of the annual income. Naturally, this can be attributed to the 'urbanization' of the countryside, with attendant opportunities for employment. While recognizing this, we must also take note of the fact that such wage-type income increased by a mere RMB 69 every year over the past seven years.

At this point, it is necessary to spend a moment analyzing how and whether 'farmers' are enjoying the benefits of urbanization. The number of rural laborers 'migrating out' to find employment is roughly 120 million. Some of these men take their families with them, which swells the numbers to an estimated 150 million people. As measured by where they are actually living, these people are included within the scope of 'urban inhabitants,' which has contributed markedly to the level of what we are calling 'urbanization.' In 1995, we calculated our rate of 'urbanization' at 29 percent, and by 2004 that figure had gone to 41.8 percent, or an increase of 12.8 percentage points over the course of nine years.

However, actual conditions are quite different from what these figures would seem to indicate. The reason is that the rural population that 'migrates' into cities does not in fact turn into [what our system defines as] 'urban residents.' If measured by their *hukou,* or the household registration of rural migrants, that is, if a person's native place defines his 'residence,' then our country's rate of urbanization was 23.6 percent in 1995 and 27.5 percent in 2004, an increase of 3.9 percentage points over the course of nine years. Seen in this way, 'urbanization' has gone up by less than one-half of one percent every year, specifically by 0.43 percentage points per year.

If we want farmers to enjoy the benefits of urbanization, not only do we clearly have a long way to go, but we will need to put serious thought into the ways in which we are attempting to industrialize and urbanize. During our planned-economy period, industrialization and urbanization relied on what was called the 'scissor-price differential' between farming and industry, whereby agriculture essentially subsidized industry by helping build up the necessary capital investment [i.e., the State requisitioned grain at very low prices, in order to feed urban populations who developed industry]. Right now, what we are essentially relying on for industrialization and urbanization is cheaply priced agricultural land and a rural labor force. Without reforming this whole structure, we will not fundamentally resolve the issue of sluggish growth in farmers' incomes [and we will continue to have a massive social problem].

II. Grain: The issue of national food security

Changes in the supply and demand equation for grain have again brought the issue of food security into focus in our country. Average annual grain production was 995 billion *jin* [497.5 billion kilograms] in the five years between 1995 and 1999. In the four years that followed, however, between 2000 and 2004, average annual grain production declined to 908.8 billion *jin.* Supply is now clearly not enough to meet demand. The severity of the problem relates not just to declining production but to such critical issues as the amount of land under cultivation, the amount being planted in grain, stocks of grain on hand in our granaries, and so on. These indicators all show dramatic declining trends. As a result, our entire society should become highly aware of and seriously concerned about the issue of food security.

Naturally, we can always consider simply importing more grain, particularly given the backdrop of a globalizing economy and our own country's entry into the World Trade Organization. A number of factors influence just how much we can import, however. First, total annual grain trade in the world currently stays steady at between 220 million and 230 million tons. This amount is not even half of what we as a country require every year. Within this figure, the total trade in rice is only some 20 million tons, which is less than 20 percent of our country's annual consumption.

Second, when supply cannot meet domestic demand, the necessary consequence is a rise in price. This has happened twice already in our country, in the late 1980s and mid-1990s, with a highly unfavorable impact on low-income groups, not to mention the stability of our entire economy.

Third, what are our farmers going to do for jobs as we start importing large quantities of grain? The first thought is to restructure what our farmers are producing so as to capitalize on comparative advantages. In the context of WTO considerations and the potential for a resurgence of protectionism, however, it is not so very easy to open up new international markets on a major scale.

Fourth, the minute China starts importing relatively large amounts of grain, international market prices will rise, triggering reactions that go well beyond the scope of grain itself, and even of the economy itself.

In addressing food security, we therefore are not going to be able to rely primarily on international markets. We are going to have to base our main response on increasing domestic grain production capacity.

III. Land: The issue of the fundamental rights and interests of farmers, as related to their production capacity

1   Household-contracted operations are the basis for our two-tiered system that integrates both 'centralized' and 'decentralized' [i.e., land ownership by the collective but dispersed operations by households]. Stabilizing and improving upon this system touches upon the whole issue of better implementation of our 'basic system' for rural areas, as mandated by our constitution.

Among all the 'factors of production,' land is unique. It is immoveable and yet it can be improved upon through 'inputs,' thereby improving productivity. Under favorable conditions, the fertility and productivity of land can continue to increase, while misuse of land can turn productive fields into wastelands. If land tenure is too brief, in terms of operating rights, not only are farmers not encouraged to maintain fertility but they may adopt exploitative practices that rob the earth of fertility. Making sure that agricultural operators have long-term, stable, usage rights to land is vital in ensuring that they are motivated to protect the land, use it properly, maintain it as a sustainable resource.

There is no doubt that supporting the transferability of land-use rights and the consolidation of parcels is desirable in terms of using land in an economically efficient way. These improve land utilization rates when taken to an appropriate degree. Nevertheless, we must remember that land issues affect the livelihood of several hundred million rural people. We absolutely cannot force the majority of farmers to leave their land in order to consolidate usage rights, merely for the sake of seeking higher economic efficiencies. This would be equivalent to repeating yet again the cycle of land annexation [and then rebellion] that recurs throughout our history.

Farmers must be allowed to share in the benefits of industrialization and urbanization, and rural populations must gradually shift into secondary- and tertiary-industry occupations and into cities, before land-usage rights can gradually be channeled into more consolidated parcels. We do not want to incur the kind of social conflict that erupts when farmers lose their livelihood. Only if we align our policies with socioeconomic development and shift rural populations in a measured and incremental way will we be able to avoid the terrible phenomenon that has recurred throughout history, namely, mass migrations of people caused by annexation of their land. Given our country's specific conditions, the process of shifting our rural population can only be gradual and undertaken over a long period of time.

Our law bestows upon farmers the legal right to determine whether or not to transfer land-use rights and operating contracts to farmland. Only farmers themselves may exercise these rights; no other person may take these fundamental rights away from them, 'expropriate' their rights and interests. These rights constitute a fundamental guarantee of social stability as well as of sustainable agricultural development.

2   With respect to how to conserve and protect farmland in the context of accelerating urbanization and industrialization, the issues involved include national food security and sustainable socioeconomic development, but also social security and employment prospects for farmers once they have lost their land.

One consequence of attempting to promote industrialization and urbanization in the country is that the process necessarily takes over some of our farmland. At the same time, our 'many-people little-land' situation dictates that we must implement one of the most stringent land-protection policies on earth. The extent to which farmland is wantonly being 'occupied' and used for other purposes has by now reached alarming proportions in certain areas. In the eight years between

1997 and 2004, we have seen a loss of farmland on the order of 114 million *mu* [76.038 million square kilometers]. In 2003 alone, the number of 'development zones' being constructed around the country reached 6,015, of which 70 percent were being built without permission. If the loss of farmland continues at this rate, any talk of 'national food security' will be illusory.

In addition, however, in the course of wholesale 'occupation' of farmers' land, the rights and interests of farmers themselves are being infringed in many places. Standards at which farmers are meant to be compensated for their land are too low and policies meant to relocate rural populations are not being properly followed. This means that, in fact, many farmers are being deprived of all means of livelihood. This is sowing the seeds for a calamitous impact on social stability.

Aimed precisely at this problem, the Third Plenary Session of the Party's 16th explicitly confirmed that we must reform our existing system with regard to requisitioning land, and it defined the principles by which we must control the extent of land requisition and preserve the rights and interests of farmers. Such reform affects the entrenched interests of a number of different parties and is enormously difficult. If we want to realize sustainable socioeconomic development, however, and if we intend to enable rural and urban areas to develop in tandem, we have no alternative but to press on with this reform.

IV. People: The issue of improving the caliber of farmers and establishing a 'Moderately Prosperous Society in an All-Round Way'

Any evaluation of disparities in social development must take into account people's opportunities for all-round development and must not focus solely on levels of income and consumption. The gap between urban and rural situations with respect to income and consumption is quite large, but with respect to what could be called 'social development,' the gap is even larger.

First, rural education opportunities lag far behind those in urban areas. In 2002, total spending in the country on education came to RMB 548 billion. Of this figure, 77 percent was spent in urban areas and 23 percent was spent in rural areas. Within budgeted figures for compulsory lower-school education, the per student spending was as follows: RMB 95 was spent on every grade-school student in urban areas while RMB 28 was spent per student in rural areas, RMB 146 was spent on every middle-school student in urban areas while RMB 45 was spent per student in rural areas. From these figures, it can be seen that the gap between urban and rural is pervasive in terms of educational opportunities.

Second, in terms of healthcare: There is still a pronounced lack of medical facilities and medicine and an inability to pay for healthcare in a large percentage of rural areas. The average number of 'sickbeds' per capita in the country is 2.34 for every 1,000 people. Most of these facilities are concentrated in urban areas. In cities, the rate is 3.67 beds per 1,000 people, while in rural areas it is 0.76 beds per thousand people. Urban areas have 4.83 times the number in rural areas, while eight times more medical equipment goes along with each sickbed in urban areas (RMB 88,000 per bed in urban areas vs. 11,000 per bed in rural areas). One can understand the paucity of hospitals and medical care in rural areas just by taking a glance at the number of farmers who died from illness while actually in a hospital, and the number of children who were actually born in a hospital.

If education and health issues are not addressed properly, we cannot come to terms with the overall issue of advancing the lives of farmers. Moreover, if we do not lift the general caliber of culture and science and technology in rural areas, we will find it very hard to realize any kind of 'moderately prosperous society' among farmers in the next 10 to 20 years. Therefore, while focusing on rural economic development and farmers' incomes, it is equally necessary to pay attention to issues related to health, education, and welfare in rural areas. Only by providing public services in these areas in an effective way will we be able to cultivate a 'new type of farmer' who is cultivated, understands technology, and has operating skills.

V. Rights: Ensuring farmers' rights, and consolidating political authority at the grassroots level

In summing up the lessons learned over the course of our country's past few decades, the Third Plenary Session of the 11th Central Committee of the Communist Party of China set forth basic principles to be followed in the 'new era' with respect to farmers. Those included protecting and ensuring farmers' material interests when it came to economic issues, and respecting democratic rights and interests of farmers when it came to political issues. Since that time [1978], the reason farmers have been so supportive of the Party's rural policies in the process of reform and opening up has been that the Party has steadfastly adhered to these principles in formulating specific policies.

At the same time, it should be recognized that the establishment of grassroots-level democratic systems [institutions] [*minzhu zhidu*] and the practice of self-governance by villagers [*nongmin zi-zhi zhidu*] has been poorly executed, in that there are still no adequate guarantees for democratic elections by farmers, democratic management, and democratic supervision [oversight]. It should also be recognized that administrative management systems [institutions] in rural areas are patently inappropriate to the needs of rural socioeconomic development. One pronounced problem is redundant staffing of local government offices, a 'bloated' number of people on the rolls, who must be paid for. In certain places, this has led to the so-called few people out there producing food and many in there ready to eat it [i.e., a situation in which the number of government officials exceeds the number of farmers]. The consequence is an ever-heavier tax burden on farmers and intensifying conflict between 'cadres' and 'the masses.'

From this perspective, if we want to ensure farmers' economic interests and respect their democratic rights, the key is going to be reform of rural institutions. First, we must change the functions of grassroots-level government and go further in overall rural reform. We must undertake in-depth research into how to differentiate between different levels of political authority and the institutions that should apply to each, as well as address the whole issue of the institutional framework for government. We must clearly delineate the authorities and respon-sibilities of governments at the rural level, in terms of their spending authority and their actual responsibilities. We must reduce the administrative operating costs of local government so that public services and agriculture itself can be funded more effectively.

The backward situation in rural areas has been developing over a long period of time and it is going to take an equally long time to change the 'backward' aspect of rural life and create a 'new socialist countryside.' We must therefore follow Central's various dictates in terms of 'a scientific approach to development,' 'a coordinated approach to urban and rural socioeconomic development,' and the 'need to construct a socialist and harmonious society.' On an enduring basis, we must put the 'three agricultural issues' at the forefront of all of our [Party] work, and hold firmly and unremittingly to that focus. Five issues surround this whole concept of 'promoting the building of a socialist new countryside,' which should serve as our starting point in setting up the right solutions.

First, we must truly aim for building up a more modern form of agriculture. We should increase government spending on basic agricultural infrastructure, on applying scientific and technological advances, and on guaranteeing the protec-tion of farmland. We should change the mode of agricultural growth in terms of improving the capacity of agriculture to carry out integrated production, particu-larly of grain, in order to ensure national food security.

Second, we must achieve real increases in farmers' income. While continuing to tap greater potential in basic agriculture, we should accelerate the establishment of secondary and tertiary industries as well as the establishment of 'small cities.' We should continue to restructure national income distribution and strengthen support for agriculture so as gradually to turn around the widening gap between rural and urban incomes.

Third, we must resolutely break through the 'great divide' between urban and rural realities. We have to set up unified and open market systems that incorpo-rate urban and rural areas, and this process means enabling both our rural labor force and capital to flow without restrictions. We have to optimize the structure of markets, so as to be able to inject new vigor into both urban and rural economic development.

Fourth, we must increase public services in rural areas.

Fifth, we must securely protect the rights and interests of farmers.

In both institutional and legal terms, taking all these reforms to a deeper level should indeed help protect the rights and interests of farmers, and thereby stimulate their tremendously creative capacities.

Note

* This article was originally published in *Learning & Study*, volume 1, 2006.

11 Several issues that deserve attention with respect to our current rural land policies*

(August 2006)

We have recently conducted surveys into land issues in a number of places, including locations in Anhui, Jiangxi, Henan, Shandong, Hunan, and Hebei provinces. Our overall view is that existing policies with respect to rural land use are basically stable but new problems have emerged that should be addressed. We note our findings and recommendations below.

I. On land contracting issues

In recent years, with the implementation of more complete laws, regulations, and policies with respect to rural land contracting, the situation in overall terms can be regarded as stable. Among those places we surveyed, we found that the rate of implementing 'rural land contracts' and having 'authorizations for contracted operations' actually reach households was already over 85 percent. Transfer of 'land operating rights' was basically carried out according to the principle of being 'voluntary, according to the law, and for compensation.' The implementation of the 'two exemptions and three subsidies' policy was particularly beneficial, in that different interest groups affected by land issues were now resolving disputes in accordance with Centrally dictated procedures. This had the effect of preserving rural stability and stimulating agricultural production.

However, our investigations also uncovered instances in which contracted rights to land were not being respected and land transfers were being conducted in irregular or unauthorized ways, to the extent that farmers were being involuntarily forced to give up their land. These instances were reflected in the following three main ways.

1. Some places were continuing to make what are called 'minor adjustments' to land contracts [as contrary to stated policy]. Our investigations discovered that quite a few areas have long adopted a practice of what they call 'a small adjustment every three years and a large adjustment every five years' in the amount of land that farmers may have under contract. These places are therefore not abiding by the policy requirement that land contracts be respected on an 'unchanged basis' for 30 years, nor are they abiding by laws and regulations that state that the issuer of contracts may not withdraw contracted rights or adjust land contracts within the stated contractual period.

Three main factors are causing this kind of situation. The first relates to a misinterpretation of laws and regulations with respect to land contracting. Back in 1984, Central decided to extend the contracted period for land to 15 years and Central's *Document No. 1,* issued in that year, stipulated,

> 'Before the extension of contracts takes place, if the masses need to make any adjustments they must abide by the principle of "basically keeping things stable *while allowing minor adjustments*" [italics added], if such adjustments are done through adequate consultation and are made through coordinated determination by the collective.'

Some places interpreted this to mean that minor adjustments could be made during the actual term of the contract, rather than only prior to when contracts were made. The second factor relates to the typical propensity of farmers not to want to be left out and suffer negative consequences. In places that habitually conduct 'minor adjustments,' many farming households feel that they have to participate as well, since family members are constantly increasing and they might get left behind. Once the first minor adjustment is made, the next becomes imperative, forming a vicious cycle.

The third factor is brought on by self-interest of those who are involved. Cadres at the grassroots level in some areas are constantly adjusting land contracts during the period in which they are supposed to be unchangeable. This is sometimes done in their own interests or those of friends and relatives, sometimes in order to gain control over the money known as 'land requisition compensation,' sometimes to avoid being exposed for various other problems. In addition, some provinces took it upon themselves to extend the circumstances under which 'minor adjustments' could be made when they formulated their own provincial laws and regulations. In the category of 'special circumstances,' they included not just 'natural disasters and so on,' but added 'population increase' and 'need to requisition the land for other purposes.' These extraneous conditions are making it even harder to implement the 'no change within 30 years' provision of the land-contracting law as originally intended.

2. Industrial and commercial enterprises are entering into the sphere of agriculture in some areas, triggering new problems and also leading to disputes over land. One of the main routes to transforming and modernizing agriculture is to enable the entry of industrial and commercial enterprises into what had been family operations. Most countries in the world encourage such enterprises to provide services in the course of the agricultural process while still placing restrictions on, or outright prohibiting, the purchase or rental of farmland altogether. They do this out of concern that major capital will displace small farmers and squeeze them out of the business. Once our own country's agriculture began to 'industrialize' in the early 1990s, much closer relationships developed between the agricultural, industrial, and commercial sectors. What are known as 'dragon-head' enterprises began to appear in certain districts. These rented the land that farmers had contracted to operate. They then 'hired' the farmers, for wages, and began to participate directly in the process of agricultural operations. The main reason this former equation of 'company + farming household' evolved into one in which the company now rented the land directly and hired the farmers was that, first, farmers lacked any understanding of modern markets and how to deal with them. Second, the 'dragon-head company' recognized that it was not economical to have to deal with each household on a separate basis, in terms of organizational and transaction costs, but instead was far better to consolidate. This also made it easier to standardize in terms of using technologies and making a uniform product.

The 'company' and the 'farmer' in point of fact represented two different interest groups, however. The forms by which 'renting' and 'employment' relationships evolved between companies and farmers were inevitably skewed in favor of the companies. For the farmer, they carried a certain degree of risk and complications. First, companies were mostly unwilling to deal directly with farmers. The leasing of larger areas of land generally came to be handled through the village organization, by setting up agreements called 're-renting of land and flipping of contracts.' Farmers' interests suffered in the process. Second, once companies had rented land actually contracted to farmers, they were able to spread their own market risk over the wider group of farmers from whom they were renting the land. Third, once companies rented the land from farming households, they often changed the use to which the land was put. If the company then pulled out for any reason, the farmer found that it was hard to restore the land's fertility and the irrigation works and so on needed for viable agriculture. Fourth, once a formerly independent farmer became a 'hired hand,' profound changes began to occur both in the psychology of that farmer and in the entire social fabric of a given area.

Because of the complexities in having companies move directly into agricultural production, and the recognition that farmers would be vulnerable in the process, Central [the Central Committee of the Party] issued *Document No. 18* in 2001. This explicitly stated, 'We do not encourage industrial and commercial enterprises to rent or operate farmers' contracted land over a long period of time, or an extensive area of land.' The document emphasized that such methods as 're-renting' and 'flip contracting' had to be stopped.

Circumstances differ throughout our countryside, however, and in many places grain production has not been profitable for farmers, especially given onerous taxes and fees. Quite a few farmers have been more than willing to let their land be operated by others. Meanwhile, local governments have been glad to allow companies or big-time farmers to take over household-contracted land in order to gain the agricultural tax levies and miscellaneous charges.

Once our country initiated tax reform policies and subsidies for raising grain, farmers have again become far more motivated to work their contracted land. They are now demanding that village organizations who rented their land out to enterprises or 'big-time farmers' retrieve it and give it back to them. Disputes and complications have been the result. In sum, one of the urgent problems we need to address is how to handle the entry of enterprises into the agricultural sector, how to 'regularize' their behavior, and decide on the optimum scope of their operations.

3. In some areas, land is being consolidated in a 'blind' or irrational fashion and land contracted to households is being taken through 'forced transfers,' seriously impacting farmers' interests. Land transfers in general have been on the increase in recent years, given the migration of rural labor 'out' to other areas to find jobs. The percentage of land already transferred is much higher in more economically developed areas along the coast; in the Quanzhou municipality in Fujian Province, over 20 percent of all land has already been 'transferred.' From an overall perspective, such transfers are in accord with the trends of migratory labor and the need to satisfy rural economic development. They are basically in alignment with the principle of 'voluntary, in accordance with the law, and for compensation.' Some areas, however, are disregarding the wishes of farmers and are forcefully taking their land. At the same time, in the majority of cases, irrespective of whether they are voluntary or involuntary, land transfers are following processes and procedures that are unclearly defined. There are more verbal agreements than there are written contracts. Farmers generally agree to what is demanded of them without careful consideration and there is very little in the way of management services being provided [to farmers]. This is setting up a recipe for disaster later, in terms of the potential for future disputes.

Stabilizing rural land contracts is a very significant matter, and toward that end we recommend the following.

First, intensify the amount of publicity aimed at the subject. Provide comprehensive, accurate, and broadly disseminated information on the policies, laws, and regulations that relate to our land-contracting system.

Second, intensify efforts to assure full implementation of the Law on Rural Land Contracting, so that the party issuing the contract cannot make adjustments within the contracted period and so that legal stipulations forbidding withdrawal of the contracts are respected. When special circumstances dictate that individual households truly do need to make appropriate adjustments, these must be undertaken under strict compliance with procedures as defined by laws and regulations.

Third, any participation or investment in agriculture by an industrial or commercial enterprise should focus on preproduction and postproduction services or on developing previously undeveloped 'wastelands.' Such participation should adopt methods that incorporate the farmer as a direct participant and should be 'order-based' farming so that it helps the farming household move in the direction of more industrialized or large-scale production. We do not encourage the long-term direct participation of enterprises in agriculture, or the large-scale renting of land and of operating land contracted to farmers. Enterprises that have already signed contracts for transferring land must deal directly with farming households in meeting the terms of the contract; the village collective is not allowed to keep back any portion of the land-transfer payment or of the resulting rent.

Fourth, large-scale land operations must be predicated on circumstances that allow for a shift in rural labor employment. At present, given our actual situation in most rural areas, our country's conditions do not allow for adopting extensive large-scale farming operations. Even though the degree of our urbanization went quickly from 18 percent in 1978 to 43 percent in 2005, this does not mean a comparable decline in absolute numbers of people in the countryside.

Due to the large base upon which the rural population is growing, and the speed with which it is growing, even though the percentage of the rural labor force involved in agriculture has dropped from 92.9 percent in 1978 to 59.5 percent in 2005, the absolute number of people involved has not actually declined but instead has gone up. It went from 284.56 million people in 1978 to 299.76 million people in 2005. (During the same period, the numbers of people in the rural labor force involved in nonagricultural jobs has also increased, from 21.82 million people to 204.12 million people.)

Despite the fact that the amount of land being cultivated has declined, the number of people trying to cultivate that land has therefore increased. Given this, conditions for large-scale operations simply do not exist in most places. For those more developed regions, areas around large- and medium-sized cities, and areas that do indeed have the conditions for large-scale production, enterprises should focus on providing middleman services. They should proceed only according to the principle of 'voluntary, according to the law, and for compensation.' Farmers should make decisions themselves, on a voluntary basis. They should proceed on the basis of standardized and orderly land operations and transfer, and engage only in an appropriate degree of land consolidation.

II. On issues to do with 'village planning' and the building of 'rural residential areas'

Since Central [the Central Committee of the Party] put forth the policy guideline about 'building a new socialist countryside,' quite a few places have quickened the pace at which they undertake 'village planning' and 'rectification.' This year's *No. 1 Document* [2006] pointed out that this task of building a new countryside is both a complex and very long-term historic mission, and as a result, 'we need to persevere with scientific planning, make sure we allow our policies to fall on fertile soil, and that we provide guidance that depends on different approaches for different categories.' From the current situation with respect to building activity and 'planning,' however, many places have inadequately clear understanding of the Central directive. Such lack of clarity is expressed in the following two ways.

1   Several 'tendencies' have surfaced in the course of formulating plans, including deviating from the right course, aiming for overly high results, and being too hasty. One problem is that in the face of no alternative way for farmers to make a living, in order to resolve very real and urgent problems, various places are resorting to what is called 'rectification,' demolishing old homes and then building new housing. This deviates from our core task of rural economic development. Another is that [the authorities] of a given place make plans that exceed the funding capacity of local taxpayers. They blindly compete with more developed areas in trying to build up their own turf by engaging in unaffordable construction. A third is that a minority of places attempt to proceed too quickly and set deadlines that are unrealistic for the building of roads and new housing in a 'campaign to rectify and reform within a certain period of time.' They tear down the old housing and displace former

residents. This not only damages the interests of farmers but incites a negative emotional response on the part of farmers.

2   In the process of promoting the merging or annexation of what were formerly
'natural villages,' some places are proceeding in reckless fashion to construct
what are called 'new residential areas.' Once the policy of 'building up a new
countryside' was announced, some areas have accelerated this process, calling
the resulting new areas by various names, new residential areas, core towns,
new districts, and so on. The differences among localities can be very great and
not all methods work for all, so we cannot be overly sweeping in our recommendations. Still, we discovered three primary problems in our investigation.

One is that merging natural villages leads directly to 'adjusting' the ownership rights of rural land. In the early 1960s, people's communes implemented
a program called 'ownership by the three levels, based on the team [*dui*].' This
meant that ownership of the great majority of rural land resided in the small production team [*shengchan xiao dui*], which is now the level of government called
the 'villagers' small group' [*cunmin xiao-zu*]. That system has been quite stable.

When the Land Management Law described 'ownership rights over land of
farmers' collectives,' it specified three different categories of land. One 'belonged
to the village farmers' collective' [*cun nongmin jiti*]. The second 'belonged to the
villagers' small groups of the farmers' collective' [*cunmin xiao-zu nongmin jiti*],
and the third 'belonged to the township government of the farmers' collective'
[*xiang (zhen) nongmin jiti*].

According to statistics of the Ministry of Land and Resources, more than 90
percent of rural land is currently [2006] owned by villagers' small groups [*cunmin xiao-zu*] (previously known as small production teams [*shengchan xiao-dui*]),
about 9 percent is owned by 'village committees' [*cun wei hui*] (previously known
as production brigades or literally 'large teams' [*shengchan da-dui*]), and less
than 1 percent is owned by the 'township collectives' [*xiang zhen jiti*] (known as
'people's communes' in the past [*renmin gongshe*]).

On August 28, 2004, a revision to the Land Management Law ruled that land
belonging to rural collectives

> 'if it is already divided into ownership by two or more farmers' collectives
> within the village as represented by rural collective economic organizations,
> should be operated by or administered by each respective rural collective
> economic organization or the villagers' small group.'

Farmers are extremely clear about this and fully acquiesce in the provisions. However, merging natural villages means that a considerable number of farmers take the
opportunity to leave the 'small group' of their own village and set up residence on
land of other villagers' small groups, which leads to changes in already existing land
ownership. This situation also involves changes in the ownership of housing.

We should remember that once the Central Committee of the Party had fully
absorbed the disastrous lessons of the early period of people's communes, a period

known for 'equalizing' everything out among people and 'transferring' resources at will, Central strictly forbade any new change in the ownership system of the productive resources of rural collectives. The intent was to avoid a repetition of what had been known as the 'poor transition.' The result was that our country failed to make any legal or policy changes in ownership rights to land held by rural collective organizations. We did not want to destabilize the situation.

In the context of no real legal or policy guidelines, the practice of large-scale mergers and annexations among 'natural villages' is now going to lead to a whole series of economic disputes in rural areas in the future. It is going to have a very unfavorable impact on social stability.

Second, merging natural villages is unavoidably going to impact the stability of rural land contracting. The Law on Land Contracting in Rural Areas rules that,

> 'land that is owned by farmers' collectives by law belongs to the farmers' collective *of the village* [italics added]. Contracts are issued either by the village's "collective economic organization" or by the "Party committee of the village." If land [in a merged village] has already been divided into ownership of two or more [former] villages, each economic organization or [Party] "small group" [of the former village] should be the issuer of the contracts.
>
> Underlying ownership rights to land that is collectively owned by a village's collective economic organization cannot be changed by the group that is issuing the contracts, whether that is the village collective economic organization or the village's [Party] committee."

This regulation notwithstanding, when natural villages are merged, the process at the very least triggers changes in the ownership rights to the places where people live, which consequently also leads to adjustments in ownership rights of a portion of cultivated land. The final result is that the practice in fact undermines the stability of farming households' contracted relationships to specific land.

Third, in certain places the real motivation behind wanting to merge natural villages is to increase the amount of land that can be put into nonagricultural purposes, namely, that can be built upon. In such places, farmers may be given a new home 'for free' or for a very small amount of money, and asked to leave their former homes and land. They may even be allocated new homes that have two or three rooms, but at the same time their former land is declared to be within the 'quota' required for construction. The reality is that the merging of natural villages is done in order to increase a locality's potential scale of investment.

We recommend the following in order to address the two issues noted above.

First, there must be better handling of the process of 'demolition' and 'construction' in the course of village planning and 'rectification.' Building must be done according to a unified planning process and must be carried out in proper stages without extreme haste to finish the job. In most rural areas currently undertaking this process, the main task in fact should be improving the basic living standards of farmers and providing people with more sanitary conditions. The main asset of a farmer's household is his home. Demolishing old dwellings and building new ones should only be done in accordance with the desires of farmers and in a way they can afford. When there is a need for new housing among farming households, the households should be led to understand the process, the regulations with respect to use of land, the requirements of any village in undertaking new construction. The process should be gradual and never be imposed on farmers in an involuntary or forceful way and massive demolition and reconstruction campaigns should not exceed farmers' ability to endure or pay for the process.

Second, the formation of new residential areas as old village structures age and decay is a result of socioeconomic development and should be seen as a very long-term process. As it occurs, the merger of natural villages should be done only when a minimum of the following three conditions are satisfied. First, it should be in accord with scientific laws of socioeconomic development. Second, it should be done only when adequate legal and policy guidelines are in place to adjust ownership patterns of private and public assets in a legitimate way, particularly with respect to rural land. Third, it should only be done when there is sufficient economic backing or capacity within an area for the requisite demolition and rebuilding.

At present, most rural areas lack the simultaneous ability to fulfill the above three considerations. As a result, we feel that, with the exception of those urban areas that have been authorized to undertake specific plans, local governments should not give any timetable for undertaking mergers of natural villages or provide any quantitative targets for the work to be done when they announce their 'plans to build a new countryside.' This is to avoid triggering psychological 'panic' among farmers, and to avoid any ideological confusion in farmers' minds. In urban planning areas that are already authorized, the rebuilding work itself should be expedited once a village is declared to be an urban neighborhood. We should take to heart the lessons of having 'villages within cities,' and avoid the waste that accompanies a repetitive process of demolishing and rebuilding.

III. On issues to do with land being used for housing

Our investigations show that most provinces (including autonomous regions and municipalities directly under the Central government) have indeed formulated policy regulations with respect to locations designated for rural housing, what are known as 'buildable land sites in rural areas.' They have specified that a system of 'one dwelling per household' is to be the limit, and they have specified procedures for permits for building in such locations, with relevant administrative procedures. Numerous problems nonetheless persist in the actual process of using rural land for housing districts. Most notable among these are that certain households gain multiple dwellings, new dwellings are built but old ones are not demolished, buildings are constructed that exceed prescribed floor space limitations, and farmland is illegally occupied for building construction.

In the long run, our current policy of 'one dwelling per household' is going to be unsustainable in the face of a growing rural population. In 2005, our country's rural population as measured by rural household registration [rural *hukou*] had increased by 18.16 percent since 1978. That was an average annual increase of 0.62 percent. During that same period, however, the 'number of households' increased by 45.4 percent, at an average annual rate of 1.39 percent. The rate of increase in number of households was 2.24 times the rate of increase in numbers of people registered in rural areas.

In 1978, the average number of people in a household was 4.63, a figure that had dropped to 3.76 by 2005 or an average decrease per household of 0.87 'persons.' This phenomenon is directly related to improved quality of life of farmers, increasing life expectancy, an aging population, an increase in nuclear family structures, and so on. It is also, however, closely related to the 'one dwelling per household' system.

Under our current 'one dwelling per household' system, rural housing can be obtained quite easily and for no compensation. That has stimulated behavior on the part of farmers to try to obtain or 'occupy' as many 'dwellings' as possible. At the same time, there are many vague aspects about the 'one dwelling' policy that enable the widespread practice of occupying more land than is officially allowed. The result is the phenomenon of multiple dwellings per family and 'villages with hollow centers.'

The whole aim of the 'one dwelling' policy was to prevent 'multiple dwellings per household.' Actual implementation has run into problems, however. First, the concept of a 'household' is not explicitly defined. Newly married children can request their own dwelling, and indeed feel deprived and left out if they don't get their own home and start their own nuclear family. This has led to the practice of dispersing family members and changing family structure, just in order to be assured of new housing. Second, the quantitative limits involved in a 'dwelling' have also not been explicitly defined. Depending on the amount of available land in a given area, mostly the amount or 'standard quota' of space allocated per household is between 120 and 200 square meters. The great majority of farmers take this figure to apply to the floor space of the actual living quarters, however. They do not include in it any supplemental buildings such as storage sheds for firewood, courtyards, and so on. Objectively speaking, it actually is not realistic in most places to try to limit farmers' living space and the space they need for 'sideline production' to between 120 and 200 square meters. Nonetheless, the lack of any specified guidelines means that farmers try their best to occupy as much land as possible for living as well as nonliving purposes, as a kind of security for the future.

According to statistics, if land used for public construction purposes in rural residential districts is included, in 2004, rural residential areas in Zhejiang Province covered a total of 361,000 hectares, meaning that per capita 'dwellings' covered 164 square meters of land. This was in contrast to 122 square meters occupied per capita only eight years previously, in 1996. In Hunan Province, rural per capita use of land for construction purposes came to 187 square meters per capita. In Jiangsu Province, Jiangyin city, per capita rural use of dwelling areas came to 61.3 square meters. In Qingyundian township within the municipality of Beijing, per-household dwellings covered 1.2 *mu* [0.8 square kilometers] of land and each household had an average of 1.15 courtyards as well. Some 1,400 cases violated regulations in terms of the Beijing municipality's 'one household one dwelling' rule, and 59 percent more land was used than was allowed under the regulations.

Dongguan city in Guangdong Province has a registered population of somewhat over 300,000 people, yet it has built over 900,000 residential dwellings. Among 9,792 'natural villages' in Jingshan County of Hunan Province, over 50 percent display the practice of 'building new but not tearing down the old.'

When one looks at the remaining evidence of urban planning in Ming- and Qing-dynasty towns in our country, in which land was clearly seen to be as precious as gold, one can see that we have now reached a point at which our current rural housing-construction system must undergo radical reform.

We therefore recommend the following.

First, we should use our existing system with respect to housing-site construction, and our original policies with respect to examining and approving applications, to carry out a wholesale 'clean-up' of rural housing-site locations. Given that this whole issue touches upon a wide range of issues and directly impacts multiple interest groups, we must be very careful to have a full grasp of the laws, regulations, and policies that pertain to the subject, including an understanding of their limitations. We must take full advantage of democratic supervisory [*minzhu jiandu*] functions among villagers, and institute open and impartial proceedings. At present, the immediate task is to deal with the problem of 'one household multiple dwellings,' the problem of 'building the new but not demolishing the old,' and the problem of taking over farmland for the purpose of building housing. The issue of exceeding allowable space during housing construction can be addressed gradually in the course of implementing rural building regulations.

Second, as land-human ratios have become increasingly tight, such places as Beijing, Tianjin, Shanghai, Jiangsu, Zhejiang, and Guangdong have long since stopped the system of providing residential housing to rural areas on the basis of 'one household, one dwelling.' The experience of these areas should be used as a resource in developing nationwide policies that lead to an overall reform of how we handle the approvals for and controls over rural housing developments.

IV. On issues to do with land that is being occupied illegally and buildings that are not in compliance with regulations

Illegal occupation of land and construction that is not in compliance with regulations is currently being done throughout rural areas in many different ways and forms. One of them is the so-called using rent to substitute for requisition; another is the sale of what is called 'rural authorized housing' to the public at large, which means selling [for a profit] to other people welfare housing that was intended to be for those with the required welfare certificates. A third is building and renting out to the public 'up-to-standards factory space' that was built on land that is meant to be used for farming.

Some of these problems are the legacy of encouraging localities to develop township enterprises in the past. Some are the legacy of allowing rural collectives to build on land 'in their own possession,' but other problems have sprung up only in recent years as we began to institute strict controls on the use of land. A notable example is the way in which so-called building land owned by the farmers' collective has evolved into something akin to a real estate asset used to get funding from companies for real estate development. At the very least, two severe problems will emerge once these practices become even more prevalent. One is that a large amount of high-quality farmland will be lost to development, gutting our so-called most stringent land-protection policy on earth of any real meaning. The other is that we will lose control over the 'sluice gates' that regulate the supply of land for nonagricultural purposes, which means we lose control over the total size of investment funds and hence the ability to utilize macroeconomic controls to regulate the economy.

As a result, we recommend the following.

First, all forms of illegal land occupation and transgression of building regulations as noted above should be thoroughly investigated, differentiated by category and severity, then dealt with promptly with reference to explicit regulations and policies.

1 Forbid the authorization under any kind of pretext for converting farmland into nonagricultural purposes and building on it, by calling it 'using rent to substitute for requisition.' When land has already been converted and built upon in this fashion, in addition to pursuing the offenders and dealing with them, land so occupied should be figured into the total quota of land allowed to the area for future construction, in other words that future quota should be docked by the corresponding amount.

2 Forbid the sale of rural housing in any way, shape, or form, to nonrural members of the public. Among 'planned districts' of municipalities that do have the required authorization for 'turning villages into urban districts,' any districts planned for residential areas should be incorporated into the overall urban planning of the larger municipality. Any requisition of land from farmers and modification of land use away from farming must be done according to laws. When farmers are displaced from their land, they are meant to be provided with housing, rented out at cost-of-construction rates, in order to assure that their standard of living does not decline and that they have a long-term form of security. When this housing is instead sold as a real estate commodity at market rates to the public at large, those who built it and are selling it must compensate the State for the cost of the State-owned land, as well as any other taxes and fees. If such compensation is not forthcoming, permissions will be denied for transferring ownership of the housing and for carrying on real estate transactions. In districts that are outside the bounds of 'planned urban areas,' in addition to requiring that housing be provided to farm households as dictated by policy, it should be made explicit that neither individuals nor collective organizations are allowed to build and sell housing as a form of real estate commodity. Other than to members of the collective organization itself, housing used by farming households cannot be 'sold' and can only be 'rented out.'

3 Other than land that has already been approved for building purposes by the farmers' collective as according to law, no individual or collective organization is allowed to build or lease to the public any kind of structure built for operating a business, such as a so-called up-to-standards factory space. Cooperative projects that are underway with investors from outside a given district must comply with all regulations and undergo all procedures for 'examination and approval' if the project relates in any way to transferring land out of agricultural use, unless the proper permits have already been received

as according to law. If authorized, the amount of land used must be entered into the annual 'land-usage plan.'

Second, considering that the nature and functions of township-and-village enterprises have already changed considerably since their inception [in the early 1980s], we recommend that new guidelines be formulated that restrict the scope of what can be done with 'farmers' collectively owned buildable land.' Laws, regulations, and policies should be improved toward that end. Various kinds of roadblocks should be put up to prevent illegal occupation of farmland, and to block any loopholes that allow for the unauthorized renting out of farmers' collectively owned farmland.

V. On the link between an increase in the amount of land going into 'Urban' construction and a decrease in the amount of land going into 'Rural' Construction

As industrialization and urbanization proceed, it is inevitable that there should be an increase in urban populations and a decrease in the overall rural population. Therefore, the general line of thought that links an increase in the amount of land used for urban construction to the decrease in the amount of land used for rural construction is, in principle, correct. Trying to take this general tendency and apply it indiscriminately to the formulation of concrete policy and regulations might lead to biased results, however, when it comes to trying to regulate the amount of land being put toward urban and rural construction.

First, under the way in which we currently define these things, the expansion of 'cities' and the reduction in 'rural populations' are not in sync. Although the number of people migrating into cities in order to work as laborers increases every year, the number who actually can take up permanent residence in cities is essentially nil. This is due to systemic obstacles created by our 'dual economic structure' and by the inadequacies of our social welfare system. As a result, many authorities call our ostensible 'urbanization' over the past 10 years a form of 'urbanizing the land but not the population.' Up to now, this form of urbanization has not created the conditions that allow for using less land for rural building purposes and more for urban purposes. Nor has it allowed for a permanent migration of farming households into cities.

Second, our country's laws dictate that two altogether different 'ownership systems' apply to land that is within city jurisdictions and land that is in 'the countryside.' If urban construction needs to occupy neighboring farmland, procedures must be followed that, according to laws, call for examination and approval of the transfer of 'farm-use land' to other purposes as well as procedures that authorize the 'requisition' of land. A simplistic 'link' that allows specific policies to increase the amount of land used for urban construction not only has the potential to infringe upon farmers' rights and interests but can easily lead to a de facto loss of control over the amount of land actually going into construction.

Third, if 'linkage' [between more building land in urban areas and less in rural areas] is translated into specific policy, this can very easily encourage such practices as demolishing and annexing neighboring villages in order to create 'residential districts.' Our investigations discovered that many places have formulated large-scale plans to do precisely that in order to expand the amount of land available to them for 'urban-building' uses. Often these plans are promoted under the guise of being in line with the government's stated policy of wanting to 'build a new countryside.' Massive campaigns to 'demolish and build' encourage behavior that is illegal with respect to land use and irregular with respect to building regulations. It enables the so-called building of a new countryside to diverge substantially from what was originally intended by Central policy makers [i.e., by the Central Committee of the Party].

As a result, we recommend the following.

First, we should clarify that any 'linkage' between land use for construction purposes in urban and rural areas relates to a general trend in land usage and reflects socioeconomic development overall. It is a way of looking at things that facilitates the strategic formulation of land-use policies but is in no way related to any concrete policy. In particular, it is not to be used in order to rationalize the forceful annexation of neighboring towns in order to increase the amount of land put to construction purposes for so-called rural residential districts.

Second, we must place stringent restrictions on those areas already undertaking pilot programs that use this 'linkage' concept. We should make it clear that any further actions can only be done within the bounds of urban planning districts, projects that are meant to transform what are known as 'villages within cities.' Pilot programs outside the scope of urban planning districts are not allowed to carry out any sort of 'linkage' programs.

Third, any land that is conserved in rural areas as a result of applying the 'linkage' concept to areas within urban planning districts can be applied to the quota for that city's 'buildable land,' if land requisition procedures are followed as according to law. In principle, any land outside of such urban planning districts that is conserved through various methods, whether those methods be 'land reorganization,' 'rectification of so-called hollow villages,' or reasonable consolidation and merging of rural residential districts, should be returned back to farmland.

Land issues directly affect the personal interests of hundreds of millions of farmers. They affect the stability of our basic method of governing rural areas. They also affect our ability to use macroeconomic measures in regulating the economy, and whether or not we can achieve sustainable socioeconomic development. Our basic premise is that we must put in place strict procedures for conserving farmland and for guaranteeing the rights and interests of farmers. Given that, we must adapt to new situations as they are upon us and take urgent steps to institute the appropriate laws and policies.

Note

* This is a report submitted by the author to the leaders of the State Council on August 9, 2006.

12 Recommendations with respect to setting up more universal coverage of the minimum living allowance system in rural areas*

(November 28, 2006)

After several years of testing and actually implementing a 'minimum living allowance' system, our understanding is that our work in setting up such a system in rural areas has made considerable progress. Coverage now extends to 21 provinces, autonomous regions, and municipalities, eight of which are in the east, eight in the central part of the country, and five in the west. A total of 2,080 counties are now covered. We have begun pilot projects in the remaining 10 provinces (including autonomous regions and direct-jurisdiction municipalities), and among four of those we will have initiated the system by the end of this year, namely, in Shandong, Yunnan, Guangxi, and Qinghai. Going into 2007, a total of 25 provinces in the country (including autonomous regions and direct-jurisdiction municipalities) will be covered by a minimum living allowance in rural areas.

I. Estimate of total numbers of rural people in need of assistance

Departments in charge of this program estimate that a total of 36 million people qualify for receiving assistance nationwide. Deducting the roughly 5.7 million who are already covered by the 'five-guarantees' program leaves a total rural population of 30 million people that should be getting minimum living allowances. Right now, around 13 million people are actually getting assistance in rural areas. Another 7 million are covered by the 'periodic fixed-sum aid for especially impoverished rural households,' subsidies that come to a per capita amount of RMB 16 per month. Local governments in the areas involved are arranging for public-finance expenditures of around RMB 4.6 billion for this latter purpose. There are still, therefore, some 10 million people who are not yet covered by the minimum living allowance system in rural areas [30 − 13 = 17, − 7 = 10]. The 7 million receiving subsidies from the 'especially impoverished household' aid system should now also have those switched over to the minimum allowance system.

II. Our targets for administering minimum living allowances and the actual situation in rural areas

By September of this year, actual subsidies being administered to recipients of minimum living allowances in the 20 provinces implementing the system came to an average per capita amount of RMB 36.6 per month, or RMB 439.2 per year. The target amount of assistance as prescribed by the system is an average RMB 1,045.4 per year.

In eight of the eastern provinces (including autonomous regions and municipalities), the average prescribed target amount came to an annual total of RMB 1,572, with Shanghai being the highest at RMB 2,560, and Liaoning being the lowest at RMB 853. Actually realized subsidy amounts, however, came to an average annual sum of RMB 642, or RMB 53.5 per month. Beijing's actually realized figures were highest, at RMB 82 per capita per month or RMB 984 per year; those of Liaoning Province were lowest, at RMB 20 per capita per month or RMB 240 per year.

In the eight provinces in the central part of the country (including autonomous regions and municipalities), the average annual target amount per capita was RMB 725, with Jiangxi's target being highest at RMB 840, and Shanxi's being lowest at RMB 668. The actual amounts of subsidies administered were RMB 294 for the year, or RMB 24.5 per capita per month. Hainan's actually delivered subsidies were highest, at RMB 32 per person per month (RMB 384 for the year), and Jilin's were lowest, at RMB 20 per month (RMB 240 for the year).

In the four western provinces, including autonomous regions, average prescribed target amounts for subsidies were RMB 630 per capita for the year, with Sichuan's targets being highest at RMB 668 and Gansu's being lowest at RMB 600. Actual per capita subsidies came to an average of RMB 295.2 per capita for the year, with Gansu's being highest at RMB 432 per capita for the year or RMB 36 per month, and Sichuan and Shanxi's being lowest, at RMB 180 per capita for the year or RMB 15 per month.

III. The time is now ripe for setting up a more universal system of minimum living allowances in rural areas

By 2007, we will need to establish minimum living allowing systems in only six more provinces, namely, Anhui, Hubei, Guizhou, Tibet, Ningxia, and Xinjiang. We recommend that Central provide the appropriate amount of subsidies to these areas on the basis of low prescribed amounts per capita but extensive coverage. We hope to be able to provide such basic coverage nationwide by the end of 2007, in order to help resolve basic subsistence issues for the most impoverished populations in our rural areas. Moreover, in actual implementation of programs in the year 2007, through more in-depth investigation and careful calculation of need, we hope to formulate a system whereby the Central budget provides fair and standardized public-finance assistance to the provinces in the country's central and western areas.

IV. The connection between rural minimum living allowance systems and development-oriented poverty alleviation

The 'minimum living standard' in nine of the provinces in which we are already administering a 'rural minimum living allowance' is defined as having a per capita annual net income of RMB 683 [a net annual income of $100 would be roughly RMB 700, so this is slightly less than USD 100 per year]. We currently have a rural population of 23.65 million who are 'hyper-impoverished' and live below that level of annual net income. The problem we face in carrying out poverty alleviation, however, is not only to assure that these people have food and clothing but to make sure that an additional group of people, more than 40 million, can be extricated from poverty in a stable and permanent way.

This larger number of people has more than an average RMB 683 per capita income per year, but still less than an average RMB 944 per capita income per year [i.e., 40 million are living on less than USD 135 per year]. We believe that our country is now in a position to resolve basic subsistence problems for this larger poor segment of our population, given our increasing budgetary strength as a result of socioeconomic growth. As a result, we feel that development-oriented poverty-alleviation type programs should shift focus. They should incorporate not just the more than 23 million 'hyper-poor,' but the 40 million who are also extremely poor.

Programs should move in the direction of preventing populations who are already above subsistence level from slipping back into dire poverty. We therefore should gradually ensure that we extricate a total of more than 60 million people in rural areas from poverty. Once we set up a comprehensive system for minimum living allowances in rural areas nationwide, therefore, we will still have a very tough task ahead.

Although the level at which we provide basic subsistence subsidies is very low, we nevertheless have now created systemic [or institutional] procedures [*zhi-du xing de*] for equalizing the treatment of people in rural and urban areas. We have set up a minimum living allowance system with universal coverage. We have also basically achieved our annual target objectives in addressing fundamental food and clothing needs of the most impoverished people in rural areas. Not only does this have very practical significance with respect to the policy objectives of 'building a new socialist countryside' and constructing a 'socialist harmonious society,' but it inevitably will have a tremendous political impact both domestically and abroad. The benefits to the public are considerable.

Note

* This is a report submitted by the author to the leaders of the State Council.

13 Coordinate socioeconomic development in urban and rural areas and set up enduring mechanisms that enable industry to propel the advance of agriculture and that enable urban areas to 'bring along' rural areas*

Finding proactive ways to build up a new socialist countryside

(2007)

Unbalanced development between rural and urban areas is one of our country's most pronounced socioeconomic problems. Changing the backward state of both our agriculture and our countryside is a major challenge and a strategic issue when it comes to the entire question of socialist modernization.

With constant improvements in our socialist market-economy system and with ongoing increases in our 'comprehensive national strength,' we have already basically reached a stage of development that enables our industry to 're-nurture' agriculture, and that enables urban areas to 'bring along' rural areas. The 16th National Congress of the Communist Party of China presented the need to 'coordinate socioeconomic development of urban and rural areas.' This was grounded in an appreciation of the major contradictions in our current stage of social development, and in a scientific analysis of the main features of our current situation.

The Third Plenary Session of the 16th Central Committee of the Party then went further in setting forth policy guidelines, including the application of scientific analysis to the issues, the 'five coordinations,' and 'setting up systems that move away from our current dual system [or bipolar structure] with regard to urban and rural areas.' The Fifth Plenary Session of the 16th [Central Committee] mandated the historic mission of 'building up a new socialist countryside,' and the Sixth Plenary Session of the 16th set forth the strategic task of 'constructing a socialist harmonious society.'

All of these policy guidelines helped clarify the underlying thinking with respect to coordinating urban and rural development, and provided the necessary political support.

In recent years, the Central Committee of the Party has employed what we call a 'scientific outlook' on problems in implementing a whole series of major policy measures to support agriculture and benefit farmers. Accompanied by growth in our overall national economy and changes in our society, these have resulted in many positive changes with respect to agriculture and rural development.

Nonetheless, it must be recognized that the path to industrialization, urbanization, and modernization in our country is going to be very long and complex, given what are the unique circumstances of a massive population, inadequate resources, and a system that has unusual features. It is of ultimate importance, therefore, that we truly do apply scientific analysis to our situation, that we understand the considerations facing our current stage of development, that we set up long-range effective mechanisms to accomplish the policy guideline of 'using industry to spur agriculture and using urban areas to bring along rural areas,' and that we pick up the pace of a real coordination between development of urban and rural areas in our country.

I. Major issues facing coordinated urban-rural development

Five main issues confront our attempt to realize a more balanced form of socio-economic development in urban and rural areas. They include the underlying conditions for improvements in agriculture, the 'basic operating system' [for land use], township governance structures, the disparity between urban and rural areas, and the appropriate route to urbanization.

1. Serious constraints on agricultural development

Per capita agricultural resources in our country are quite limited and are also embedded in a fairly fragile ecosystem. With considerable difficulty, we have been able to accomplish a basic balance between supply and demand of such main agricultural products as grain. As we say, 'in good years, we enjoy a surplus.' Nonetheless, both our population and food consumption continue to grow, while agricultural resources in contrast are on the decline. Environmental problems are intensifying and agriculture is still undermechanized and inadequately supported by science and technology. For a certain time to come, we face severe challenges in meeting our goal of being basically self-sufficient in major agricultural products such as grain.

1. Resource constraints are intensifying. The amount of our remaining arable land is declining by the day. Statistics show that the quantity declined by 120 million *mu* [80.04 square kilometers] in the years between 1996 and 2005. Our arable land resources are already down to 1.4 *mu* per capita, which is 40 percent of the world average. The current estimate is that over the period of the 11th Five-Year Plan, building construction will take over more than 4 million *mu* of land every year, of which some 2.8 million *mu* will be farmland.

Water resources are in short supply. Fresh-water resources in our country come to 2,098 square meters per capita, which is one-quarter the per capita average in the world at large. Precipitation is extremely uneven both in terms of time of year and distribution around the country. Some 80 percent of our water resources are concentrated in the south, and rainfall is plentiful in the summer and fall but scarce in winter and spring. Droughts and water shortages are increasingly becoming a bottleneck constraining agricultural development.

The ecological context for agriculture continues to deteriorate. Desertification of land is increasing at a rate of 2,400 square kilometers per year, and 2.62 million square kilometers of our land is now regarded as 'desert.' Severe soil erosion now afflicts 1.62 million square kilometers, and the problem of severe degradation of land is ongoing. Discharge of industrial effluents (the so-called three waste discharges), the massive use of chemical fertilizers in agriculture, refuse from animal breeding operations, untreated garbage in rural areas, are all contributing to intensification of environmental pollution in the countryside. A total of 150 million *mu* of farmland has already been affected by pollutants, while the polluting of rivers, streams, lakes, and ponds is constantly getting even worse.

2. Basic infrastructure for agriculture is 'flimsy' [i.e., inadequate]. Effective irrigation systems cover only 840 million *mu* out of a total of 1.83 million *mu* of arable land. This is 46 percent of all arable land. Less than half of our small-scale irrigation systems and ditches are in good shape; around 100 million *mu* of land that is meant to be irrigated is actually not irrigated due to breakdowns in systems, antiquated equipment, or changes in water flows due to drying up of the source of water. Land that is low to middling in productivity comes to 68 percent of our total arable land resources. Our ability to withstand natural disasters is low, to the extent that we lose in excess of 60 billion *jin* [30 billion kilograms] of grain every year to disasters. Fully mechanized agriculture produces only 36.5 percent of our total nationwide production. Mechanized cultivating comes to 50.7 percent of the total, mechanized planting comes to 31.2 percent of the total, and mechanized harvesting comes to 22.7 percent of the total.

3. Agricultural utilization of science and technology is inadequate. In 2005, the 'rate at which science and technology contributed to agriculture' stood at 48 percent, which was 30 percentage points below that in developed countries. The rate at which scientific advances translates into products is also low, only 30 percent, which is 40 percentage points below that in developed countries. Investments in R&D in agriculture come to some 0.36 percent [of total budgets]. The Central government's publicly funded research and development in agriculture is a mere 5.24 percent of all publicly funded research and development. This is far below the percentage of agriculture's contribution to the country's GDP. Agriculture's ability to undertake research and development, to transform research results into products, and to make applied technologies more widespread is relatively weak and the educational level of our farmers is low, all of which will be creating a long-term bottleneck in agricultural development.

4. Our agriculture is not internationally competitive. The small scale of operations at the household level prevents us from increasing productivity to any great
extent, our basic infrastructure is poor, grasp of science and technology is weak,
degree of underlying organizational support is low. State-funded systems for supporting and protecting agriculture are inadequate. All of these contribute to our
lack of international competitiveness.

Only some 9.8 percent of all farming households currently participate in any
kind of cooperative organizations. Between the years 2000 and 2003, we estimate that only 1.8 percent of all agricultural income was derived from governmental support for producers. In OECD countries, governmental support for
producers can be as much as 30.8 percent. Between 2000 and 2004, our country's agricultural exports stayed consistently at around 3 percent of the world's
total agricultural exports, but during the same period, our agricultural imports
went from 3.3 percent to 5.1 percent of the world's total imports. Exports are
increasing at a relatively slow pace, while the burden of imports is constantly
increasing. Since 2004, we have seen three consecutive years of negative trade
balances in agricultural products. In 2005, we imported 26.59 million tons of
soybeans, which constituted 60.5 percent of our total domestic demand. We
imported 2.65 million tons of cotton, which represented 31.8 percent of domestic demand.

2. Over the short term, it will be hard to contain the growing
   disparity between urban and rural situations

In recent years, the Central Committee of the Party has adopted a series of powerful policy measures to accelerate socioeconomic development in rural areas. The
disparity between urban and rural continues to widen, however, given our bipolar
[or dual] economic system in the country and given the stage of development in
which we find ourselves. We now face a formidable task in trying to achieve harmonious development of the country as a whole.

1. Maintaining sustainable growth in farmers' income is going to get harder. Since
2004, farmers' incomes have been increasing at over 6 percent a year, but this has
been based on a rebound in agricultural prices and also on all kinds of subsidies
in support of farmers. Keeping up this rate of increase is going to be harder in the
future. In 2005, the portion of additional income that was derived from agriculture
fell to 22.46 percent. There is not much margin left in which to increase selling
prices of agricultural products over the short run, while inputs are becoming ever
more expensive and this trend is not easy to change. It therefore will be hard if
farmers try to rely on agriculture alone to raise their incomes. In 2004, direct State
subsidies to farmers came to RMB 14.522 billion, which included direct subsidies
for grain, for better seeds, and for purchase of equipment. In 2005 and 2006, these
sums went up by RMB 2.73 billion and RMB 1.618 billion. The amount by which
subsidies are increased every year is now declining. In 2006, the 'three taxes'
on agriculture were abolished, miscellaneous fees for compulsory education will

soon be entirely done away with, and any remaining ways by which we can 'take less' from and thereby increase farmers' incomes are contracting.

The great bright spot for farmers over these past few years has been indus-trial-type income from nonagricultural activities. Between 2000 and 2005, such income as a percent of total income went up from 31.2 percent to 36.1 percent. By 2005, industrial-type income was already 55.3 percent of any additional income farmers were making. However, young people are increasingly wanting to find alternative employment 'outside' either on a seasonal or permanent basis, and the speed at which urban areas can absorb additional migratory labor is slowing down. As a result, increasing industrial-type income of farmers will be more and more difficult.

2. Disparities in income between urban and rural areas continue to grow. Both urban and rural incomes have grown at a fairly fast pace since the start of reform and opening up, but the gap between the two has also grown at a fast pace. In 1978, the ratio was 2.57 to 1 (urban to rural), and by 2005 that had grown to 3.22 to 1. Realistically, it is going to be very hard to change this overall trend for a long time, given our stage of economic development and given systemic constraints brought on by our dual-economy structure.

Our country is currently in the midst of a period of rapid urbanization and indus-trialization. Market mechanisms are drawing all factors of production toward urban centers, including capital, land, and human resources. The result, necessarily, is a gap in the level of development between urban and rural areas. This has been the universal experience of all developing countries in the course of industrialization. Nonetheless, our situation is unique in one regard. The fundamental reason our urban-rural gap continues to widen is that our long-standing dual-structure system imposes systemic constraints on our economic development.

The main features of this system are that it has focused investment on fixed assets in urban areas at the expense of rural areas, it has focused on industry at the expense of agriculture, and it has focused on employment and social security measures for urban residents at the expense of farmers. This has led to a situation in which socioeconomic development in urban and rural areas is diverging even as we enjoy a fairly high degree of industrialization.

During the tenth Five-Year Plan period, investment into fixed assets in rural areas came to RMB 4.9419 trillion, which was 16.73 percent of the nation's total. In 2005, investment into fixed assets in rural areas grew by 18 percent over the previous year but this was 9.2 percentage points lower than the investment into fixed assets in urban areas. Investment in the basic infrastructure for agricultural industries, including agriculture, forestry, fishing, and animal husbandry, came to only 5 percent of the nation's total in 2005. Systems that keep urban and rural employment strictly separate, and social security systems that handle the two pop-ulations separately, have not yet changed in any fundamental way.

3. The development of basic infrastructure in rural areas is falling behind. In recent years, the State has focused on remedying this problem through increasing investment every year, but deficits built up over years of neglect mean that great expanses of our countryside 'lack roads, potable water, electricity, and gas.' At the end of 2005, the country still had 40,000 local administrations or villages that were unconnected to any roads. Some 79 percent of counties and townships had roads ranked at 'grade four' or below, while 98 percent of roads connecting villages were at grade four or below.

The drinking water of some 320 million people in our rural population is either unsafe or hard to get. More than 50 million of these people are drinking water with fluoride and arsenic contents that exceed our nationally mandated health standards, and 130 million of these people are drinking water with both pollutant and microbe levels that radically exceed allowable standards. Close to 40 million people are drinking brackish or salinized water; more than 90 million are finding it hard to get any drinking water at all.

We currently still have a rural population of 20 million people who have no access to electricity, and around 150 million people who have insufficient fuel for both cooking and staying warm.

4. Development of public services in rural areas is falling behind. Health, education, culture, and social security are radically underfunded, which serves as a fundamental constraint on developing rural areas and improving the lives of rural people. In 2002, total public spending on education nationwide was RMB 548 billion. Of this amount, 77 percent went into municipalities while 23 percent went into the countryside. In 2005, primary and middle-school buildings categorized as 'dangerous' in the countryside still came to a total of 36.7 million square meters. Only 39.1 percent of our rural population had received the equivalent of a middle-school education. This was 26.3 percentage points lower than the situation in urban areas. Between 2000 and 2005, the number of health professionals per every thousand people in urban and rural areas worsened with respect to rural areas. It went from 2.15 to 1 in 2000 to 2.30 to 1 in 2005. Health facilities in central and western parts of our country are housed in unsafe buildings – as many as 33 percent are at a 'dangerous' level. In 2004, total public expenditures on 'cultural endeavors' in the country came to RMB 11.36 billion, of which 26.5 percent went to rural areas. There are still some 4,000 towns in the country without any kind of 'cultural station' at all. Our social security systems covering minimum living standards and also rural health facilities are highly imperfect. Only some 54 million people out of our total rural population participates in old-age pension systems. 'Social emergency assistance funds' for rural areas total less than 0.2 percent of our GDP, one of the lowest percentages of any country in the world.

3. The basic operating system [governing land use] in rural areas is in urgent need of being stabilized

Our country implements a system of land use that is dictated by our underlying national situation and by the unique features of agriculture. That system is based on the household as the 'operator,' with a two-tiered operating system that is both 'centrally coordinated or centralized but also decentralized' [in that decision making is dispersed to households]. Stabilizing this system can have the effect of providing a firm foundation or platform on which to build a harmonious society and propel economic growth in rural areas. At present, however, a number of destabilizing factors are affecting the contractual relationships over land in rural areas. We should be extremely concerned about the situation.

1. Our underlying national situation and the unique features of agricultural production require that we persist in our system of having households contract to operate land. The fact that we have very scarce land resources per capita, given our population, means that the scale of operations per household is quite small. In 2005, our country's 'level of urbanization' had already reached 43 percent, yet according to *hukou* registration figures, 950 million people are still registered as rural residents, and hence are treated as such under our dual system. There are around 250 million 'rural households,' and each has an average of only 7 *mu* of land.

Not only is that far below the average amount of land per capita in Europe and America, but it is also below the average amount in such Asian countries as Korea and Japan. For a considerable time to come, despite the ongoing shift of our rural labor force into nonagricultural sectors, our rural population will remain enormous and the sharp contradiction between amount of land and numbers of people will remain pronounced. The very small scale of farming operations per household, a consequence of our human and land-resource endowment, is simply going to persist.

Our basic national conditions also dictate the fact that any shift in the rural labor force into alternative employment is going to be a very long and slow process. During this process, we cannot expect to expand the size of farming operations per household in any major way.

Household-based operations in agricultural production are in accord with the inherent laws of the industry, which is why the standard practice worldwide has been to adopt this 'household' mode of operations. It meets the needs of how agricultural production is organized. On top of that basic foundation, our own country's two-tiered system is one of the most important systemic results of our entire process of economic reform. It provides an integration of 'centrally coordinated and dispersed.' Granting autonomous operating rights to households released tremendous productivity among rural areas and greatly motivated farmers to produce. Keeping on with that system, and stabilizing the contractual relationships of households to land, is therefore not only a matter of necessity but also of great practical significance.

2. Destabilizing factors now exist that are altering contractual relationships to land in rural areas. Frequent adjustments to contracts are being made in some areas, rampant consolidation is happening in other areas where farming households are forcibly being required to 'transfer' their contracted land. Many industrial and commercial enterprises have entered the sphere of agriculture and are farming on a large-scale and long-term basis by leasing land, and so on. These things are affecting the livelihood and the production modes of farmers, and they are infringing upon the legal rights and interests of farmers. They are affecting the stability of the basic operating system in rural areas, inciting new forms of socioeconomic conflict.

Three main 'causes and effects' are leading to these destabilizing factors. First, they are enabled by loopholes and inadequacies in our current laws and regulations. Our existing law defines rural land as being owned by 'farmers' collectives.' There is no explicit definition that governs the 'membership of collective organizations,' however. More than 90 percent of rural land is owned by 'villagers' small groups.' A 'villagers' small group' lacks any independent legal standing, however.

Second, destabilizing factors are enabled by the fact that our policy with regard to adjustments in contracts has not been formalized in laws and regulations and therefore can be misinterpreted. Many grassroots-level cadres take the stated policy principle of 'overall stability but [allowable] small adjustments' to mean that they can carry out 'adjustments' of farmers' contracted land every three to five years. In addition, many places use the practice of 're-renting and flipping contracts' as a means of attracting investment, which allows commercial enterprises to lease extensive amounts of farmers' land on a long-term basis.

Third, in recent years we are seeing a considerable rise in the practice of forcing farmers to transfer their land, against their wishes. This infringes upon and damages the rights and interests of farmers.

4. Township governance structures are far from perfect

Since we began the process of reform and opening up, our country has abolished the system of people's communes throughout our rural areas. In its place, we have gradually set up a basic framework for new rural governance structures. In looking at the reality of how these are actually functioning, however, we find a number of problems and contradictions.

1. The functions of township governments are not clearly defined. It is of ultimate importance to define township governmental functions in a reasonable way, to set up national administrative governance systems that enable grassroots levels to operate properly and to provide services efficiently. At the end of 2005, there were a total of 35,509 township governments nationwide. Under our existing laws and regulations, the functions and responsibilities of these governments are to protect the personal safety and property of township inhabitants, to guarantee social and political rights of the people, to execute development plans and budgets for socioeconomic development within their jurisdictions, and to carry out such administrative tasks as managing economic, social, civil, public security, justice, and birth-control endeavors.

At the same time, township governments are to perform fund-raising requirements for the next level of government up [to which they are administratively responsible], they are to make any necessary adjustments in agricultural structure, and to engage in other such social and economic development projects. In our parlance, this is known as 'one thousand threads to upper levels, and one thin needle at the lower level' [meaning that they are the sole body responsible for handling all the stitching demands of all those threads at the upper level]. The greatest drawback in 'positioning' our township governments as being 'full-function governing bodies' is that they both lack authority and are able to overstep authority. It is very easy for them to execute their intended functions badly, while involving themselves in all manner of things that are outside their proper role.

Functions that they are performing badly, quite realistically speaking, include providing public services and public goods to their constituents. In terms of public services, there is a clear lack of adequate information on marketing, on technology, on communications. In terms of public goods, their capacity to provide health, education, and welfare to farmers is extremely weak. In terms of social administration, their capacity to ensure public safety, to defuse social conflict, to ensure rural stability in general is in urgent need of being addressed.

On the other side of the coin, overstepping authority is involving township governments in many unintended spheres of activity. The phenomenon of not separating out business endeavors from governmental authority and social issues is widespread. Some township governments engage directly in production, providing services that should be rendered by social service organizations. They involve themselves in the business operations of enterprises, and some even force farmers to undertake structural adjustments in their farming operations for various purposes.

The fact that township functions are not explicitly defined translates into functions that are not carried out. At the same time, it is hard to streamline personnel, which means that payrolls expand and operating costs soar. The budgetary burdens on local people are too great to cover, resulting in ever-larger township debt.

2. The relationship between township governments and villagers' 'self-governing' [or autonomous] organizations has always been left highly vague. The Law on Organizations Called 'Villagers' Committees' states,

> 'The 'people's government in the three jurisdictions of townships [*xiang*], ethnic-people's townships [*minzu xiang*], and towns [*zhen*] shall provide guidance, support, and assistance. It must not interfere in endeavors that legally fall within the scope of villagers' committees. Villagers' committees may cooperate in helping people's governments perform their roles in townships, ethnic-people's townships, and towns.'

In point of fact, the law has not specified any 'endeavors that legally fall within the scope of villagers' committees.' In addition, the provision that villagers' committees should 'cooperate in helping' people's government is overly abstract. It serves only as a kind of principle. Township governments can essentially sweep all responsibilities into the scope of their own control. There is no corresponding regulation that provides legal remedy to farmers when villagers' autonomous rights are infringed upon by township governments.

Villagers' 'self-governing [or autonomous] committees' and township governments therefore co-exist in a relationship that is highly vague. Township governments are meant to provide 'guidance,' but in fact such guidance can turn into control, such that the relationship becomes one in which a 'controlling body exerts influence rather than mere guidance over a body that is controlled.' Village affairs are then handled by administrative fiat.

Township governments directly undertake such tasks as receiving money, taking in grain, taking in materials, and directing the labor force. Some township governments wield control over the election of village committees. Some even brazenly appoint members of village committees in direct opposition to legally mandated procedures. Some township governments interfere in business operations, as well as the construction activities associated with public facilities. Using administrative-fiat methods, they tell farmers what to plant, and how much. Some places disregard farmers' wishes, and also their capacity to pay for such things, and undertake building projects that put the local government in debt. Some reinforce their control over village committees by 'taking over the villages' fiscal resources.' Such actions are damaging the autonomy of villagers, they are infringing upon the rights and interests of farmers, and they are in essence affecting social harmony.

3. The relationship between 'village committees' and 'villagers' small groups' is obscure. 'Villagers' small groups' are a 'level' of governance within the 'self-governance' of villagers. In the great majority of villages, they are the entity that holds, or 'represents,' ownership rights to land. By all rights, they should be responsible for operating the land, and managing collectively owned land and other assets that belong to the 'villagers' small group.' Since many places have not clarified the lines of responsibility between 'village committees' and 'villagers' small groups,' however, we have the pervasive practice of village committees infringing upon the rights of villagers' small groups. In some places, village committees have supplanted villagers' small groups in contracting out land, to the point that they forcibly make adjustments to farmers contracts at will, essentially expropriating the land ostensibly 'owned' by villagers' small groups. This is extremely detrimental to social stability in our rural areas.

5. Acute challenges facing how we are urbanizing the country

Our country is in the midst of a period of rapid urbanization. In the course of this process, our rural population will gradually decline but the tremendous bulk of our population will continue to live in what is basically a rural situation. Given that the size of our population is unique in the world, we have no ready-made model to follow in trying to urbanize. Our mode of urbanization must rely not only on our specific situation but we should recognize that it is going to take a long time. During this extended period, our economic growth and modernization are going to be affected if we do not adopt transitional policies that are formulated in accordance with scientific analysis. Among other things, that means that we must fully eliminate all institutional barriers that isolate rural areas and populations from urban centers.

1. Our current stage of urbanization could be called 'quasi-urbanization,' or 'aiming at urbanization.' A large number of rural migrant workers who have moved into cities are now the primary labor force as wage earners in industry. They are an indispensable force driving economic growth. Nevertheless, people defined as 'farmers' who have come into cities are still not defined as 'urban' and so are still not 'urban residents.' The widespread phenomenon at this stage in our country's urbanization is that farmers who live in cities are not able to take up permanent residence in cities with all of the rights and privileges that such residence entails. Therefore we are only at a stage of quasi-urbanization.

In 2005, as measured by where people are registered by their official *hukou* location under the household registration system, 949.08 million people were registered as 'rural.' This figure was 72.6 percent of our total population. As measured by where people were actually living, in 2005, 745.44 million people were *actually* 'rural.' That is to say, more than 200 million 'farmers' have left their *hukou* location to take up jobs that place them in cities for more than six months out of the year. Despite their presence in our cities, they cannot take up permanent residence, 'settle down.' Despite having left their villages, they cannot 'cut the root.' Their cost of living and the risks that they are undertaking are heightened not only by our existing system of household registration but by our system of administering welfare and social security benefits.

This makes farmers even more 'marginal' as a fringe population in our cities. Housing costs are expensive in large- and medium-sized cities, rents are high, and barriers to entry for incoming rural people are particularly high. Millions upon millions of farmers can only, therefore, exist in a kind of well-traversed space between rural and urban. In its rightful sense, industrialization and 'urbanization' do not refer merely to the ability of rural people to migrate into and work in cities but to their ability to truly be absorbed into cities and become urbanized themselves.

2. The migration or 'flow' of factors of production into cities has unique qualities when it is within the context of 'quasi-urbanization.' The fact of rural migrant labor finding jobs in cities has increased the mobility of the labor force in rural areas. According to the fifth population census, conducted in 2000, labor mobility that remains within a province constitutes 65 percent of all human movement, while cross-provincial mobility constitutes 35 percent. More than 70 percent of all migrant labor is within the age bracket of 15 to 35. In 2005, 125.78 million people went 'outside' to find work, and hence were defined as rural migrant labor. This figure constituted 23 percent of the total labor force of rural areas. Around one-fifth of these people, or 25.4 million, took their families with them.

Meanwhile, other factors of production, including financing and land, are also seeing an accelerating trend of increased mobility. In recent years, along with rapid national economic growth, the speed at which land is being put to other uses is shocking. Between 1996 and 2005, the net decrease in our arable land came to 120 million *mu*. Of this amount, 16.8 million *mu* went into urban construction. Conservative estimates show that between 1978 and 2000, land actually worth more than RMB 2 trillion went into urban construction since compensation, the 'requisition' being compensated at overly low rates.

The outward flow of rural funds is also intensifying by the day. In 2005, savings deposits in four different banking institutions, the Agricultural Bank of China, the Agricultural Development Bank of China, rural credit cooperatives, and the Postal Savings Bank of China, exceeded RMB 10 trillion. In that same year, however, the entire sum of loans made for agricultural purposes came to RMB 4 trillion, a mere 40 percent of the deposited amount. Loans made by financial institutions at the county level and below stand at roughly 56 percent of total savings on deposit, which is 13 percentage points lower than the national average. According to estimates, a total of some RMB 4.5 trillion in rural funds has flowed via various channels into cities [where they earn a higher return].

On the one hand, such massive flow of the factors of production into cities, including labor, land, and money, should be regarded as a natural consequence of market forces and a favorable trend that accelerates the process of industrialization and urbanization. On the other hand, however, the one-way flow of these factors leads to highly unfavorable consequences. Accelerating industrialization and urbanization is occupying more and more arable land. It is exacerbating the contradiction between too many rural people and too little land. It is bringing into sharp relief the problem of [not] compensating for 'requisitioned land' and the problem of settling displaced farmers down in adequate alternative situations. Migratory labor is also triggering social problems, such as how to handle women, children, and old people who are left behind, ever-lower educational levels of those people who remain engaged in agriculture, and so on.

3. Our country's 'quasi-urbanization' is going to require a very long transitional period. The common international experience is that industrialization occurs in tandem with urbanization, that industrialization stimulates structural changes in industry, which then spur structural changes in employment. The percentage of people engaged in primary industry production declines and nonagricultural employment rises, eventually leading to increasing urbanization.

[Our path is somewhat different.] From the founding of our country, we have followed a course that strictly separates the systems governing urban and rural areas. Despite accelerating trends [to unify systems], a long interim period of quasi-urbanization is still going to be necessary, due to stage-specific features in our economic development and the ongoing impact of 'switching tracks' from one form of economic structure to another.

In the mid-1990s, once per capita GDP in our country exceeded USD 1,000, our industrial structure began to undergo rapid change and we have now entered into what can be called the 'middle stage of industrialization.' In 1978, primary industries contributed 29.1 percent of our GDP. By 2005, this figure had dropped to 12.5 percent. However, it should be recognized that in 2005 44.7 percent of our total social labor force was still engaged in primary-industry production. In developed countries, the normal percentage of the labor force engaged in primary industries at this stage is below 10 percent. With structural changes in employment being out of sync with structural changes in industry, we are seeing deviations in our form of urbanization.

According to World Bank data, using 'permanent residence' as the statistical measure, China's urbanization rate of 32 percent in 1999 was 14 percentage points lower than the world average. It was 18 percentage points lower than the average of countries with medium-range average incomes and it was 45 percent below countries with high average incomes. Internationally, the ratio of urbanization to industrialization generally falls between a range of 1.4 to 2.5. In the year 2000, our country's ratio was a mere 0.8. It is quite apparent that our degree of urbanization is falling behind our industrialization.

The fundamental reasons for our slow rate of urbanization have to do with the dual-structure of the systems we apply to urban and rural areas. The first reason has to do with our employment policies. These are still separate and distinct for urban employment and for rural employment to a broad extent, which serves as an extreme constraint on any shift of the rural population into cities. Planned-economy models still pertain with respect to employment in many areas. Practices formed over years of upholding that former system now serve as a deterrent to economic efficiencies and seriously damage overall social welfare. Such things as 'first [develop] cities, then later the countryside,' 'first the core, then the periphery,' assure that discriminatory practices against rural migrant workers continue. They create unequal employment opportunities and unfair distribution of benefits, and they enhance the already fragmented nature of the labor market.

The second reason has to do with our social welfare system. We are currently in the process of improving that system for urban residents, but any safety net for rural people still, to a very large degree, depends on land. Rural people who come into cities to work are already absorbed into industrial structures in the sense that they are making enormous contributions to urban economic development, to tax revenues off urban enterprises, and so on, but they are unable to join in any urban social welfare systems.

A third reason has to do with our system of household registration. The system as it is currently practiced has the effected of reinforcing the outside or inferior social status of rural migrant laborers. The household registration system enables these people to be discriminated against when it comes to supplying affordable housing, providing publicly funded healthcare, educating children, and so on. A whole series of discriminatory policies directly limits their personal growth and prevents them from taking up permanent residence in urban centers.

4. Our country will continue to have a large rural residence for a long period of time. Our rate of urbanization will continue to rise along with sustained and stable economic growth, but that does not mean that rural populations will decline overall. Since our form of urbanization is 'quasi,' when very large numbers of rural people enter cities and are unable to live there permanently, quite a few have no alternative but to return to their hometowns. The actual rural population is therefore very much higher than the ostensible 'urbanization rate' of 43 percent would lead people to believe.

According to World Bank forecasts, our country's population will reach 1.366 billion by the year 2010, and the 'urbanization rate' will be 47 percent by then. [The country will be 47 percent 'urbanized.'] By 2020, our total population is expected to reach 1.449 billion, at which time we will be 55 percent 'urbanized.' By these projections, in the year 2010 our rural population will be 642.02 million, however, and by the year 2020 it will have continued to grow to a total of 796.95 million. These fundamental facts about our situation dictate that we will have a large rural population for some time to come. The 'three agricultures' will continue to present a huge strategic challenge to formulating national policy. These facts also lead to the unavoidable conclusion that our country's path to 'modernization' is going to have to be unique.

II. 'Guiding Ideology' and 'Basic Principles' in coordinating the development of our urban and rural areas

1. Guiding ideology

In coordinating the socioeconomic development of urban and rural areas, we must adhere to the guiding ideology of 'Deng Xiaoping theory' and what are, in shorthand, called the 'three represents.' We must firmly keep to a 'scientific outlook' in everything we do to guide socioeconomic development. The core task of all the key work undertaken by the entire Party must be to address and resolve the 'three agricultural issues.' We must ensure that industry 're-nurtures' agriculture, and that cities now in turn support the countryside. We must stick to policy measures that 'give more and take less' from farmers. We must vigorously pursue the elimination of any vestiges of a dual structure with respect to urban and rural systems. We have to set up long-range effective mechanisms that enable 'industry to stimulate agriculture and enable urban areas to "bring along" rural areas.' We must promote social justice and the establishment of democratic and legal institutions, consolidate, improve, and strengthen policies that support farmers, find definitive ways to increase farmers' income, promote the building up of a more modern agriculture, strengthen public facilities and services in rural areas, deepen comprehensive reform of governance structures in rural areas, and promote the building of a new countryside on a stable and incremental basis. We undertake all of these guiding ideologies or policy guidelines for the aim of ensuring social harmony.

2. Basic principles

1. We must reinforce the inclination to put more public goods into rural areas, and to invest more of all factors of production into rural areas. The basic guarantee for coordinated socioeconomic development of urban and rural areas is making sure that supply of public services for the two is equalized. It lies in promoting greater investment of both funding and human resources in rural areas. One fundamental reason for the severely retarded nature of rural development is that public-finance expenditures are egregiously inadequate, including those for social security, those for the building of basic public facilities, and those for health, education, and welfare. Agriculture is underdeveloped not only because funding and human resources are insufficient but because they are flowing out and away from rural areas on a massive scale. Therefore, we must truly shift the focus of infrastructure building and social endeavors in the direction of rural areas. We must be proactive in restructuring public spending and all spending on rural fixed assets, and on restructuring the issuing of credit. We have to set up stable mechanisms for furthering resolution of the three agriculture problems, so that we have a steady source of funding for forming a new countryside. We must formulate effective policies, establish necessary mechanisms, channel funds, and mandate spending and delegation of personnel to rural areas. We should reorganize the way funding sources for education, health, and wealth are handled between rural and urban areas. We must support the building up a 'new countryside.'

2. We must adhere to the policy of implementing coordinated urban-rural development during the transitional period to urbanization. Formulating transitional policies that are proactive yet prudent, incremental, and staged, will be the most effective way to balance urban-rural development. Our country's basic situation includes the following: a massive population and resources that are inadequate relative to that population, unbalanced development between urban and rural areas on top of an entire economic system that is 'switching tracks' from one mode to another, economic patterns in rural and urban areas that will be in flux for a long time to come as population structures shift. For these reasons, unifying our cities and countryside into one integrated unit is impossible to do in one fell swoop. As a result, while seizing the moment to do what we can to spur urbanization and industrialization, we must also take steps to support farmers, rural areas, and agriculture over the long run. We must find every means possible to do this, through proactive transitional policies. We must concurrently promote urbanization and the 'building up of a new countryside.' While picking up the pace of modernizing the country, we must also take necessary steps to promote social harmony.

3. We must stick to the policy of attempting to resolve the 'food issue' basically through domestic supply. That means assuring basic self-sufficiency in such major agricultural products as grain. This is a fundamental prerequisite for ensuring economic development, social stability, and national security. For a rapidly developing country such as China, grain and other similarly major agricultural products are not merely commodities but a strategic resource. They are a bargaining chip in the international political contest. Overreliance on international markets for grain can easily lead to being put in a disadvantageous position. It cuts our ability to make strategic decisions from a position of strength, which is a very unfavorable position to be in with respect to international competition.

Therefore, in order to adhere to the policy of maintaining basic self-sufficiency in major agricultural products, we must begin to see that conservation of water resources, arable land, and healthy ecosystems are critical as the foundation for assuring the very survival and ongoing development of our State [as a political entity] and our nation [as a people]. Food security in terms of assured supply of grain and major agricultural products requires that we speed up the pace at which we are modernizing agriculture and improve the comprehensive productive capacity of our agriculture.

4. We must adhere to the policy of stabilizing the basic property system in rural areas. In political terms, this means respecting the democratic rights of farmers; in economic terms, it means guaranteeing the property rights of farmers. These are the institutional cornerstones when it comes to stabilizing social harmony and promoting rural economic development. Stabilizing the 'basic operating system' in rural areas through assuring the rights of farmers to land that they have contracted to operate, and to their own homes and their own means of production, are basic rights bestowed upon farmers by the constitution. These cannot be modified or changed by any organization or individual at any time.

In the course of promoting the whole process of industrialization and urbanization, therefore, as well as the program of 'building up a new countryside,' we must fully respect the authority of laws and regulations, and indeed must improve those parts of the legal system that need to be addressed, in order to lay a very firm foundation for socioeconomic development in the countryside and for the overall modernization of the country as a whole.

III. Basic measures to take in coordinating urban-rural development

Given that we are in an era of fast industrialization and urbanization, it is vital that we address the 'building of a new countryside' concurrently with the attempt to urbanize, that we adhere to our policy of coordinated urban-rural development. We must avoid the phenomenon of urban slums through taking proactive measures to address farmers' inability to 'set down roots' once they move into cities. We must handle the departure of farmers from their homeland in stable fashion. At the same time, we must curb the ever-widening disparity between rural and urban situations, make sure that 'industry promotes agriculture, while cities bring along the countryside,' and that 'we give more, take less, and invigorate [agriculture].' We must increase investment and support for rural areas and agriculture, make sure that the transferability of such factors of production as land, financing, and labor is truly benefiting rural development and agricultural development. We have to improve the underlying conditions that enable agriculture to move forward, by strengthening public services in rural areas, stabilizing the 'basic operating system,' and improving rural governance structures.

1. Put major effort into modernizing agriculture

Given that natural resource constraints are only getting worse, our sole option in trying to improve agricultural efficiencies, yields, and competitiveness lies in building up more modern agricultural practices. This is especially true when you consider our fairly low level of agricultural mechanization and technology. Modernizing agriculture should be seen as both a strategic move and a substantive part of the effort to build up a new countryside.

1. Strengthen our infrastructure for agriculture by improving the underlying conditions that enable agriculture to move forward. In order to ensure national food security and sustainable development, we must set a lower limit on the amount of arable land left to the country [beyond which we should not allow the situation to get worse]. We must improve the quality of the soil on that land, improve the conditions for agricultural production, and protect agricultural resources, including the ecosystem surrounding agriculture. We must have long-standing and strict requirements that protect arable land, that prohibit any reduction in basic farmland, that improve soil quality, and that speed up the development of higher-quality fields. We should put very considerable effort into setting up irrigation systems, and improving the capacity and efficiency of existing systems. We should guide farmers and the rural public in general in the direction of building water conservancy facilities.

We should continue to expand environmental protection efforts, so as to improve the ecological context for agricultural production.

2. Accelerate the pace of scientific innovations in the field of agriculture, and find ways by which to transform agricultural growth. Scientific and technical innovations are key to increasing overall productivity and competitiveness in agriculture. They are the essence of transforming agriculture and ensuring sustainable development. In raising innovative capacity, we must set up national-level mechanisms that encourage scientific personnel to focus on agriculture; we must set up an 'innovation base,' mobilize 'special projects' and 'key projects,' with an aim to making breakthroughs in critical areas.

We must increase the strategic preparedness of agricultural science and technology, increase the rate at which results are translated into practice, increase the productive capacity of agriculture, improve resource utilization and the efficiency with which inputs are used. We should cultivate a 'new type of farmer' through training and education, improve technical skills in agricultural production through large-scale training programs, shift the way the labor force currently relies mainly on physical strength and experience to the use of technical skills and scientific methods.

3. Improve our market systems and regulatory mechanisms [with respect to agricultural goods], lift efficiencies in how goods are circulated, ensure market stability. More advanced systems relating to the logistics of moving agricultural products and more advanced marketing systems are the best guarantee of a more modernized agriculture. Setting up effective regulatory mechanisms is a necessary measure in maintaining market balance and assuring that the market is orderly. We must build up basic infrastructure in the countryside that can handle the logistics of moving agricultural products. We must develop new methods and forms for moving products, create entities that are more diversified and multifaceted. We must enhance the degree to which farmers organize themselves into specialized cooperatives and processing and trading enterprises. We must raise the 'socialized' level of small-scale farming production through 'socialized' services at each link in the process of agricultural production and through improving systems that provide socialized services for agriculture. We must strengthen supervisory controls over the quality of agricultural products and over the environment in which they are produced. We must improve marketing services. We should determine and make explicit which products are in our strategic national interest, in terms of both production and trade, and set out long-term plans for developing certain industries and certain kinds of products. We should improve the effectiveness of our regulatory mechanisms over imported and exported agricultural products.

2. Strengthen provision of public services in rural areas

A key aspect of gradually bringing rural and urban socioeconomic situations into a more balanced alignment relates to equal provision of basic public services in rural areas. This is also a substantive component of 'building a harmonious society.'

1. Strengthen the building up of basic infrastructure in rural areas and improve living conditions for farmers as well as their working [production] conditions. Changing the 'backward' aspect of the countryside and resolving issues in most urgent need of attention will involve improving basic infrastructure in the areas of irrigation, transport, energy, and information. It will mean speeding up solutions to the drinking water problems of 320 million people, giving special priority to providing safe water for small-population ethnic minorities, for those people being displaced due to the building of reservoirs, for districts in which schistosomiasis is prevalent, and for rural schools. [It will mean] strengthening road construction and maintenance in rural areas, making sure that all areas of the countryside are connected via roads as fast as possible, and assuring that the road system among counties and townships is networked. It will mean continuing to press for construction and improvement of telecommunications systems in the countryside, for development of hydropower resources and for more widespread use of methane as an energy source. It will mean accelerating the process of 'informatizing' the countryside, that is, making sure that all villages and all households have access to information.

2. Promote efforts in rural areas that lead to the overall advance of farmers. Efforts in such areas as health, education, and culture [general welfare] not only impact rural development and the improvement of agriculture but also impact the course of our industrialization and urbanization. They are part of the strategic task of improving the general caliber of our nation. [They include] consolidating the results of our nine-year system of compulsory education, improving the quality of education, putting in place effective measures that advance rural vocational-technical education, strengthening the efforts to set up a three-tiered network of health service centers, steadily and firmly implementing the program for new rural healthcare services, setting up a system of basic healthcare and medical security that conforms to the needs and realities of rural areas, expanding cultural facilities that are of a public nature, making sure that all villages and households have access to radio and television, gradually setting up a system of public cultural services that extends to both urban and rural areas, incrementally establishing a minimum-living allowance system in rural areas, improving emergency relief systems in the countryside, and taking a more proactive approach to exploring the establishment of social security systems [old-age pensions] in rural areas.

3. Stabilize and improve upon the rural land system

Stabilizing our 'basic operating system' in rural areas, protecting the rights and interests of farmers with respect to land assets, and conserving farmland in terms of land-use practices, all directly impact our country's long-term prospects for industrialization and urbanization. They do not merely affect the sustainable development of agriculture or the personal interests of farmers.

1. Stabilize 'cheng-bao' *relationships in rural areas [contracted rights to land], and improve upon the property rights system and land-use system with respect to land.* Stabilizing the contractual relationships of farmers to land [*cheng-bao* relationships] is the core of the Party's basic policies with respect to rural areas. It is also fundamental to achieving a stable and harmonious society and to achieving sustainable economic growth in our country. Right now, our emphasis must be on intensifying publicity about the Law on Land Contracts in Rural Areas, together with relevant policies, laws, and regulations, and on making absolutely sure that these policies, laws, and regulations are in fact fully implemented. We must assure that contractual terms are not adjusted during the term of the contracts, and that land is not withdrawn from those to whom it is contracted. In accordance with actual circumstances in rural areas, and with the need to protect the rights and interests of farmers, we should revise relevant articles of the Land Management Law and other relevant laws and regulations in such a way as to formulate detailed provisions for the actual implementation of the Law on Land Contracts in Rural Areas. This must be done as soon as possible. We must set up the underlying systems for resolving disputes about land, including an improved method of registering property rights with respect to land (including contracted land-use rights). This includes formulating standardized registration methods that apply to both cities and rural areas. As soon as possible, we must promulgate a Law Covering Arbitration of Land Disputes in Rural Areas.

2. Encourage a market in which operating rights to rural land can be transferred to others, promote the development of a market for the farmland factor of production. We should allow market mechanisms to play a fundamental role in allocating land resources, on the basis of [our stated policy principle requiring that all transactions be] 'voluntary, legal, and for compensation.' In order to protect the rights and interests of farmers, to improve land-use efficiencies, and to realize fair land transactions, we should establish a market for standardized [regulated], fair transfer of land-use rights to farmland. In order to improve the functioning of such a market, we should also encourage the development of intermediary organizations. We should set up a legitimate 'platform' for dealing with a market in farmland-use transfers, including service organizations that deal with registering both supply and demand sides, that disseminate information, that provide fair price appraisals, that provide consulting services on laws and policies. We must improve upon the legal framework for farmland transfers and make sure that they are conducted according to laws and regulated management practices; we must step up the pace of reforming the system of land requisitioning [i.e., government appropriations of land] and go further in protecting the legal rights and interests of farmers.

3. Improve policies that relate to rural housing locations and to village planning, conserve land that is going into rural construction. One of the most important principles that we must adhere to on a long-term basis as we pursue modernization is the conservation of scarce land resources. Intensive use of land must be practiced. The effective course of action has to involve a scientific approach to planning and 'deployment' in rural areas, to policies regarding where housing is to be located, and to use of land for construction purposes. We must therefore reform our existing system with respect to location of housing, modify policies regarding how permissions are given, take a firm approach to the problems of 'one household many homes,' 'building up new sites without tearing down the old,' and profligate and illegal use of farmland for new construction. We must explore concrete methods to put a stop to the system that enables land to be used under the 'one site for each household' policy. We should launch pilot projects that reform the rural housing-site system. Village planning should be conducted according to specific situations which can be categorized. Within districts that fall within the scope of 'urban-area planning,' village planning should be integrated into the overall urban planning and implementation should be carried out on a unified basis. Building should proceed in stages and residential districts should be concentrated in certain areas. [In the planning process,] issues of farmers' employment should be addressed, as well as the education of children, the provision of public facilities, social security systems, and so on. Within districts that are meant to remain permanently 'rural' (in which farmland is being protected), strict provisions should be followed that preserve nationally designated 'basic farmland.' Village plans and construction should be carried out in such a way as to conserve farmland, to facilitate [agricultural] production, to reflect the special nature of the countryside, to improve basic infrastructure, and to benefit the cleanliness and hygiene of the village. All plans should be in alignment with laws of socioeconomic development, and all approaches should be suited to specific circumstances and needs. No approach should be taken that exceeds the 'carrying capacity' of the local people or that does not respect their wishes.

4. Enhance the support of agriculture through various forms of financing, through public expenditures, and through industry

We must be proactive in adjusting the income allocation structure of the country. To do this, we should continue to adhere to the policy of 'giving more, taking less, and invigorating.' We should increase coverage of public finance in rural areas, and guide financing from both public and 'social' [or nongovernmental] sectors in the direction of rural investments. We should encourage the extension of both industry and commerce into rural areas and fundamentally alter the existing situation, namely, an extreme paucity of financial, technical, and human resources in rural areas.

1. Enhance financial and fiscal support for rural areas by setting up enduring mechanisms that 'enable industry to spur the growth of agriculture,' and 'enable cities to bring along rural areas.' We should accelerate the process of extending public funding to rural areas, of adjusting the structure of public-finance expenditures, and of establishing stable and enduring mechanisms that now allow industry to 'repay' agriculture by supporting rural areas. Annual increases in State [national] public expenditures for such things as health, education, and culture [general welfare] should be put to rural areas, as well as to investments in rural fixed assets. A greater percentage of funds that the State derives from land transfer fees should gradually go to rural areas. We should go further in financial reform in rural areas, improve upon the system of financial institutions in rural areas, create new forms of financing operations, improve financial services, encourage financial institutions to increase their credit lines to the 'three agricultures,' guide funds that have flowed into the postal savings system to start flowing back into rural areas. We should use fiscal [tax] and financial [funding] policies to guide investment funds in the direction of rural areas and agriculture; we should accelerate legislation to do with investing in agriculture, so that there are legal guarantees for funding sources that make investments in agricultural and rural development.

2. Improve systems that support and protect agriculture; raise the yields and the competitiveness of our agriculture. In line with our increasing national financial strength but also in accord with WTO rules and regulations, we should create subsidy programs for agriculture that have clearly defined objectives, are easy to manage and implement, are diverse in nature, and benefit farmers directly. We should continue to provide direct subsidies for grain production, for improved varieties, and for purchase of agricultural machinery. We should continue policies that provide comprehensive subsidies for prices of means of production and for a minimum price support on grain purchases by the State. We should continue to provide incentive awards to counties that are mainly involved in agriculture and counties that are facing financial difficulties. We should accelerate the setting up of risk-mitigation mechanisms for agriculture, and improve our early-warning systems for predicting natural disasters and problems caused by both harmful insects and noxious weeds. We should actively promote adoption of policy-type agricultural insurance, and provide financial subsidies for those farming households that participate.

3. Guide industry in the direction of supporting agriculture; create a more optimal industrial structure in the country's economy. To an appropriate degree, we should encourage processing industries that relate to agriculture to shift their operations from urban to rural areas. This is an important move in terms of our stated policy directives of 'having industry spur agriculture,' and 'having cities bring along rural areas.' We should formulate policies that incentivize this process, in order to persuade processing industries for agricultural products to concentrate in 'county' areas. Through such means as mergers and acquisitions, technology transfers, product transfers, outsourcing and processing, we want to support urban processing and manufacturing industries so that they can participate in upgrading and reforming local-level industries. We want to spur the development of small- and medium-sized enterprises, and increase the margin for local, *in-situ,* employment of farmers as a way to increase their locally earned income.

4. Encourage social [nongovernmental] investment as a way to spur rural development. We must constantly seek to open up new channels for investment in agriculture, by using such measures as subsidies, share participation, discounts, loan guarantees, and other things, to create a beneficial environment for greater social [nongovernmental] investment. We should gradually develop diversified investment mechanisms that enable widespread public participation. We should encourage people from all walks of life to contribute to the creation of better facilities in rural areas for both agricultural production and improved life in general. We should mobilize people to join in civic activities that contribute to farmers' training, medical services, and exposure to culture.

5. Improve services for rural migrant workers and provide them with a [social] security system

Rural migrant workers are a specific social phenomenon associated with our country's urbanizing process. In the course of trying to create a 'new countryside' as we both industrialize and urbanize, we must formulate and implement transitional policies that are appropriate to their situation. Policies must be in line with rural development in its current stage, and with the way farmers are currently entering cities to seek work. The immediate task at hand is to realize and fully implement the State Council's *Opinion on How to Strengthen Our Work with Respect to Rural Migrant Workers.* This relates to resolving immediate and very real problems of rural migrant workers, and to our efforts to realize a more coordinated development of rural and urban areas.

1. Strictly enforce a system of using contracts when hiring workers; protect the legal rights and interests of rural migrant workers. The fundamental prerequisite for ensuring the rights and interests of farmers who enter cities to find jobs is full adherence to the [existing] labor contract system as well as strengthening relevant legislation. [We must] also increase supervision over those units that hire workers and that are meant to carry out labor contracts. We must ensure that workers' wages are being paid, that safety standards are met, that injury insurance is being covered, and that other such basic rights and interests of workers are being respected. We should set up a system of reserve funds to guarantee that there is money for workers' wages; we should establish and constantly improve long-range mechanisms that address the problem of contractors being in arrears on wages. We must strengthen protection of rural migrant labor through making sure that liability insurance is carried for them as according to law; we forbid child labor but in addition we must protect the special rights and interests of female workers and minors.

2. Improve training programs that enable rural migrant workers to gain technical skills, and improve the ability of workers to shift into other [nonagricultural] jobs. The key to improving the overall quality of the labor force is training. It lies in covering the costs of training, in improving the quality of training, in constantly enhancing the conditions under which training occurs, in strengthening training measures and broadening the scope of training. [We should] encourage enterprises who hire labor to carry out targeted training in places from which the labor is being 'sent out.' [We should] 'organize and mobilize' social forces to participate in training on a widespread basis, of the sort that enables a shift of employment [away from agriculture]. To meet the needs of upgrading industries, we should train up a group of mid-level and senior qualified technicians from among rural migrant workers.

3. Provide basic public services for rural migrant workers; improve their quality of life and their social standing. In line with [the principle] of integrating urban and rural situations and ensuring fair and equal employment, [we should] provide basic public services to rural migrant workers. We should go further in strengthening the infrastructure for service systems, and provide such services as information [on jobs], agencies, and security considerations. In drafting regulations, formulating public policies, and creating public facilities, we should take into full consideration such things as the living conditions for rural migrant workers, their housing, education for children, health services, and social security. When workers who have 'gone away' for work come back to set up their own businesses, we should provide them with funding, information, technology, marketing, and other such services.

For those workers who qualify to stay on in cities and 'put down roots' in an urban environment, we should do our best to research and then formulate policies and measures that enable them ultimately to become 'urban residents' and that enable 'urbanization' in a real sense. Not only will this be beneficial in improving the treatment of rural migrant workers, but it will assist those workers who 'go away' to truly disengage from [a reliance on] the land. It will thereby enable expanded farming operations for those farmers who remain on the land.

6. *Develop and boost county economies*

County economies are an important force in propelling our country's overall economy. They hold the potential to allow a greater shift of 'farmers' away from agriculture into other forms of employment, and they are vital when it comes to trying to improve farmers' income.

1. Build up the 'pillar industries' of county economies and strengthen the foundations for growth of local economies. In strengthening our planning for more coordinated development of urban and rural areas, and our policy guidance for industry, [we should] create conditions that help counties 'take on' appropriate industries and enterprises. We should actively explore the creation of a system whereby provinces have direct jurisdiction over counties. [We should] expand the margin for growth of county economies [i.e., the 'space' within which they can operate]. In planning for industrial growth of counties and [a more] rational and scientific allocation of industries, we should focus on industries that process agricultural products as well as industries that serve urban enterprises as part of the manufacturing process. [We should] adopt preferential policies with regard to tax, financing, commercial, and industrial considerations that serve this purpose. We should support a shift of urban industries into rural areas.

2. Encourage the development of specialty industries as new 'pillars' of county economies. We should enable each locality to make use of its own natural and human resources in the optimum way by encouraging the production of 'leading' products and 'specialty' products and improving the regional allocation of industries. We should prescribe solutions that are specific to unique situations, and enable areas to focus on producing things that have long traditions, or that are ethnic in nature, or that are particular to a given place. These can either be goods or services, such as tourism in rural areas, gardening and horticulture, breeding of certain species, and so on. Through planning and policy guidance and support, [we should] enable villages to focus on their unique strengths. We should cultivate a whole range of diversified localities that build their economies around 'pillar industries.'

3. Develop service industries and [build up] flourishing county economies. One key means to helping farmers create their own businesses, that thereby expand employment, lies in developing service industries that are directly related to agricultural production and to farmers' lives. Focusing first on county seats and 'core towns,' and making sure that actions are in line with the real needs of farmers, [we should] develop service industries such as trade, food and beverages, transport, travel, information, and financing, as well as all kinds of services that assist farmers with agricultural products such as marketing, means of production, daily necessities, and the full range of services involved in science and technology, information, law, and accounting.

7. Strengthen grassroots democracy and the 'building up' of party organizations

In order to integrate planning of urban and rural areas, including economic and social situations, and in order to create a 'new countryside' that is harmonious, peaceful and orderly, fair and equitable, and full of vitality, we must go further in strengthening the establishment of basic Party organizations. We must improve self-governance mechanisms of villagers, and advance the establishment of democratic and legal institutions at the grassroots level.

1. Strengthen Party organizations at the grassroots level and go further in enabling the core functions of Party organizations. [We should] consolidate and maintain the results of the 'progressive education' campaign undertaken by Party members. [We should take actions] that enable the 'role' of grassroots Party organizations in pulling together the will of the people, in promoting development, and in furthering 'harmony.' This should all be within the context of a more coordinated approach to urban-rural growth and the policy of 'building up a new countryside.' We should select certain Party members to become members of 'leadership groups' in grassroots Party organizations, namely, those who are highly qualified in terms of their politics, who have strong working ability, and who are generally recognized by the public as being 'good' Party members. We should explore effective pathways to selecting ['electing and appointing': *xuan ren*] outstanding village cadres to public positions in townships and to recruiting township civil servants. We should improve the physical conditions of Party organizations and address any difficulties Party members face in terms of their actual living situation. We should put more investment into constructing facilities for grassroots Party organizations. We should improve the harmonious coordination between Party branches and village committees.

2. Improve self-governance mechanisms of villagers and enhance stability in villages as well as economic growth. [We should] improve the self-governance mechanisms of villagers and invest them with vitality, under the guidance [leadership] of village Party organizations. We should spur rural [economic] development and build a 'harmonious countryside.' In improving villagers' self-governance mechanisms, the emphasis should be on assuring a system of democratic procedures and openness in village affairs. The great mass of farmers themselves should have the right to, and be truly able to, know what is going on. They should have the right to participate, the right to manage, and the right to supervise or oversee. We should go further in actually realizing good democratic elections, democratic policies, democratic management, and democratic supervision. We should improve self-governance capacities of villagers and the level at which those capacities are exercised.

We should explore setting up new mechanisms in local areas that enable self-education, self-management, and self-servicing. We should improve governance structures in townships. We should assure that farmers' service organizations can play their proper role in terms of administering village social and economic affairs. We should further advance the legal systems that support democracy [the 'legalization' of democratic processes], improve self-governance bylaws among villagers, standardize self-governing behavior among villagers, as well as administrative procedures. We should assure that 'villagers' meetings' [*cunmin huiyi*] and 'villagers' representative meetings' [*cunmin daibiao huiyi*] are able to fulfill their key function in villagers' self-governance.

Notes

* This is an important special report submitted by the author according to the instruction of the Central Committee of the CPC as a preparation for the 17th Congress of the CPC.
1 Agricultural socialization is the process through which agriculture production mode changes from an isolated one into a collaborative, open-ended one with clear division of labor. Specifically, agricultural socialization means collaboration and division of labor are more prominent in different aspects of agricultural activities, including infrastructure construction, material input, the process of planting, harvesting, processing, and selling. Aside from the input on the part of family, government, the collective, and specialized service departments are also included in the production process. Close collaboration and clear division of labor have proved to significantly increase agricultural productivity.

14 Several noteworthy issues with respect to the recent increases in agricultural prices*

(June 2007)

The prices of quite a few agricultural products have been on the increase since autumn and winter of last year, causing considerable concern on all sides. Looked at overall, these price increases can be attributed to such general factors as changes in supply and demand and differences in cost structures, but they can also be traced to more fundamental underlying causes. Because of this, they deserve our close attention.

I. The precursor to the recent increases in agricultural prices was a sustained 10-year period of depressed prices

Commodity prices reached their highest point since the start of reforms [1978] in the year 1994. After that, we adopted two rounds of policy measures to increase the prices at which the State bought agricultural products, in order to keep farmers enthusiastic about raising grain. As a result, by 1996, prices of most agricultural products in our country were at their highest levels in history. For the ensuing decade, however, prices of agricultural products remained depressed. The following statistics use *May* 1996 prices as the baseline figures. By May 2006, the price index for nationwide grain was 0.9873 [i.e., around 1 percent less than the baseline figure 10 years earlier]. The price index for meat and poultry and associated products was 1.0155. That of egg products was 0.6925. If one uses the baseline figure of *December* 1996, the price indexes of these three items one decade later were as follows: 1.0606 for grain, 1.1284 for meat and poultry, and 0.9872 for egg products.

[For one decade], prices for agricultural goods remained depressed but in that same period the production costs of agricultural products went up markedly, as well as income levels of the population as a whole. Those increases can be seen in the following statistics. Using 1996 as the baseline figure, by 2006, the overall index for the cost of producing agricultural goods had gone up to 1.096, while feedstocks specifically were 1.168. It should be noted that cost increases were actually already appearing by the fall of 2003.

Starting in 2004, Central adopted a whole series of policies that were aimed at supporting agriculture and farmers. These were known as the 'four reductions and four subsidies.' To a degree, the measures ameliorated the effect of ongoing cost increases for farmers and therefore helped curb increases in agricultural prices. However, starting in 2006, the incremental impact of these policies was beginning to decline while farmers now faced a dramatic rise in energy costs associated with agricultural production. Since fall and winter of last year, therefore, we have been seeing a new round of price increases in agricultural products.

II. Causes of recent price increases in domestic agricultural products

This time, the price increases for agricultural products are different in that causes have varied, depending on the product.

This round of price increases started as we entered winter last year, with price increases in wheat. The harvest was good last year, with total production coming to 208.94 billion *jin* [104.47 billion kg], which was a 7.2 percent increase over the previous year, and inventories were relatively well stocked as well. The cause of price increases was mainly due to temporary blockages in grain 'circulation.'

Next came a rise in the price of edible oils. The main cause here was an increase in consumption coupled with a decrease in the amount being produced domestically, while soybean prices rose on the international market. In 2006, our country's oil-plant production declined overall by 0.6 percent, while production of rapeseed went down by 3.1 percent and production of soybeans went down by 2.5 percent. At the same time, international prices of these products rose dramatically. From December 2006, the wholesale price of soybeans in the country began to increase dramatically, going up more than 10 percent per month, or increases on the order of RMB 260 per ton.

The 'third wave' came in the spring of 2007, with increases in the price of pork. Prices for feed had been rising, contributing to increasing costs, but in addition two particular factors were at play. One was that epidemics among live-pig-raising operations were fairly severe last spring, resulting in a decline in the number of sows that has led to a corresponding decline this year in the number of marketable fattened hogs. The second factor relates to a lack of valid statistical reference, given the distortions of prices that were previously overly low. In May 2006, the price of pork was at its lowest point in the previous 33 months, since September 2003. The rebound in prices this spring is therefore clearly of a 'recovery' nature. In May 2007, the average price of pork in 36 large- and medium-sized cities was RMB 9.54 per *jin*. This was 30.9 percent more than it had been in May 2006 (RMB 7.29 per *jin*), but only 5.9 percent more than it had been in October 2004 (RMB 9.01 per *jin*).

Finally, the price of edible oils has also begun to rise most recently. The main cause here is that estimates of domestic production of rapeseed and soybeans continue to be lowered, while international prices for both edible oils and soybeans continue to rise. Right now, the new crop of rapeseed is already coming to market and the 'production price' is ranging from RMB 1.5 to RMB 1.8 per *jin*, which is an increase of some 50 percent over last year's prices. Indications are that the prices of processed rapeseed oil are going to be up significantly.

III. Grain prices in international markets are notably increasing

Given a reduction in the amount produced [globally] combined with lowered stocks and increases in demand, international grain prices continued to increase as we entered 2007.

Wheat: In March, the FOB cash price for wheat was USD 211 per ton (hard red winter wheat) and USD 221.5 per ton (hard red spring wheat). These showed increases of 13.9 percent and 13.4 percent over the previous year. The average price for first-quarter futures was USD 181.3 per ton (hard red winter wheat) and USD 185.2 per ton (hard red spring wheat), which was an increase in price, respectively, of USD 29.3 (19.3 percent) and USD 35 (23.5 percent).

Corn: In March, FOB cash prices were USD 173 per ton, 61.3 percent over the previous year. Futures prices were USD 162.7 per ton, 80.4 percent over the previous year.

Rice: In the first quarter of this year, FOB prices for *man-gu* rice kept increasing every month: They were USD 282 per ton in January, USD 290 per ton in February, and USD 297 per ton in March. These prices were 12.7 percent higher than the same period last year, and were the highest rice prices have been since August 1997.

IV. Our country's two great 'weak points' are soybeans and edible oils, since they are so subject to international price volatility

In terms of supply and demand over the short term and medium term in our country, the impact of international price volatility on our grain will not be as great [as it is on soybeans and edible oils]. The production and demand situation in 2006 shows that we have a slight surplus in the 'harvest-year' of wheat in 2006, while the total amount of rice will show a close balance [between supply and demand]. If we restrict the amount of corn going into ethanol fuel production to within reasonable limits, we should basically have enough corn to meet demand.

So long as we adhere to policies that enhance production conditions for agriculture, including promoting further scientific and technological advances, forming rational prices, and so on, we should be able to increase grain production overall at a rate of 1 percent per year per *mu*. In addition, so long as we maintain strict controls over conserving the existing amount of arable land, and maintain the amount of acreage put into grain production, we should be able to limit the impact of international grain prices on our own grain. [Literally, 'there is a possibility we can limit the impact.']

However, we are feeling an ever-greater impact of international prices on our soybeans and edible oils. The main reason for this is that our domestic production is not meeting demand, and we are constantly in need of increasing the amount we import. In 2006, our country produced 15.9 million tons of soybeans and 30.59 million tons of the plants producing edible oils. We imported 28.27 million tons of soybeans and turned 5.1 million tons of that into oil while using the pulp as an important source of feedstock protein. In addition, we imported 6.71 million tons of edible oils.

More than 60 percent of our domestic consumption of soybeans and edible oils is currently imported. (This includes oils produced from soybeans that we process after importing.) As a result, our domestic prices for both feedstocks and edible oils are to a great extent determined by international market prices. We should therefore put all due consideration into the difficulties we already face in trying to regulate prices of livestock and poultry products, and edible oils.

V. The new feature in this current round of international price increases for agricultural products is that there is now a direct relationship between such prices and the prices of energy products

A certain relationship has always existed between the prices of agricultural products and energy, but in the past the relationship was always indirect. For example, it was reflected in the cost of chemical fertilizers and so on. Our current situation shows a dramatic change. In researching the causes, one can be traced to the way petroleum prices exploded upward after the United States occupied Iraq. A second can be attributed to the way in which the Bush administration strongly advocated the use of processed biofuels, leading to a dramatic rise in the price of corn.

The union of these two factors led to a situation in which corn and oil now are in a direct price relationship. At current standards of processing, around 3.3 tons of corn is required to produce one ton of ethanol fuel. This sets the direct price relationship between the two. It is not hard to imagine that corn will increasingly be processed into ethanol under the impetus of higher returns, given the way oil prices are remaining high. This may then give rise to changes in the price relationships among not only grains but all agricultural products. Further, it may spur a rise in international-market prices of all agricultural products, but especially prices of grain. We should therefore give full consideration to all potential ramifications.

VI. Several further thoughts

1. From a global perspective, this particular round of price increases in agricultural products is directly related to increases in the prices of energy. In the context of high energy prices, it is going to be hard to get agricultural prices back down overall, and prices may even rise to the level of a new 'platform.'

Therefore, when it comes to evaluating the supply and demand and the pricing of agricultural products, we must take a global and a long-term view. Research of a comprehensive nature on existing trends, with analysis of underlying causes, should be done in order for us to form policies that are effective over a medium- to long-term timeframe.

2. From a domestic perspective, price increases of agricultural products are ben-eficial in that they motivate farmers to produce more, and they improve farmers' incomes. International markets have differing impacts on the prices of our domes-tic grain, poultry, egg products, and edible oils, however, which means that we must adopt specific policies to protect the interests of different groups of people. With respect to farmers, we should continue to adopt policies and measures that encourage farmers to increase production. We should consolidate, stabilize, and strengthen our policies of 'supporting agriculture and giving preferential treat-ment to farmers.' With respect to the majority of urban inhabitants, given that incomes are continuing to increase quite rapidly, people should be able to absorb increases in the price of food products on their own. With respect to low-income groups in cities (such as college students), when called for, we can implement appropriate price subsidies.

Overall, having a certain degree of price stimulus is beneficial in encouraging domestic production of grain, and gives us the ability to form a competitive advan-tage in terms of our domestic prices versus international prices of grain (which include cost of transport). Greater production not only helps reduce the impact of international markets on our domestic grain prices, but may also increase our power over the grain-importing needs of our neighboring countries (such as Japan and South Korea).

3. Increases in pork prices are helpful in restoring and stabilizing our pork produc-tion industry and its market prices, but we still need to adopt comprehensive mea-sures in order to create stable mechanisms that are effective over the long run. First, we must strengthen preventive measures against animal diseases and epidemics, in terms of increasing funding, facilities, and people to implement policies. Second, we should speed up the process of providing policy-type insurance mechanisms for the poultry-breeding industry. Third, as soon as possible, we should formulate poli-cies that encourage large-scale raising of livestock and especially hog production. Fourth, we should strengthen the gathering and dissemination of information on market conditions for the livestock and poultry raising industries. Fifth, we should set up the necessary regulatory mechanisms in large- and medium-sized cities with respect to the preparation of meat and poultry products.

4. Several other products in our country are heavily influenced by international prices, in addition to soybeans and edible oils. Those include the agricultural and forestry products listed below. (See Table 14.1.)

Research that is of a strategic nature should be carried out on these products, in order to evaluate not only how to improve domestic production but how to

Table 14.1 Imports of various agricultural and forestry products into China in 2006 (in units of 10,000 tons and 10,000 square meters).

	Cotton	Natural rubber	Timber	Sawn timber	Wood pulp	Woolen
Imported amount	364.3	161.2	3215	607	759	29.96
Domestic production	674.6	53.8	6112	2984	370.8	42.92
Imports as a percentage of domestic production	54%	300%	53%	20%	205%	70%

Note: Data for wood pulp is for 2005.

support it and protect it against changes in international markets. The aim is to avoid serious price and market volatility by preventing domestic industries from being overly subject to large destabilizing impacts from abroad.

Note

* This is a proposal report submitted by the author to the leader of the State Council.

15 On the current socioeconomic situation with respect to agriculture and to rural areas, and major policy considerations*

(September 6, 2007)

I. Current status of agriculture

In our discussions [at this meeting], we have all been quite conscientious in how we analyze the country's agricultural situation in the first half of this year. Everyone is in agreement that the situation looks quite good for both agriculture and rural areas, especially since the convening of the '16th' [i.e., the 16th National Congress of the Communist Party of China].

Like everyone else, I too see grain production going up every year and farmers consistently earning more. Moreover, the extent of the increased yields and incomes is something that we have not seen in years. We should give full recognition to the good side of the situation. At the same time, we cadres involved in rural affairs also have a sense of foreboding. We also see a side of things that is very grave. We therefore should have a new approach to our work, be more mindful, adopt new forms when appropriate in terms of our working methods and policy measures. We should adapt to what is in fact a new situation.

1. Our country's demand for agricultural products has already entered a new stage of accelerated growth

On the one hand, the situation looks extremely good. On the other hand, we should be aware of impending problems. For example, even as we confirm the steady increase in grain yields, we have to recognize that the supply and demand equation is still extremely serious.

A few statistics are sufficient to tell the story. First, grain yields went up for three consecutive years between 2004 and 2006. In the first year, production increased by more than 77 billion *jin,* in the second year by more than 29 billion *jin,* and in the third year by more than 26 billion *jin.* Over these three years, increased grain production came to 133.5 billion *jin* altogether, something rare in our history and a most laudable achievement. Second, when comparing the output in 2006 of 994.9 billion *jin* to the output in 1998 of 1,024.6 billion *jin,* which was the highest in history, we see that 2006 production was in fact 29.7 billion *jin* less than 1998 production. Third, statistics show that total national consumption of grain in 2006 was 1,015.4 billion *jin* whereas production was only 994.9 billion *jin*. The gap between production and domestic supply came to 20.5 billion *jin*.

Putting these three statistics together shows both good and bad news. Increased production came to 133.5 billion *jin* over three years, but the highest yielding of those three years was still 29.7 billion *jin* behind the historic high of 1998. Moreover, it was not easy to achieve last year's production of 994.9 billion *jin* yet that production was still 20.5 billion *jin* below actual demand. [Note: divide *jin* figures in half to get kilograms.].

This then is our current basic situation with respect to the supply and demand of grain. If we do indeed aim to 'construct a new socialist countryside' and 'build a moderately prosperous society in an all-round way,' then we face a pressing demand to increase agricultural production and stabilize grain production in particular.

In recent years, our country has entered a stage of rapid increase in demand for agricultural products. Two major factors are influencing this situation. One is the relative increase in demand for agricultural products as incomes of urban residents continue to rise. The second is a corresponding increase in demand for 'commodity agricultural products' as urbanization accelerates.

China's total population increased by 90 million people in the decade between 1996 and 2006. The increase in our population over this past decade therefore exceeded the total population of Germany, which is around 80 million. On top of that demographic change, the distribution of our population has also undergone major changes as evidenced by an increase of 200 million people now living in 'urban' areas.

This increase in the urban population signifies that those who were once producing food are now those who are consuming it. Prior to entering cities, the food that most farmers consumed was supplied by themselves. The moment they entered cities, these people instead became purchasers of what are called 'commodity agricultural products.' After 'farmers' become 'urbanites,' their consumption of grain goes down but their consumption of other agricultural products rises noticeably. For example, in 2006, our country's urban residents on average consumed 15.5 percent more vegetable oil than farmers on a per capita basis, 47.7 percent more meat and poultry, 133.3 percent more eggs, and 200 percent more aquatic products.

Another important factor driving the increase in consumption of agricultural products is the structural change in what farmers are producing and how they themselves are living. Many farmers are now engaged in specialty production. They themselves produce no grain or vegetables but instead buy these things at a market. Some places do indeed produce grain but of types that are not for human consumption. For example, farmers in the northeast grow feed corn and sell it, then take the proceeds to the market to buy rice and flour.

In brief, the changes in demand for agricultural products caused by various socioeconomic changes are highly complex. Overall, one can say that demand is increasing quantitatively and there is also a demand for higher quality. Meeting both these demands presents farmers with a formidable challenge, which also means that we cadres involved in agricultural and rural affairs bear a very heavy responsibility.

2. Any ability to supply more agricultural products is circumscribed by environmental and natural resource limitations

Confronted with the changes in demand as described above, what is the situation with respect to our supply capacity? Many of our agricultural products are global leaders in terms of the total amount produced. A closer analysis does not permit much optimism, however. The main issues relate to the natural environment and to resource constraints.

The first resource constraint is that of land. Our amount of arable land is diminishing every year due to industrial development, urban construction, the building of basic infrastructure [roads and so on], adjustments in the structure of agricultural production, replanting of forests on what was farmland, and so on. In the decade between 1996 and 2006, arable land declined by 124 million *mu* [82.708 million square kilometers]. There are currently only six provinces whose arable land exceeds 1 million *mu* in total. What's more, in the short term there is no way we are going to reverse this trend of declining amounts of farmland, given that industrialization is not yet 'finished' and we have not yet passed even the halfway mark in urbanization (in 2006, our rate of urbanization was 43.9 percent).

Our country currently has the strictest land-administration system in the world, in order to try to preserve arable land. The State Council authorizes land-use for construction on [only] 4 million *mu* of land every year, of which some 2.8 million *mu* is land that was formerly farmland. During our discussions yesterday, we heard from cadres in some provinces who are complaining that their quota of construction land-use permits is too low, only 180,000 *mu*, which is far below the existing demand in their provinces for construction land.

In fact, this is not an insignificant figure when you consider that the entire country only authorizes 4 million *mu* altogether. By the end of 2006, we had 1.827 billion *mu* of arable land left in the country in total. If we want to hold the line [literally the 'red line'] at 1.8 billion, below which we will not go, that means that only 27 million *mu* is available nationwide for construction purposes. This amount will be used up within 7 to 10 years, if we calculate on the basis of 4 million *mu* authorized annually of which 2.8 million is former farmland.

In reality, however, requests to the State Council that come in every year for authorizations to build on farmland are totaling between 12 and 13 million *mu* of land. The State Council only authorizes 4 million *mu*, but we all know perfectly well that this does not mean the land is not taken over for construction purposes anyway. There are cases of going ahead with building even when authorization has been denied, and there are also cases when authorization was never requested in the first place. Land is the primary 'factor of production' in agriculture. Without conserving our land, our agriculture is in trouble.

In addition to trying to conserve land, we must constantly seek to improve yields per unit of area by improving the technological content of our agriculture. In these past few years, our increases in total production have come primarily from this side of the equation. In 2007, the total area planted in grain crops came to 1.58 billion *mu*, which was an increase of 90 million *mu* over 2003. From now on, however, it is going to be increasingly difficult to expand farm acreage. Only through constantly improving yields are we going to be able to satisfy the demand for grain and other agricultural products.

We are now operating under a market-economy system and the government cannot and should not coerce farmers into planting this or that by administrative fiat. Just now, one of our 'small groups' described this extremely well in its report, in saying that market forces are beginning to perform their proper role. Why then is it so hard to increase the amount of land planted to grain? Because returns on planting grain are low. The amount of land being planted to vegetables and other 'economic crops' is increasing, even without requiring that this happen, and the reason is that there is a market demand and the comparative returns are higher. We have a steadily declining amount of arable land and a steadily increasing demand for agricultural products – how to meet that demand is therefore an increasingly stiff challenge.

The second resource constraint is that of water. Water conservancy specialists tell us that there are three types of circumstances when it comes to water shortages. One is a 'resource-type shortage,' such as in the northwest where many places essentially have no water at all. A second is a shortage due to a lack of facilities or projects channeling the water. The water exists but cannot be used until irrigation channels are cut or wells are dug. A third type relates to the quality of water, when water is so severely polluted that not only is it undrinkable by humans but it cannot even be used to irrigate. All three types of 'water shortages' exist in our country.

Water resources themselves are scarce in much of the northern part of the country; facilities are lacking in much of the southwest, while water quality issues face many of the more developed parts of the country. Water is the source of life and is of ultimate importance to agriculture. Under normal conditions, our water resources per capita come to some 2,100 cubic meters. Globally, water resources per capita total some 8,000 cubic meters; we therefore have only a little more than one-quarter of the world's average amount of water per capita.

Just now, I was talking about land resources and noted that we have a total of 1.827 billion *mu* for a population of 1.314 billion people. That equals out at 1.39 *mu* per person, which is roughly 40 percent of the world's per capita average. Our water resources per capita, however, are even less, just 26 percent of the world's per capita average. Our extreme scarcity of water resources is therefore even more pronounced than our scarcity of land.

Moreover, the timing, and the spatial distribution of our country's water resources is extremely uneven. In terms of location, most resources are in the southern part of the country, while in terms of seasons, most water is available in the three months of July, August, and September. If too much water is upon us, we face floods; too little, and we can't find a drop. Throughout history, the situation has led to a 'production and demand' scenario in which the south produces grain that is then shipped to the north. The Grand Canal, which passes through the country from Hangzhou in the south to Tongzhou in the north, was built primarily to transport grain.

Historically, grain transport northward via 'maintaining the canals' was always a major part of making sure that the 'realm was peaceful.' The 'cutting through' of the Grand Canal was begun in the Sui dynasty, which signifies that prior to the Sui there was already a pattern of transporting grain from south to north. The reasons for such a pattern were quite simple: The combination of water, soil, sunlight, and temperature was better in the south [for agriculture] than it was in the north. People of my generation still remember that many places 'south of the river' were a kind of paradise in terms of 'fish and rice' [i.e., food], while anyplace in the north that had moderately good farming conditions was always described as being a 'south-of-the-river type place.'

In the past 20 to 30 years, however, this situation has been entirely reversed. We now have northern grain being shipped to the south. One cannot simply characterize this as being 'good' or 'bad,' 'correct' or 'incorrect,' it is simply the result of the way things have changed. The fundamental reason for this has been that coastal regions in the southeast moved far more quickly in 'reforming' and 'opening up' than the rest of the country. The process of industrialization and urbanization was faster and therefore the amount of land occupied for nonfarming purposes increased, to the point that grain production in these areas declined.

Between 1998 and 2006, grain production nationwide declined by 29.7 billion *jin,* but in the 10 provinces along the coast, grain production declined by the far greater amount of 61.4 billion *jin.* This indicates that the difference was made up by grain production in the central and western parts of the country. And what is wrong with that? If production declines in places where conditions are ideal in terms of soil, sunlight, precipitation, and so on, and has to be made up for in places where conditions are less than ideal, one has to question the sustainability of such a pattern of production.

Paddy rice is a clear example. People living in what was once considered the 'paradise for fish and rice' are increasingly eating rice that was grown in the far north, in Heilongjiang. Naturally, there is still a great deal of potential in Heilongjiang grain production, especially once the water conservancy project in the 'two rivers and one lake' district is completed (the Heilongjiang River and Ussuri River, and Lake Xingkai). Once that happens, it may be possible to increase grain production by 30 billion *jin.*

Nonetheless, we encounter two problems. First, the rivers and lakes define the border of the country, which immediately complicates the issue of the right to use water resources. Second, the long-term environmental impacts ['changes in the ecosystem'] of putting large swathes of land into rice production in the far north are unclear at this time.

Now, I am not saying that the south should not industrialize and urbanize, nor that we should restore fields in the south and again plant them to rice. What we are discussing here is simply a fundamental fact: If we increasingly shift grain production toward the north, the glaring problem becomes not a lack of land but a lack of water.

From the lessons of history and from international experience we know that it is not beneficial to attempt large-scale agriculture, and particularly horticulture, in areas that have 400 mm or less of rain. In China, a line of 400 mm of precipitation falls diagonally across the country, from Mohe in Heilongjiang Province [in the far northeast] to Tengchong in Yunnan Province [in the far southwest]. Areas to the north and west of the line generally have less than 400 mm of precipitation; those to the south and east have 400 mm or more.

Naturally, this has been the case historically. Today, with global climate change, this line may be shifting. By world standards, places that have less than 400 cubic meters of water resources per capita are said to suffer from extreme scarcity of water. Israel has around 400 mm of precipitation per capita per year and can only engage in irrigated 'precision' agriculture, or agriculture grown with special facilities. The cost of this kind of farming is quite high.

Given these considerations, one has to give serious thought as to whether or not the path we have chosen, that of relying on the northwest to make up for deficiencies of grain production elsewhere, is a path that is sustainable in the long run.

Another factor that should be taken into consideration is that urbanization and industrialization are pushing on into the inner regions of the country. No longer can any area live under the expectation that it can peacefully continue to enjoy a traditional agrarian existence. In this respect, we are still in the midst of exploring a path of agricultural development that is suited to our national conditions, including our environmental considerations and our resource endowment. Trying to accomplish all three things in tandem, industrialization, urbanization, and modernization of our agriculture, remains a daunting task.

We have just entered the threshold of what is called a 'moderately prosperous society,' but in doing so we already face severe problems in terms of our agricultural self-sufficiency, water and land resources, and environmental impact. Moving further into what the 16th [National Congress of the Party] has termed a 'moderately prosperous society *in an all-round way*' [italics added] will place even greater pressure on all of those factors.

Therefore, even as we recognize the challenges being imposed by increased demand, we should be even more clearly aware of challenges being imposed by natural resource and environmental constraints. This is a major reason our Central leading cadres are constantly emphasizing that we should approach the country's agricultural issues with a sense of impending crisis, with an awareness of the grave risks that are involved.

3. International markets for agricultural goods are in the midst of dramatic change

Capitalizing on the multifunctional nature of agriculture is fine, but it also shifts agricultural production in the direction of industry as opposed to food production. This is particularly true when it comes to biofuels and other biologically based materials. The change is now leading directly to substantial increases in world prices for grain.

In addition, after the war in Iraq erupted in March 2003, the price of oil more than doubled, going from 20-some US dollars to more than USD 70. The minute oil became so expensive, the possibilities of using corn, sugarcane, and other materials for combustion increased. In 2006, the United States proposed to replace

20 percent of all fuel derived from petroleum with fuel derived from biologically generated ethanol. To promote this effort, the country offered substantial subsidies. This had a direct effect on pulling prices ever higher.

With corn prices rising, farmers naturally planted more corn, which affected the production of other agricultural commodities and led to a rise in their prices as well. Our own country cannot be considered tardy in developing the technology for transforming biomass-based energy. In 2006, producing 1.02 million tons of ethanol required 3.6 million tons of corn. The ratio generally held that 3.3 to 3.5 tons of corn could be transformed into 1 ton of fuel. Naturally, the process remains dynamic [in that the process is constantly being improved], and as the price of oil continues to rise, the ratio should get better. If the price of oil goes down, enterprises with lower levels of technology will have to exit the scene.

Most recently, increases in the price of pork could be attributed to various reasons including epidemics, production cycle, and so on, but increasing feedstock costs was one of the factors. We currently have a greater supply of corn domestically than we have demand for corn, so are not in need of large-scale imports. The direct impact of increases in feedstock prices is therefore still not all that great.

This round of global price increases for agricultural products can mainly be attributed to a direct price relationship between the price of grains and the price of oil. In the past, grains and varieties of corn were purely a source of energy for humans and animals. Now they can be transformed into fuel and serve as a source of energy for industry. The determining factor in whether humans or pigs eat corn or whether it is used to propel automobiles will lie in production efficiencies. This change brings profound and long-term consequences to the supply and demand for agricultural goods in general and to their prices.

Right now, fluctuations in prices of agricultural goods inside the country can be attributed in part to a 'reasonable restoration' of where prices were before the recent escalation. It should be recognized, however, that there are limits to our ability to adjust agricultural prices. The reason is that we have two weak points when it comes to allocating resources and adjusting the structure of what our farmers produce. One is soybeans. In 2006, our country planted more than 140 million *mu* of land to soybeans and harvested 16 million tons, but we also imported 28.27 million tons.

In 2007, we planted 1,000 *mu* less in soybeans and the harvest came to less than 15 million tons; we estimate that our imports [next year in 2007] will exceed 30 million tons. Of total domestic demand for soybeans of 45 million tons, some two-thirds is now being supplied from international markets overseas.

Using a conversion to oil ratio of 18 percent to 20 percent, importing 30 million tons of soybeans allows us to press more than 5 million tons of soybean oil and get 24 million tons of soybean protein. Due to the excessively large influence of international prices, many uncontrollable factors influence our domestic prices of soybean oil and feed.

The second weak point we face when it comes to allocating resources and adjusting agricultural structure is the oilseeds crop. Consumption of vegetable oils in our country currently comes to around 23 million tons this year. We produce around 10 million tons (including rapeseed oil, soybean oil, and peanut oil), and we need to import 13 million tons. We can derive more than 5 tons of soybean oil from the imported soybeans but we still need to import between 6 and 7 million tons of vegetable oils every year. In 2006, we imported 6.7 million tons. Of a total consumed quantity of 23 million tons of oils and fats, we need to import 13 million tons annually, which means that our domestic market prices are clearly influenced by international markets.

The current international price for soybeans is around USD 380 per ton, which is one-third higher than it was in 2006. The international price of such things as palm oil and rapeseed oil has also risen some 30 percent to 40 percent over 2006 levels. Given this, naturally the price of domestic vegetable oils is bound to rise.

Given this situation, our major task is to figure out how to use our own comparative advantages, to improve China's agriculture in order to satisfy our basic needs. An overall calculation shows that imported agricultural goods are essentially equivalent to using some 400 to 500 million *mu* of other people's land. At our current levels of technology, growing 30 million tons of soybeans requires roughly 250 million *mu* of land. This is roughly the amount we currently use in producing vegetables.

The land required for producing the 6 to 7 tons of oils that we import comes to around 100 million *mu*. In 2006, our country produced more than 6.7 million tons of cotton, which was the highest harvest in history, but we also imported more than 3.7 million tons, which was also a record. At our current production capacity, we would require more than 40 million *mu* of land to produce that 3.7 million tons of cotton.

Then there are various other products that we are tightly controlling inside the country in order to protect our environment, such as timber. We keep tight controls over supply from domestic sources but the demand is multiples of what we can produce. Imports can only go up. Right now, more than 40 percent of our demand for logs and sawn boards has to rely on imports; our annual imports now exceed 40 million cubic meters per year.

Paper pulp is a derivative of cellulose fibers, and if you want to produce high-quality paper, you must use wood fibers. Our country only has the capacity to produce 4 million tons, however, so we import around 7 to 8 million tons every year. Two-thirds of our demand for wood pulp relies on international markets.

In addition, our annual demand for rubber comes to around 2.5 to 2.6 million tons per year while we only produce something over 0.5 million tons ourselves. The same general situation holds with wool. Given our extreme scarcity of land and water resources, it is naturally a good thing to import agricultural products since we lack those resources ourselves, but this also subjects us to considerable risk. It is easy for unfavorable international prices to affect our own markets.

One of the policy considerations that we urgently need to take up is how to use our own agricultural resources in a scientific way in order to minimize the risk of the impact of international markets. In addition to imports, we also export quite a few commodities, including vegetables, fruit, livestock products, aquatic products, and so on. As we have all been discussing over these past few days, the environment for exports is also getting tougher. Technical barriers are constantly being lifted ever higher. In the context of economic globalization, our agricultural development faces both beneficial circumstances and those that are not so beneficial. In formulating policy, we have to put serious thought into how to expand upon the opportunities and avoid the pitfalls.

Over the long run, China's agriculture does not allow for much optimism. Our enduring attitude must be one that is prepared for problems. Cadres who are engaged in rural affairs should approach them from the high ground of the State's interests and the nation's interest. They should ensure that agricultural production maintains stable growth, a prerequisite for preserving the economic security of the country. This also constitutes our most fundamental responsibility. We should look upon the issues we are facing from a global perspective and think of them in strategic terms, and we should address them as per the requirements of the Central Committee of the Party. Only if we recognize the long-term nature of the challenges and pressures we are facing can we hope to safeguard sustained and stable growth in our agricultural sector.

II. Profound changes currently occurring in the rural economic situation

Since the start of the new century and a new stage of development, all aspects of socioeconomic 'reform and opening up' have been stimulating profound changes in rural areas. These are requiring that we keep up with the times in terms of liberating our thinking, taking 'reform' to deeper levels, being innovative in our theoretical approaches and our actual implementation. The aim is to ensure that the social and economic administrative systems in rural areas, as well as operating mechanisms, are more in tune with the actual situation.

I could use three specific terms to encapsulate the many profound changes occurring in rural areas. They are: the 'hollowing out' of villages, the tendency of farming to become a 'sideline operation' while other jobs are also pursued, and the 'aging' of farmers.

These three aspects differ from region to region but mainly only in degree. They can be seen most pervasively, perhaps, in those provinces that are 'exporting' the greatest amount of rural labor. The 'hollowing out' of villages stems from many causes, including the whole issue of our system of authorizations for housing sites. When new housing is built, the old housing is often not torn down, and the large-scale 'out-flowing' movement of the agricultural population to other areas is exacerbating the trend. The 'earned wages' component of the average farmers' income is increasing and will probably exceed 40 percent in 2007. Agriculture is rapidly becoming a sideline occupation, and the percentage of households that do nothing but farm the land is declining. Any young and able-bodied labor in rural areas 'goes out' to find work elsewhere, so that the extent of an 'aging population' in rural areas is already higher than it is in urban areas.

Our theoretical circles have been debating the issue of exactly when we will see a turning point in terms of our surplus of labor becoming a shortage of labor. Cai Fang, the director of the Institute of Population Studies at the Chinese Academy of Social Sciences, believes that this turning point has already been reached. He believes that our country is already experiencing a shortage of labor. Many disagree, however, and his research results are controversial. In point of fact, what he defines as a 'shortage of labor' specifically relates to nonagricultural labor and is under conditions of no change in wages and benefits.

The reality right now is that young, able-bodied labor from rural areas is flowing 'out' in massive numbers, while those staying behind to do the farming are mainly older people and women. One can't judge this phenomenon as either 'good' or 'bad.' It is simply a fact, and a natural result of the whole process of urbanization and industrialization.

In theoretical terms, there are two main types of agriculture. One exists in more 'traditional' countries that were relatively early in their development, such as Europe and Asia. Archaeological discoveries indicate that farming on our own Loess Plateau began more than 8,000 years ago, including the planting of millet. Rice production in the middle reaches of the Yangtze River also dates back some 7,000 years. Generally speaking, countries that have a long history of cultivating the land are also countries with a dense population, which means that their scale of farming operations is relatively small.

The second main type of agriculture exists on the 'new continents,' mainly North and South America and Australia, which have developed in the past 500 years following the discoveries of Columbus. Agriculture in these places has been going on for a shorter time and, relatively speaking, enjoys a greater amount of land per capita. One notable difference between this type of agriculture and that in 'traditional' countries is that rural areas do not have the same 'village' structure. Farming is undertaken by much larger-scale family operations.

A look at the development process in countries with more traditional agriculture shows that all three aspects noted above are generally present, including the hollowing out of villages, the increasingly sideline nature of farming, and the aging of the farming population. Industrialization and urbanization in our own country naturally must proceed, and at a certain point we too must face the challenges that they present. At the very least, this raises the following three considerations.

1   Shifting employment patterns among farmers and the problem of urbanization.

Although very substantial numbers of rural laborers have already taken up jobs in cities and live there permanently, they exist at the margins of municipal systems. This is seen most clearly in the fact that not a single governmental department can even say exactly how many people have migrated into cities and exactly what their situation is.

Statistically, our 'rate of urbanization' in 2006 was 43.9 percent. The 'urban population' had already reached 577 million people. Correspondingly, the 'rural population' had declined to 737 million people and now constituted 56.1 percent of the total. However, by the classification of people by where their households are registered, that is, by where their *hukou* is located, 949 million people are still classified as 'farming households.' This means that around 212 million people do not, in fact, live in their registered location. How many of these have migrated to urban areas is, however, unclear.

In addition to uncertainty about the fundamental status of these people, we also are quite unclear about what to call them. Some people think that the term 'rural migrant worker' is pejorative. But is our treatment of these people any different just because we don't call them by that name?

One important reason for using the term 'rural migrant worker' as opposed to 'farmers who have taken up jobs in cities' is that many of these people are not in fact in cities. Many are engaged in working for town-and-village enterprises in jurisdictions that are below county level. Such enterprises employ some 140 million people. It therefore is not sufficient merely to protect the rights and interests of farmers who have indeed taken up jobs in urban areas – we also must protect the rights and interests of those farmers who are working outside of cities.

Exactly how are we to protect the rights and interests of those who have already come into urban areas? The most fundamental way is to provide oversight over the contracts that enterprises are supposed to sign with rural workers. The lack of a contract fundamentally deprives the worker of all rights, since there is no documented evidence of who is responsible when a problem occurs. Starting with contracts, we must improve all of our work relating to worker security, including proper payment of wages, workplace conditions, living conditions, social security, assurance that children go to school, and so on.

A host of new issues derives from the fact of having so much rural labor 'go out' to other places. Such large-scale migration of people unavoidably creates wholly new situations that must be dealt with, from such services as pre-job training and job advice to the protection of rights and interests once people have found jobs, and especially to how to take care of those who are left behind, mainly women, children, and old people.

Who in fact should be dealing with all these issues, and how should they go about it? Once our whole concept of 'coordinated development of urban and rural areas' really began to penetrate people's consciousness, a number of urban departments began to realize they should focus on these things, but for departments working on rural issues, it is an inescapable responsibility to deal with such issues. Rural work departments must also actively participate in the efforts. At the very least, they must first get a clearer idea of just how many people have actually 'gone out.' They should know the situation of these people once they arrive in cities, for only then can we formulate policies to do with rural migrant labor that are backed up by data and have some real teeth.

In 2006, the State Council issued *Document No. 5,* which set up a 'joint conference system for rural migrant workers.' More than 30 departments are participating, and the main office is in the Ministry of Human Resources and Labor, and Social Security. Having this system, versus not having it earlier, is truly like night and day.

How patterns of migration will develop in the future depends to a large extent on the path we take in urbanization. In 2000, 'Central' [the Central Committee of the Party] raised a key comment with respect to the proposed 10th Five-Year-Plan.

It said that the country should adopt a process of urbanization that included linking in smaller towns to all sizes of cities, including large, medium, and small. Our theoretical circles continue to debate this issue. Some of our macroeconomists wonder why we should even make the attempt to 'build up a new countryside.' They feel that farmers' problems will be addressed by the process of urbanization. Trying to promote development in small towns will, in their view, simply waste resources so the more effective course of action is to focus on large cities.

Looking at the rest of the globe, but particularly developed economies, we can see that the bulk of the population in such places, as well as economic production, lies within 200 kilometers of the coastline. Some of our cadres therefore feel that we should focus on developing coastal areas, use large cities as magnets to draw in large numbers of rural people, and thereby ultimately resolve their problems. We can explore these things to the *n*th degree in academic terms, but when it comes to creating actual policy and dealing with the real world, setting up methods and long-term regulations for dealing with things, we have to base ourselves on China's specific conditions.

There are very few countries in the world that can be described in the same light as China. Among the more than 200 countries and political entities on the globe, fewer than 10 have populations that exceed 100 million. Only 2 have populations that exceed 1 billion, namely, India and China.

Naturally, we should take advantage of the experience of other countries, but the numbers are of a whole different order when it comes to population. We can always look to the United States and say that that country's population is clustered around coastal areas, but America's population has only recently gone over 300 million. That is still 1 billion less than our population. Some people look to Japan and note that there are only two main clusters of population, in Kansai and in Kanto. Japan's population is only 130 million, however, less than one-tenth of ours.

Recently, more people are talking about the lessons to be drawn from Korea, but Korea in its entirety has a population of 40 million, while the Seoul area holds close to one-half of the total. Yes, we should draw on the experience of others, but simply copying over any kind of model will not resolve our problems. Our problems are of a different magnitude. Our solutions must be derived from our actual situation – not only must we recognize that urbanization is going to be a very long process, but that for a very long time, we are going to have a substantial population living and working in rural areas.

In recent years, the pace of our urbanization has been accelerating, going up 1.3 percentage points per year. If the rate were to go up annually by 1 percent, we would be at a 'rate of urbanization' of 55 percent by the time we accomplish what we define as being a 'moderately prosperous society in an all-round way.' By 2050, when we will have completed what we define as 'basic modernization,' our rate of urbanization may come to 60 percent, perhaps even 70 percent. Even then, we will still have 30 percent of our population living in rural areas.

Experts predict that China's population will peak at around 1.5 billion. If that is the case, 30 percent of that number will be 450 million people. What does it mean to have 450 million people living in a rural situation? What it means is that the rural population will be roughly the same as it was when the People's Republic of China was founded [in 1949] [i.e., we will be back where we began].

Many other complex issues must be addressed in the course of China's urbanization. The three great problems that specifically relate to rural people migrating into cities are housing, employment, and social security. If half of our 250 million rural households migrate into cities, that means we must provide housing for 125 million households. At an average of 50 square meters per housing unit, that means we must construct 62.5 trillion square meters of housing. This figure is roughly 10.3 times the total amount of 'commodity' housing that was sold nationwide in 2006.

Some places are recommending that farmers trade their land-use rights for the assurance of social security [insurance] as they migrate into cities. I feel we need to be very careful about this approach. People cannot live on social insurance alone, they need jobs. They should rely on social insurance only when they have no alternatives. The biggest issue for people migrating into cities is employment.

Right now, our production capacity in the manufacturing sector already exceeds demand. Market constraints are already changing our previous reliance on the old way of stimulating job creation. There are still areas of growth potential, such as banking, insurance, accounting, auditing, advertising, and so on, but most rural people are not qualified to take up such jobs and would find it hard to penetrate these industries. As a consequence, we should be crystal clear in our thinking as the pace of urbanization accelerates. First, we must not slacken in our policy of 'building up a new countryside,' for that must be done in tandem with urbanization. We cannot think that tackling the one problem, urbanization, will automatically resolve the other [rural development].

Second, we must recognize that the matter of rural migration into cities is not a simple problem. Only when we have the capacity to resolve employment, housing, and social security problems for rural migrant workers can we dare to think that we are making progress. Some of our cadres feel that the two-way flow of people between urban and rural areas is impeding the process of urbanization. Naturally, nothing would be better than to enable farmers to leave the land completely if they were able to live secure lives in an urban context. To prevent them from becoming refugees and destitute urban dwellers, however, we must first provide solutions to employment, housing, and social security issues.

These are things that cannot be resolved by simply paying people the monthly pittance of a minimum living allowance. How can there possibly be any kind of stable society if a few hundred million people flood into cities and live solely off welfare? The first thing that must be done is to create employment opportunities for farmers who migrate into cities. As they have the chance to improve their incomes, social wealth in general increases, fiscal revenues going to the State increase, and we can gradually create the underlying conditions to address the three major issues noted above.

One thing must be made very clear, however. In those cases where farmers have indeed had their land requisitioned, they must be entered into social security rolls. This was mandated by the State Council's *Document No. 28* in 2004. Many of these issues extend beyond the bounds of rural policy and what can be done by those working on rural affairs, but since they impact the rights and interests of farmers, we must do our best to see that they are handled well.

2   Improve the organizational capacity of farmers, and systems providing 'socialized' services in agriculture.

Given the aging of the population engaged in farming, and the tendency to engage in farming as only one income-producing activity among several, we now need to put very careful efforts into making sure that farmers are better able to organize and have services that provide for their needs. These two things have become an urgent imperative. From looking at the process of industrialization in such countries as Japan and Korea, where agriculture was also carried out in very traditional ways, we can see that if these two requirements are met, farmers can continue to farm even into their 60s and 70s.

In one sense, the degree to which Chinese farmers are 'organized' exceeds that of almost everywhere else in the world, in that each person is included in a 'village committee' [*cun weihui*]. Nevertheless, there are still very few collective organizations in villages that actually have much economic power. In most places, the 'village committee' is concerned with social administration and is an 'inward looking' type of organization. Under a market system, what farmers need is an organization that is oriented to the 'outside' and that provides support for economic activities.

Naturally, each place is going to be different and we should find solutions that pertain to each specific situation when we try to increase organizational capacity. Some places have more real economic clout in their village collectives, such as in southern Jiangsu and northern Zhejiang. In such places, we can rely more on the one organization to address the two key issues noted above of greater organizational capacity and better services. That means having the 'three functions' all handled within one entity, namely, serving as the Party branch, also the 'village committee,' and also the 'collective economic organization of farmers.'

In other places in which the collective economy is weak, farmers should be guided in the direction of organizing themselves, charting a course of developing cooperative organizations. With the support of the government, they should rely more on farmers' specialized cooperative organizations that provide 'self-help' services. On July 1 of this year [2007], we began to implement the Law Regarding Farmers' Specialized Cooperatives. As a result, we should take the opportunity now to strengthen the 'self-help' capacities of farmers by improving the degree to which they are organized.

It is worth our while to look at the experience of other countries in this regard. For example, one approach used by Germany is known as a 'farm machinery circle' or a 'farm machinery ring.' What this means is that farming households organize a united effort to purchase certain equipment in common and then use it as needed. Often one family or one household's operations are too small to own a full set of farming equipment. Financing everything is not possible and in any event the equipment sits idle for much of the time. Instead, several households, or even a dozen or more households, come together to form a 'farm machinery ring' in order to reduce costs and improve efficiencies. One household buys the planter, another the harvester, and so on, and then all share in the use.

Some of our grassroots-level cadres are not willing to spend any time or effort helping farmers organize this kind of thing. Faced with new issues in trying to develop agriculture, they are reluctant to think deeply about how to handle things and instead would rather simply consolidate the various contracts of farmers into larger tracts of land in order to carry out so-called economies of scale. This seems to be the easier solution, but if urbanization is still not able to accommodate so many farmers, the consequences [of taking jobs away from farmers] can be far worse.

In reviewing the experience of other countries that have a similar situation to ours, in terms of transitioning from a traditional agriculture, there does not appear to be a single country that has formulated laws mandating that household-operated land be consolidated in order to carry out so-called larger-scale operations. All other countries, such as in eastern Asia and western Europe, have gone the route of improving farmers' organizational capacity, strengthening services so that they operate more efficiently, providing them with the external conditions as appropriate to carry on their own household operations.

It is time for us to resolve to put painstaking and meticulous effort into improving farmers' organizational capacity and improving services that support their farming, in order to address the multitude of difficulties that they are facing in improving agriculture. Wheat harvests have been excellent for the past several years. This can be attributed in part to better varieties but another important reason has been that some tens of thousands of combines have been put into operation, moving from the south to north, providing the service to farming households of harvesting the grain. Without this harvesting capacity, despite excellent yields in the field, we would not have seen excellent harvests in a countryside that is now shorn of its able-bodied young men.

Given that the male population has hired itself out for labor elsewhere, one can see the importance of such services. To reiterate: The appearance of the three key issues of the 'hollowing out' of villages, the 'sideline nature' of farming, and the aging of the farming population make it all the more urgent and imperative that we focus our work on helping farmers organize and have access to services.

3   The issue of how to improve rural governance at the township and village level.

Once taxes on agriculture were abolished in 2006, the grassroots level in the countryside began to face new issues that had never been encountered before. For example, how were public goods to be supplied now [without any revenue to fund them]? How was public infrastructure to be built? If opinions differed [on spending priorities], and the ideal of one discussion for one case was not feasible, how were things to be decided?

In some places the collective economy had little real strength so that compensation for township and village cadres stayed low – as a result, competent people refused to serve as public officials while those who were incompetent were willing to serve but unable to deal with all the issues. A summary of new problems that have been arising includes the following.

1. Issues to do with the system of township and village governance. Looking back at how our rural system evolved, we can chart several major changes that followed the implementation of the 'household contract operations' system. First came having farmers contract to farm specific fields, which put the process first started at Xiaogang Village in Anhui Province into practice on a nationwide basis. That system was described by Xiaogang farmers themselves as, 'keeping what was left over for ourselves after we had handed over what was due to the State, and retained a sufficient amount for the collective.'

Next came not requiring farmers to 'hand over' anything at all to the State or the collective and also fully exempting farmers from taxes and fees.

Finally came a situation in which farmers' autonomy [in making economic decisions] was further expanded. In this stage, a large-scale movement of labor began flowing 'out' to find employment elsewhere, with many people taking their families along.

In the course of this entire process, farmers have become less and less dependent on the traditional township and village organizations. Using those organizations and the old methods to try to administer the countryside and farmers themselves is by now definitely no longer workable.

I am fully aware of just how many problems [you all] face at the grassroots level in your work, and aware of the dilemmas facing the two levels of government, township and village. Nonetheless, yearning to go back to those old days of a planned economy, when cadres held all power in one hand and all money in the other and could simply tell farmers what to do, is out of the question. Wanting to return to the time of people's communes is not only impossible but would not meet the basic needs of setting up a socialist market-economy system.

We now have a society in which farmers can freely move as they wish and 'vote with their feet.' Given a pronounced decline in their economic dependence on the old collective structures, if they are dissatisfied at any time they can simply get up and leave. As a result, we need a thorough reevaluation of rural governance in both townships and villages, from systems design all the way to specific implementation.

It is true that we have formulated plenty of laws and policies to do with rural governance, but many of the regulations are contradictory and full of loopholes. They need to be constantly improved in the course of actual practice. For example, surveys indicate that 91 percent of land ownership rights in rural areas in our country belong to 'villagers' small groups' [*cunmin xiaozu*], namely, what were formerly called 'production teams' [*shengchan dui*]. Despite possessing land ownership rights, this level of organization in our country does not in fact have any independent legal standing – 'villagers' small groups' are not legally defined as independent organizations. [In contrast], 'villagers' committees' [*cunmin weiyuanhui*] are autonomous organizations that *are* legally defined but the great majority of them do not enjoy ownership rights to land.

A contradiction therefore arises. Entities which in fact own rights to property do not have legal standing, while those which have legal standing do not in fact own property. [When farmers contract to operate land, they have to contract it from some entity.] If we authorize 'villagers' committees' to be that entity, then we authorize people who have no ownership rights over assets to administer those assets. In the meantime, entities actually holding ownership rights are rendered impotent [by having the authority removed from their control]. In the long run, this is going to create problems.

2. Issues to do with the costs of administering government in rural areas under [what we call] the rural autonomy [or 'self-governing'] system. Our constitution states that our country has two different categories of 'autonomous organizations.' One is 'farmers' [*nongmin*] autonomous organizations' [*zizhi zuzhi*] and the other is 'urban residents' [*chengshi jumin*] autonomous organizations' [*zizhi zuzhi*]. A comparison of the two reveals enormous differences in everything from their functions to how they implement their duties. Urban residents rarely find themselves in conflict with 'residential committees' [*weiyuanhui*]. Why is that? The economic interests of urban residents are not tied in to the committees. In fact, residential committees provide local residents with many benefits such as making sure the neighborhood is clean and safe and organizing sports and cultural activities. If this kind of thing is what local residents want and need, they are quite pleased with the 'work' of the residential committees. If it isn't, it doesn't matter so much since local residents are not paying the costs.

The situation is quite different in rural areas. Rural committees [*cun weihui*] need to raise all their funding from local sources, starting with the wages of committee members. All administrative costs, public goods and services, basic infrastructure, and so on are their responsibility. In places where the collective economy is doing well, these costs are not taken out of 'the hide' of farmers but instead are paid for directly by the village collective. In places where that is not the case, costs must be covered by farmers themselves and the people governing a particular area collect money from farmers in order to get things done.

This raises the critical issue of who, in fact, should be paying the costs of operating 'autonomous organizations' in rural areas? All this time, we have been hoping and expecting that the growth of collective economies will resolve the problem, and in some places that in fact has worked. Successful places have developed town-and-village enterprises. Not every village has the means to do this, however.

In most rural places, the Secretary of the Party branch and head of the villagers' committee find it extremely problematic to rely on the collective economy to cover operating costs of the villagers' committee. Why? There are no resources. Before the period of 'cooperativization' in our country, there was no 'collective economy.' Once 'cooperatization' and 'communization' ended [i.e., once the people's communes were ended], what was termed a 'collective economy' mostly involved simply taking over farmers' land and calling it 'collective property.'

When people's communes were disbanded, most places had very little in the way of any operating entities that could be considered 'collective business.' Once land itself was distributed out to households under contract, collectives owned very little in the way of any assets at all. By now, a major issue that we must grapple with and come to terms with through serious research and application is how to finance governance structures in what we call our 'new countryside.'

Who in fact is going to pay the costs of the self-governance of villagers and how indeed are self-governing structures to come about?

Another thing that should be mentioned is that while we ought to support those places that are relying on collective economies to solve governance issues, at the same time we need to make their financial affairs open and transparent. Townships and villages that truly cannot make ends meet will have to consider gradually transitioning to getting their expenditures paid through public finance. Otherwise we will increasingly see an unstable situation in which nobody at all is handling a village's public affairs.

[For example,] in recent years, the Beijing municipal government has to a considerable degree instituted transfer payments to village committees at all levels of government [under its jurisdiction]. Annual payments to any given village come to a minimum of RMB 130,000 to RMB 180,000, which can be used to help subsidize wages of cadres but also to a degree for public undertakings. In the process of improving rural governance structures, therefore, we need to increase transfer payments to the basic level of governance in rural areas.

I want to emphasize here that I am not saying we should not develop the collective economy in local areas. In fact, I feel that we should do all we can to bolster and strengthen collective economies. What I am saying is that we have to be realistic about the fact that many areas do not have what it takes to develop enterprises, and without any business to rely upon for funding they have no other resources upon which to call.

Precisely how most village committees are going to support their operations is a question that must be placed on our agenda for serious consideration. Otherwise, we will find that it is very hard to maintain stability and a hold on political power at the basic level of governance in rural areas.

3. Issues to do with the functions of government in townships and villages, and the allocation of public resources. As reform of rural governance structures has proceeded, we have been discovering more and more major issues that need to be resolved, such as the question of exactly how we are to determine the functions of government at the township and village level.

The '15th' [National Congress of the Communist Party of China, in 1997] gave official confirmation to what it called the four major functions of government. These were: 'economic regulation, market supervision, social administration, and public goods and services.'

The minute you even get to the provincial level of government, however, you find that these four functions cannot be fully applied. For example, financial regulation is an important aspect of economic regulation, whereas provincial governments have no authority to conduct financial regulation. By the time you get to the township level of government, how are 'the four' to be interpreted?

Some cadres feel that the main responsibilities of government at the township level are social administration and provision of public goods and services. Others, however, feel that township- and village-level government simply cannot function unless it is involved in business, for otherwise it has no source of funding. Over these past two days of discussions, some of our cadres here have also expressed the opinion that the aim of 'reforming and simplifying township and village structures' cannot be reduced simply to streamlining employees and organizations. Instead, they feel that the critical issue is how to transform governmental functions at this level.

That may be, but the first question that must be asked is, 'What exactly *are* the functions of government at this level?' In point of fact, they differ from place to place – one cannot use a sweeping generalization to cover them all. Townships and villages differ too greatly. The economic scale of just one village in a more developed region might exceed the economy of an entire county in another region. Through surveys and investigations, we have to proceed in each case on the basis of its specifics.

Along with the question of how to position and evolve the functions of township and village governments is the whole issue of how to allocate resources for public goods and services. One could also call this the issue of reforming local public institutions. This extends to two main areas, one of which involves social administration, for example, prevention and control of animal diseases and epidemics. Such an issue impacts not only agriculture and farmers' interests but also public health in general. Such functions must be strengthened, not weakened. They relate to mandatory functions of social administration.

The other main area involves functions relating to public goods and services, such as education, healthcare, and so on. In the past, every town had its own central primary school, and larger towns might also have a middle school, while primary schools were also located in villages. With the rise of urbanization, this pattern of resource distribution is being challenged. In order to optimize resources, the schools of villages are being consolidated. Some people think this is a good thing, others think it is not. Those who approve feel that it concentrates resources and enables students to receive a better education. Those who disapprove feel that schools are too far from children's homes, that going to school has become unsafe for children and also increases family costs.

Resources for public health in towns are also facing challenges. In the past, each town had its own health clinic but now, with improved transport into larger places, many farmers go to the county hospital if they get a serious illness. The local clinic is seeing fewer patients as a result. How to strike a balance between conserving and optimizing scarce resources and still making sure that farmers' lives are improving and public services are available is something we need to work on, through surveys and then through real improvement in our plans and guidelines.

[Our aim is] to turn 'farmers' into 'urbanites' through the process of urbaniza-tion, to improve the organizational capacity of farmers, to provide farmers with improved services in conducting their farming, as well as to gradually improve township governance structures. [It is] to provide more and better social admin-istration and more resources for public services. More than ever before, we need to focus on these issues. If we do not, it will be very hard for us to adapt to the profound socioeconomic changes occurring in our rural areas. We must broaden our perspective, intensify and improve our work, do our utmost to mitigate the chaos and confusion in the countryside during this period of socioeconomic tran-sition to new forms and structures. This must be the primary emphasis of our current work.

III. On several specific policy issues

1. On the question of providing direct subsidies to farmers

During our meeting, some cadres have noted that the list of types of subsidies we provide has been getting longer and longer. In the beginning, we just had direct subsidies for grain production, for better varieties of seeds, and for farm equip-ment. Now we also see subsidies for sow production, and we may soon be seeing subsidies for milk production and so on.

In point of fact, there have always been differences of opinion on these subsi-dies from the moment they were introduced. Some cadres feel that there are limits on how well such subsidies actually stimulate agricultural production. Others feel that the costs of administering the subsidies are too high, from deciding on the policy to creating lists to posting announcements and then distributing money, household by household. They feel it would be better to give funding to the town-ship or village – they say, 'Wouldn't it be better to concentrate funds for the build-ing of roads or public facilities?'

Many grassroots cadres expressed similar opinions to me in the course of on-site research. My feeling on it is that our grassroots cadres need to think more deeply about the issues, based on very meticulous and in-depth study. We real-ize that implementing the policy of putting production subsidies directly into the hands of farmers does indeed raise the workload of cadres considerably. At the same time, the considerable work required before we implemented our policy of exempting farmers from taxes and fees was not necessarily all that much less. It involved going around to each household, pressuring people to pay up on grain, on fees, on taxes. What's more, these days we can use modernized financial tools to expedite the subsidy payments process.

The key thing here is that we cannot afford to lose the people's confidence, their belief that the Party and the government will come through on what they have said they will do. Once we have declared a policy throughout the land, we cannot rescind it lightly.

Any policy that directly impacts farmers' interests is a policy that must be treated seriously. For example, if we were now to cancel the subsidies on planting grain, farmers might well believe that the State was worried inventories are already too high and then what would the consequences be? Protecting the reputation and integrity of the Party and government, and maintaining the continuity and dependability of policies, is of decisive importance in maintaining the stability of grain production.

[To repeat,] it is vital that we keep faith with the people. Policies can always be improved upon, but they should not be changed capriciously. We always need to sum up our experience to date and figure out how to do things better in the future.

In another respect, many of the issues raised by grassroots cadres are quite reasonable. For example, how should subsidies for grassroots officials themselves be handled, how should basic infrastructure in rural areas be built, which things should be paid for by farmers themselves and which by the State? As the economy grows, it is quite true that people at governmental levels above that of townships and villages should also be addressing the issues of how to achieve this 'coordinated development of urban and rural areas,' and of how to increase transfer payments to rural areas. They should be taking on more of the responsibility for public works and the building of rural public infrastructure.

At the same time, one thing should still be made crystal clear: The Central Committee of the Party and the State Council have decided on funding of direct subsidies for farmers, and it is absolutely forbidden for these funds to be siphoned off for other uses.

If money that was intended to go directly into farmers' hands is found to have been channeled off for other purposes, nothing good will come of it. Even if you use it [for laudable purposes], things will not necessarily turn out as you may think. Farmers themselves will voice their opinions: 'Why have you not given us the money that the Central Committee of the Party and the State Council intended as subsidies for us?' The relationship between cadres and the masses will develop even further problems.

In overall terms, we have already moved into a developmental stage in which industry is meant to repay or 'stimulate' agriculture and cities are meant to 'bring along' rural areas. The minute you talk about building a 'new countryside,' however, some cadres immediately take it to mean that farmers should rely on themselves, that rural roads and schools should be built by farmers. It is true that farmers should work industriously, use the fruits of their own labor to create a good life for themselves, so to that extent the thinking is correct. But that does not lead to a conclusion that the government bears no responsibility at all.

In urban areas, all public works and all building of basic infrastructure is paid for by the government. We haven't yet heard of a city in which parks are being built by urban residents or city people are out there paving the roads. So yes, it is good to mobilize farmers to do their duty by helping out with basic infrastructure and social endeavors, but the government itself has a greater duty to perform its duties. First, it must break through old concepts and eradicate all systems that have evolved from the way we have applied a 'dual' economic structure to urban and rural situations. It must break out of a mistaken approach that says the government is not responsible for rural reconstruction and development. Only then will we truly be able to create a situation in which urban and rural socioeconomic development move together in tandem.

2. *On the issue of rural land policies*

The Central Committee of the Party has repeatedly emphasized that the system by which land is administered is the cornerstone of the Party's rural policies. As mandated by the constitution, that system is a double-tiered operating system based on a 'union of centralized and decentralized' and expressed in terms of the household contracting system. This 'basic operating system' is directly linked to the whole issue of land management, so it is clear that we must be highly respectful of policies regarding land use. Those policies currently face three major challenges.

1   Regarding the land requisitioning system.

At present, our system of requisitioning land is still fundamentally related to the system we had under the planned economy. Under that system, farmers were quite pleased whenever the State took their land for it meant that in return they would become 'city people.' The State had to provide them with a job, with housing, with the guarantee that until death their health and old-age needs would be covered. As a consequence, the requisitioning of land did not stir up problems.

Things are quite different now. When land is taken, the people are simply discarded and the harm done to farmers is extreme. In 2004, the State Council took steps to deal with this situation by issuing *Document No. 28.* This raised the amounts of compensation that farmers were to receive, it specified policies regarding displacement and resettlement of people, and it brought displaced people under the social security system. In 2006, the State Council went a step further with *Document No. 31* in explicitly requiring that greater amounts of the 'land-transfer payment' had to go for resettling farmers who had lost their land and for restoring agriculture and doing rural reconstruction. Under our current land-requisitioning system, only if there is strict compliance with the spirit of these two State Council documents can we preserve the rights and interests of farmers.

Given the direction our development is currently taking, from now on reform of our land-requisitioning system should abide by the principles of public benefit. That is, the government should not be allowed to requisition land unless it is in the overall public interest. Land should not be requisitioned by the government for other purposes.

However, just because the government cannot requisition land for 'operating' [business] purposes does not mean that land already classified as 'operating land' can be bought and sold at will. The standard practice worldwide is that governments regulate land use by requiring that it conform to certain plans. Moreover, the process of formulating land-use plans must be open and transparent and, once passed into law, compliance with the plans must be rigorously enforced. Only when such a plan authorizes use of land for construction purposes can sale of land for construction purposes be carried out. Absolutely no unauthorized land can be entered into 'construction-land' markets.

Our own country is also moving in this direction in terms of our reforms regarding our land-use system, that is, moving in the direction of regulating land use. Some people say that in reforming our land-requisitioning system, we first must specify what we mean by 'public-interest use of land.' We must therefore standardize a list of land uses that can be regarded as 'in the public interest.' In fact, though, I have researched this issue in both the United States and Canada and found that those countries have no such 'list' of 'public-interest land use.' Representatives of the courts in these places have told me that 'public-interest land use' is a concept that relies on the common sense of a given community, and for the government to transgress this in requisitioning land is simply not done. As for land use for purposes that are not in the public interest, that depends on whether or not planning regulations permit such use, for example, the use of farmland for construction purposes. If regulations do permit it, then negotiations between the person selling the land and the person buying the land are carried out according to market-economy principles.

The key, therefore, is to have stringent regulation of land-use practices and to set up an authority that can determine land-use planning regulations. This is the only way to protect farmland through legal measures, and it is also the only way to safeguard the rights and interests of farmers.

2   On the issue of stabilizing the 'household contract operating system.'

The policies of the Central Committee [of the Communist Party of China] have consistently been crystal clear in this regard. First, they are intended to stabilize the 'basic operating system,' and to stabilize the contractual relationships pertaining to land. Second, as per the [mandated] principle of 'legal, voluntary, and for compensation,' they permit the *operating authority* of land-use contracts to be transferrable [italics added].

Operating rights can be consolidated and larger-scale operations can be carried out as appropriate in all kinds of ways. Once contracts have been signed [with farmers], however, the key issue is who decides on how the land is to be used. Whether the farmer himself plants that land or transfers it to others for farming is something that the farmer himself has the power to decide. Neither the government nor any village organization has the authority to transgress a farmer's rights and decide on his behalf. Forcing the farmer against his will to grant land-use rights is even less acceptable.

[We cadres] can guide farmers with advice on how to transfer land-use operating rights, in order to consolidate land into larger operations, for example. We can provide examples that serve as models, but we cannot use force.

An absolute prerequisite for a functioning market economy is that property rights be clear. Otherwise, nobody dares be party to a transaction. With respect to the market for land-use operating rights, 'clear property rights' are achieved by stabilizing our contractual relationships [of people and land]. Given a labor force that is increasingly mobile [going 'out'], and given increasing division of labor and occupations in villages, the more stable farmers' relationships to their contracted land are, the more willing they will be to engage in transfer of land-use operating rights. The market for those rights will correspondingly become more and more developed.

The government's role in this process, and the role of village organizations, is to provide farmers with services. It is not to usurp the decision-making authority of farmers. Some townships, for example, are setting up 'service centers' for land transfers. Some villages are setting up 'service stations,' others are setting up 'field-authorizing places' or 'land banks.' These provide services to farmers who are interested in transferring land and they help in gradually developing a legitimate land-transfer market.

3   Regarding the issue of land used for construction purposes that is the property of the village collective.

This is the third large issue with respect to our current rural land-use system. 'Collective land' used for construction purposes includes three main categories: land of town-and-village enterprises, land used for farmers' housing, and public facilities in townships and villages. If land in these three categories is in accord with land-use plans, if it is transferred in compliance with laws and regulations, then it can be used for construction purposes without going through the State requisitioning process.

In the past, this was all very clear and simple but in recent times it has been getting more complex. For example, land used by town-and-village enterprises falls within the scope of land that can be used for rural construction purposes. However, what exactly is a 'town-and-village enterprise?' The Law on Town-and-Village Enterprises is quite explicit in its guidelines. It says that such enterprises include those organized by the 'collective economic organization' of a village or by farmers themselves, and it includes collective economic organizations that undertake the obligation to 'have industry support agriculture.' In point of fact, by now most town-and-village enterprises have restructured themselves. Very few actually meet the guidelines of the Law on Town-and-Village Enterprises. How, then, is it possible that many places are still using the pretext of the old form of town-and-village enterprises to apply for land use for 'collective construction purposes'?

Our country's Law on Land Management specifies two allowable exceptions [to following land-requisition procedures]. One is that land to be used for construction purposes for town-and-village enterprises, and for farmers' housing, and for public-interest facilities does not require application to the State for requisitioning State-owned land. The second says that collectively owned land in rural areas cannot be used for nonagricultural construction through such means as 'leasing' or 'transferring,' *except* for when a town-and-village enterprise goes bankrupt or is merged with another enterprise. In such a case, its land-use rights 'follow along' with the new situation and are allowed to be incorporated into the new entity.

These two exceptions are now being expanded to allow for nonagricultural construction on land in situations that are purely used for pretext. Quite a few places are now disregarding [the original intent of the law]. Some places brazenly take over land and build factories on it, for leasing out to businesses. Others raise funds to set up so-called joint ventures that have not gone through proper application procedures [and that then appropriate collectively owned land]. Still others unilaterally act on their own to build what are called 'small property-rights hous-ing' [which means housing that lacks valid certificates of title].

Quite frankly, the reason we are unable to control the 'sluice-gates' to this kind of land use is that local [authorities] have unilaterally changed the nature [defini-tion] of 'collectively owned construction land' in order to suit their own purposes. This not only has a direct impact on our ability to conduct macroeconomic mea-sures, but it has a direct impact on our future food security. It has a direct impact on the long-term rights and interests of farmers, right now and on into the future.

We cadres who are involved in rural affairs ['work'] must cultivate a very basic quality. We must be absolutely steeped in the laws and regulations that pertain to rural land-use issues. We must have a profound understanding of all articles that relate to rural land in our various laws, including the constitution, the Law on Land Management, the Law on the Organization of Villagers' Committees, the Law on Rural Land Contracts, and the Law on Material Rights. At the same time, we must understand the relevant documents put out by the Party and the government.

For example, the document extending land contracts to a 15-year period was *Document No. 1* put out by the Central Committee [of the Communist Party of China] in 1984; the document explicitly re-extending contractual periods for another 30 years was *Document No. 11* put out by the Central Committee in 1993. Since that time, two more extremely important documents have been issued: One is *Notification No. 16,* put out in 1997 by both the general offices of the Central Committee of the Party and the State Council, that relates to stopping the 'dual-plot management system,' and the other is *Document No. 18* put out by the Central Committee in 2001 that relates to standardizing [regulating] land transfers. We must have a firm grasp of these laws, regulations, and policies. Only then can we safeguard our arable land through the use of legal administrative procedures, and only then can we properly preserve the fundament rights and interests of our farmers.

Note

* This article is organized according to the author's address at the symposium on the rural work held in Hangzhou.

16 Modernize agriculture in a way that accommodates China's specific situation*

(October 2007)

Agriculture is the foundation of our national economy. This has repeatedly been demonstrated in this country of ours, and can be regarded as self-evident in a place that has a population of over 1 billion people.

As we move into a 'new stage' in the new century, the depth and breadth of industrialization, informatization, urbanization, marketization, and globalization are increasing at great speed. Only if we also accelerate the pace of our agricultural modernization will we be able to assure that agriculture rests on a firm foundation and grows in a stable manner. Only then can we assure sustained growth of farmers' income and overall progress in our rural areas.

This has enormous practical significance in accomplishing our [stated policy goals of] achieving a 'moderately prosperous society in an all-round way' and 'accelerating the advance of socialist modernization.' To this end, the Report of the Party's 17th National Congress [2007] explicitly states that modernizing agriculture and creating a prosperous rural economy must be our main priorities as we advance the whole agenda of creating a 'socialist new countryside.' We must 'chart a course that modernizes agriculture in accordance with China's specific conditions.'

I. Building a 'Moderately Prosperous Society in an All-Round Way' requires that we accelerate the process of agricultural modernization

It is true that our agriculture has achieved remarkable things since the start of 'reform and opening up,' to the extent that the world has been amazed at our progress. Nevertheless, given our population and the per capita resources available to us, in addition to relatively backward production methods and general conditions, we still only barely meet demand for such basic commodities as grain and we have to supplement domestic production with imports to meet demand for a number of other agricultural products. In addition, our society's demand for agricultural goods is increasing by the day as the economy develops and living standards improve. Sustainable and stable growth of our agriculture is imperative if we want to achieve a 'moderately prosperous society in an all-round way.'

Table 16.1 Per capita consumption of major agricultural products by urban and rural residents
(unit = 500 g)

Year	Grains	Vegetable oil	Meat	Eggs	Milk	Aquatic products
1996	414.0	11.0	30.4	10.5	4.3	10.8
2006	297.3	13.5	40.0	14.7	22.1	17.0
2006/1996	–28%	+23%	+32%	+40%	+414%	+57%

Note: All the weights in this book are expressed in 500g.

1. Our country is in the midst of a rapid increase in demand for agricultural products

Much higher demands are being placed on agricultural production in recent years, given the ongoing fast pace of economic development and markedly improved incomes in both urban and rural areas. A comparison between 1996 and 2006 shows that per capita consumption of most agricultural products has increased dramatically in both urban and rural areas, with the exception of grain rations. (See Table 16.1.)

At the same time, we should recognize that our country is in a stage of very rapid urbanization. The total population of the country increased by 90 million in the decade between 1996 and 2006. During that same period, however, the number of people living in urban areas increased by more than 200 million. In the space of one decade, our 'degree of urbanization' went from 30.48 percent to 43.90 percent. This was an average annual increase of 1.34 percent, which means that more than 20 million people were added to urban populations every year.

The degree to which a country is urbanized is an important indicator of its socioeconomic development, and is a natural consequence of economic development. It also indicates, however, that those who were previously producing agricultural products are now those who are consuming them, and it also signifies a major increase in the per capita amount of such products that are consumed. Taking 2006 as an example in comparing the amounts of different types of foods consumed by people in urban and rural areas, we see that urban residents overall eat 15.5 percent more vegetable oil, 47.7 percent more meat, 133.3 percent more eggs, and 200 percent more aquatic products than rural residents.

As we move into a stage of even faster urbanization, and as we aim to accomplish a moderately prosperous life for everyone in the country, it is all the more imperative that we assure stable and sustainable growth in our agricultural production.

2. The constraints of scarce resources on our agricultural production are increasing by the day

As described in the *Report* of the 17th National Congress of the Party [2007], due to the combined effects of a variety of factors, 'it is becoming increasingly difficult to ensure stable growth in agriculture and sustainable increase in farmers' incomes.' The underlying conditions in which farming is being carried out 'are facing ever more severe challenges.'

The first challenge is the decrease in the amount of arable land. In 1996, the total amount of our country's farmland came to 1.951 billion *mu* [1.3 billion square kilometers]. By 2006, this had already dropped to 1.827 billion *mu,* a decline in one decade of 124 million *mu.* Given that we are still not as 'industrialized' as we aim to be, and that we are still less than 'half-urbanized,' despite the fact that we adhere to the most strict standards in our land-administration system, it is going to be very hard to turn around the trend to even further loss of farmland. At the very least, we still need to authorize an additional 4 million *mu* of land merely for construction purposes every year.

The second challenge is the scarcity of fresh water. Our total per capita fresh-water resources come to only around 2,100 cubic meters in all. This is roughly one-quarter of the worldwide per capita average. In addition, the distribution of this water is highly uneven in terms of location and also timing. In general, the northern part of the country faces a severe lack of water. Unfortunately, those areas in which we do have water, in the southern and eastern parts of the country, face faster industrialization and urbanization. This has drawn in more laborers, increasing the demand for food even as farmland declines there faster than in the rest of the country.

Grain-production capacity has been falling faster in the 10 coastal provinces and municipalities than elsewhere – between 1998 and 2005, it declined by 17.6 percent, a decline of 61.4 billion *jin* [30.7 billion kilograms] of grain. In terms of the contribution to the nationwide grain production, these areas went from 34.02 percent down to 29.67 percent. Historically, we have always seen 'a transfer of southern grain up to the north.' This has now been replaced with the phenomenon of 'northern grain going down to the south.'

The problem with this is that grain production is an industry that requires large amounts of water. We should think deeply about the sustainability of transferring the responsibility for producing an ever-increasing amount of grain to water-scarce regions in the north.

The third challenge is the aging of irrigation facilities and infrastructure on farmland. In recent years, we have seen a severe drop in necessary repairs. In 2006, only 46.41 percent of our total farmland was provided with effective irrigation systems, that is, only some 848 million *mu* of land. More than half of our arable land relies on 'nature' for its sustenance. As a result, we now lose in excess of 70 billion *jin* of grain every year to natural disasters.

3. *The basic solution for our country's agricultural issues lies in accelerating the advance of science and technology*

Our margin for improving yields by relying on natural resource inputs is growing ever smaller. Our per capita arable land and fresh water is already far below world averages, and we are facing even more pronounced constraints on these resources by the day. Moreover, our tremendous use of chemical fertilizers, herbicides, and pesticides is already preventing us from improving quality and safety standards of our agricultural goods, to the extent that agricultural polluting is becoming a critical problem.

According to statistics, we have spread around 200 million tons of chemical substances on the land since the country was founded [1949]. This includes chemical fertilizers, pesticides, and other materials. We currently use more than 46 million tons of chemical fertilizer per year. The rate at which nitrogenous fertilizers are 'taken up' in a given season is only around 30 percent, resulting in 'super-nutritious' or eutrophied surface water and polluted underground water. Nationwide use of pesticides comes close to 1.3 million tons every year, and fields that are overly polluted to one degree or another by these pesticides cover some 136 million *mu* of land. The widespread use of plastic sheeting on fields [to prevent the growth of weeds and hold in moisture] has also given rise to a new form of pollution.

The main way we are going to be able to break out of these resource constraints and achieve any kind of sustainable increase in yields is to accelerate our ability to innovate in science and technology. [We must] increase the rate at which scientific achievements are transformed into practical uses, and increase the amount of resources we put into this effort as well as the efficiency with which we use the results. Currently, the 'contribution' of science and technology to our agricultural production is only 48 percent, which is 30 percent lower than it is in developed countries. The rate at which scientific results are transformed into practicality stands at a mere 30 percent, some 40 percent below developed countries.

We absolutely must develop a sense of urgency about this issue, and an awareness of the consequences if we do not take action. In addition to improving our ability to protect our natural environment and its resources, we need to rely on the advances of science and technology to improve yields, increase the utilization rate of natural resources, and increase the labor productivity of those engaged in agriculture. This, in brief, is the path we need to take in modernizing our agriculture.

II. In taking this 'path' of agricultural modernization, we have to take our country's specific situation as our starting point and understand that we must operate within the confines of our national conditions

The *Report* of the Party's 17th National Congress pointed out that 'we still have not fundamentally changed the situation of a very weak agricultural foundation and backward conditions with respect to rural development.' This is a very realistic approach to how we must proceed in modernizing agriculture, and it recognizes the fact that our country has certain specific conditions that oblige us to chart a unique course.

1. Adhere to the basic policy guideline of 'coordinating urban and rural socioeconomic development so that they advance in tandem'

The *Report* of the 17th explicitly declared that, 'Among important tasks of the Party as a whole, the most important is to find solutions to the problems of agriculture, rural affairs, and farmers. This impacts the overall situation of building a moderately prosperous society.'

Only when the entire Party's thinking has reached a high level of unity on the subject will we be able to create the appropriate social atmosphere for pushing forward agricultural modernization. A brief glance at agricultural development in countries around the world shows that many in fact neglected agriculture in their drive to industrialize and urbanize. As a result, their agricultural production declined, their rural communities withered, and their economic development and stability in general was eventually forced to pay a heavy price. In the course of industrialization, the contribution of agriculture to a nation's GDP gradually declines and the amount of tax revenue that the State derives from agriculture also becomes modest to insignificant.

This is the natural progression in any modern country's economic development. Nevertheless, it does not change by one particle the fundamental standing that agriculture must continue to maintain in a national economy. We are a developing socialist nation, with a very large population that has a majority of 'rural' people. This fundamental reality determines the fact that the 'three agricultures' [agriculture, rural issues, and farmers] are and will remain intimately tied to the stability and growth of the nation as a whole. If we dare to neglect agriculture simply because its contribution to GDP is declining and its share of fiscal revenues is modest, then we are abandoning the basic needs of a 'scientific approach to development,' as well as the natural progression of socioeconomic development.

This can only lead to monumental setbacks in the future that will exact a very heavy price. As a result, our Party's thinking must be firmly unified around the idea that 'the most important among important tasks' is to find solutions to the 'three agricultures.' As we seek to build a moderately prosperous society in an all-round way, we must coordinate the process of urban and rural development and make sure that they advance together.

2. Regarding how to implement the policy of having industry 'repay' agriculture, and having urban areas 'bring along' [or provide support to] rural areas

One explicit requirement of the *Report* of the 17th [Party Congress] was to set up mechanisms with long-lasting effect that could enable industry to contribute to agriculture and could help urban areas 'bring along' rural areas. The declared aim was to create a new pattern of integrated development of urban and rural areas. This provided the necessary institutional and policy context for advancing our country's agricultural modernization.

The reason our agriculture and rural development have been backward for so long is that we still have not broken out of a 'dual system' approach to urban and rural areas. Socioeconomic administrative structures that have resulted from this fundamental problem remain entrenched. This leads to an ongoing loss or 'flowing out' of the factors of production away from agriculture, and to patently insufficient financial and technical support for agriculture.

Our urgent task, therefore, is to formulate systems that change the dual nature of the economic structures governing urban and rural areas. It is to find ways to actually implement the policy of enabling cities to 'bring along' rural areas and industry to facilitate agriculture. No country can rely exclusively on the strength of farmers themselves in modernizing its agriculture. Countries that have already accomplished a modernization of their agriculture generally adopt practices that include setting up public fiscal incentives, improving transfer-payment systems, establishing subsidies for farmers that are still in accord with World Trade Organization regulations but that also address their country's specific situation.

As we ourselves have pursued ever higher levels of industrialization and urbanization, we too have already taken major steps in this regard. The Central Committee has adopted a whole series of measures since the time of the Party's 16th National Congress [2002], such as abrogation of all agricultural taxes and adopting various production subsidies that go directly to farmers. The Central Committee has set up incentives and subsidy mechanisms for those counties and townships that are experiencing severe hardship as well as those counties that are major grain producers. It has established policies and systems to protect the legal rights and interests of rural migrant workers, as well as improving upon those that already existed and making sure they were followed. This indicates that mechanisms with long-lasting effect are in the formative process in our country as a means to ensure that industry does indeed support agriculture and urban areas do indeed bring along rural areas.

So long as we persist in this direction and really do abide by the goals of the Party's 17th National Congress [2007], in 'forming a new pattern of integrated socioeconomic development in urban and rural areas,' we should be able to see daily improvement in both the policy environment for our efforts and the actual creation of systems for 'modernizing agriculture in a way that conforms to China's actual situation.'

3. *Put particular effort into improving the overall production capacity of agriculture*

One basic indicator of the state of a country's agricultural modernization is what is called 'overall production capacity' or 'comprehensive production capacity.' We must put our efforts into improving this indicator in China, if we aim to develop a modern agriculture and create a 'socialist new countryside.' Many of our agricultural products lead the world in terms of the quantity of production, but in terms of the economic efficiency with which they are produced, and the output per required inputs, we are still demonstrably behind the level of advanced countries.

For example, we lead the world in output of such things as certain grains, meat, poultry and eggs, and fruit, but we also spread tons of chemical fertilizer on the ground in order to achieve that. In 2005, we spread up to 366.5 tons per thousand hectares, for example, a figure that was 3.5 times the world's average. Specifically, it was 1.6 times as much chemical fertilizer as Japan uses, 3.6 times as much as the United States uses, and 6 times as much as France uses. Not only does this keep production costs high but it contributes to environmental pollution.

Furthering our country's agricultural modernization will therefore mean putting serious effort into improving our overall production capacity.

The *Report* of the 17th Party Congress put forward explicit demands with regard to modernizing our agriculture, and dealt specifically with the various outstanding issues to do with increasing overall production capacity in particular.

First, while continuing to emphasize the building of rural facilities and general infrastructure, we must pay even more attention to efforts that relate to marketing and a 'socialized services system.' Sound infrastructure is the basis for improving the competitive edge of our agriculture as well as improving farmers' quality of life. Right now, problems relating to poor rural and agricultural infrastructure are still pronounced. The government should increase its investment in this regard, increase mechanisms by which resources can flow into agriculture from various channels, including farmers themselves but also from other social forces. We should strengthen the building and the expansion of irrigation facilities on farmland, step up efforts to fortify dams and mitigate the danger of their breaking, promote the building of major ecological projects, undertake more comprehensive mitigation of erosion problems, including both water and soil erosion, accelerate the creation of 'standard fields' that consistently produce high yields, address problems of unsanitary drinking water in rural areas, intensify efforts to build roads in the countryside, increase access to information in the countryside, promote more widespread use of renewable clean energy sources, improve facilities for centralized management of waste products in rural areas including both garbage and sewage.

In general, we must truly improve the underlying conditions for better agricultural production and a higher quality of life in rural areas. These things are all necessary but not sufficient in order to improve agricultural and rural development. In recent years, such things as soybean production have been severely impacted by imports, a situation that has led to volatility in the price of such products as pork. In addition, technical barriers to the export of such things as meat, poultry, fruit, vegetables, and aquatic products are a phenomenon that clearly indicate we will not be able to improve our agricultural efficiency and compete in international markets without developing sound rural marketing systems and better socialized servicing systems.

In this regard, the *Report* of the 17th points out that we should 'strengthen the building up of basic agricultural infrastructure, and improve rural markets and rural servicing systems.' At the same time, we should put serious effort into improving and modernizing modes of product distribution in rural areas, including new 'formats' in our logistical systems. We should cultivate multilayered and multimodal market distribution entities. We should improve socialized servicing systems that can accommodate the 'marketization' and the 'internationalization' of agriculture. We should strengthen regulatory mechanisms over both imports and exports in order to protect domestic agricultural production and ensure that we maintain basic stability in our agricultural markets. At each link in the production process, from preproduction to postproduction, we should increase economic and technical services to farming households in order to help them withstand both natural and market risks. The aim is to enable ongoing stability in production and steady improvement in economic results.

Second, while continuing to push for increases in the overall quantity of production, we should focus even more on improving the quality and the safety of our agricultural products. Our main problem in the past was an insufficient supply of agricultural goods. We are now in an era when we have a basic balance in supply and demand, and often even a surplus in prosperous years, but consumer demands have increased as people's standard of living improves.

People already have enough to eat – what they want now is better food, more nutritious food, food that is healthy. Quality and safety issues have become paramount in determining both agricultural results and consumers' health. Food safety incidents that have been occurring both domestically and abroad are evidence that quality and safety are now determining factors in the international competitiveness of both agriculture and food. The *Report* of the 17th points out that, 'while strengthening the comprehensive capacity of our agriculture and assuring that we have adequate food security as a nation,' we should 'improve all preventive and control mechanisms that relate to animal and plant diseases and improve the safety standards and quality standards of agricultural products.' This means that we must strictly enforce the Law on the Quality and Safety of Agricultural Products, and we must strengthen preventive and control measures by proactively implementing agricultural standards.

We have to accelerate the establishment of an entire system that deals with this so that infringements can be traced back to sources. We have to protect legally registered trademarks on agricultural products as well as marks indicating the place of production and the brand. We must strictly enforce a system that gives notice when products are genetically modified, including milk that is in liquid form; we should improve the production environment for all agricultural products and the means for testing and evaluating product quality and ensuring that agricultural products sold on the market are both of sufficient quality and safe.

Third, while emphasizing the improvement of agricultural yields and economic results in agriculture, we should focus even more on securing and protecting our nation's food security. The greatest challenge facing agriculture is that economic returns are low as compared to producing other products. Within agriculture, the returns on grain are especially poor, and this is a tremendous constraining factor when it comes to encouraging farmers to plant grain. Since the 16th Party Congress, the Central Committee has adopted a whole series of powerful measures that 'support agriculture and benefit farmers.' These have had a marked effect on bringing grain production back up and on motivating farmers to want to plant grain. However, the acreage under grain production in 2006 was still 125 million *mu* less than it was in 1998.

Modern agriculture means highly efficient agriculture. If we do not improve yields, then our agriculture will not be able to move forward. We therefore still need to press for strategic restructuring of our agricultural production, and develop zones in which more competitive products are raised, encourage diversified operations in agriculture, a more regional distribution of planting, and specialized production. We need to improve the degree to which agriculture is 'industrialized,' as well as its overall economic returns. In the process of optimizing our agricultural structure, we must adhere to the principles put forth by the 17th: Reinforce the policies of supporting agriculture and benefiting farmers, strictly enforce policies that conserve farmland, increase investment in agriculture, promote the advance of science and technology with respect to agriculture, strengthen agriculture's 'comprehensive production capacity,' and 'ensure national food security.'

Various policies 'supporting agriculture and benefiting farmers' should lean in the direction of assisting the major grain-supporting areas and should create sound systems in support of policies that foster and protect grain production. Through every means possible, we should lift the comprehensive economic results of growing grain, in order to motivate farmers as well as government administration at all levels in grain-producing regions. In very stable and consistent fashion, we should increase our capacity for grain production.

Fourth, while emphasizing increased investment in agricultural equipment and facilities, we need to focus even more on cultivating what we call a 'new type of farmer.' Naturally, equipment is important in modernizing agriculture but at the end of the day what we will be relying on most are 'modern' farmers. It is imperative, therefore, that we raise the caliber of our rural labor force. In 2005, among a total rural labor force of 504 million people, 34.1 percent had a grade-school education or below and, among these, 6.87 percent were either absolutely or nearly illiterate.

In recent years, the trends of an aging farming population and the tendency to view farming as a sideline are becoming even more pronounced. If we do not start cultivating a 'new generation of farmers' soon, 'farming' will soon be finding itself in need of 'farmers.'

There is a tremendous need, therefore, to cultivate a 'new breed of people' who are educated, technically qualified, and capable of operating a business. We must develop modernized agricultural operating entities. We must put far greater efforts into training that relates to market-economy systems and production skills needed for a modern agriculture. We should actively help households specialize in various parts of agricultural production such as planting or cultivating or breeding operations, and we should promote the development of both institutions and people who serve as agents in the process of moving and distributing product. We should accelerate the provision of 'vo-tech' education in rural areas as well as adult education, and increase assistance to students who are majoring in agriculture at universities, junior colleges, and vo-tech institutions, and encourage them to return to rural areas upon graduation and take up a career in modernized agriculture.

Fifth, while emphasizing production capacity, we should focus even more on innovative forms of farming operations that still are rooted in the 'basic operating system' that applies in rural areas. All evidence shows that family operations are most suited to the unique requirements of agriculture. This appear to be the case from the distant past to today, and from China to other countries. Our own experience and the lessons we have learned since the founding of the country [in 1949] also indicate that household operations are the most effective way of protecting the fundamental rights and interests of farmers.

Not one of the countries around the world that has achieved modernized agriculture is not conducting its farming through family operations. Family operations are therefore not at all in conflict with the whole idea of modernization. The crux of the matter lies in being able to infuse agriculture with modern industrialized methods and modern factors of production. The role of urbanization in the process is to enable a shift of excess population as household operations expand in scale. The role of 'marketization' is to provide better socialized economic and technical services to household operations. We therefore have to maintain a long-term adherence to our country's basic operating system in rural areas, which is, as defined by the constitution, 'a two-tiered management system that provides for an integration of the "centralized" and the "dispersed," that is based on household-contracted operations.'

Based on this fundamental system, each place must make decisions according to its own specific circumstances in terms of its degree of urbanization and 'shifted' farming population. As the *Report* of the 17th Party Congress pointed out,

> 'Always respecting the principle of doing things according to the law, in voluntary fashion, and for compensation, those areas that are qualified can develop more large-scale operations, through all different ways and means, once they have set up well-functioning contractual operating rights that can begin to be traded on a market.'

At the same time, we should explore various ways of effectively mobilizing collective economies, developing cooperative organizations that focus on a specialized aspect of production, and supporting the professionalization of agriculture as well as the growth of 'dragon-head' enterprises [i.e., leading enterprises in a given area]. On the basis of improving and stabilizing the household contract operating system, we must constantly try to improve the organizational degree of households with respect to their ability to participate in markets and to raise production.

III. Deepen rural reform, help farmers increase incomes and decrease [tax] burdens, provide institutional guarantees that will support a modernized agriculture and the building of a 'new socialist countryside'

State policies that 'support agriculture and benefit farmers' have been constantly strengthened in recent years. Nevertheless, the gap between urban and rural development is still highly apparent, given the impact of our ongoing dual economic structure and our current stage of development.

Between 1985 and 2006, the disparity between urban and rural incomes grew from 1.86 to 1 to 3.28 to 1. We therefore must deepen rural reforms, improve the coverage of public finance in rural areas, strengthen public services in rural areas, increase the 'space' in which farmers can find employment, promote an increase in farmers' income and a decrease in their [tax] burden, and basically provide the underlying conditions that enable the building of modernized agriculture and what we call a socialist new countryside.

1. Deepen comprehensive rural reform

Our country is currently in the midst of a period of very rapid development of both industrialization and urbanization. As a result, under the impetus of a market economy system, all factors of production are quickly being concentrated in and absorbed into cities. This includes financing, land, and human resources. Due to the way our economy still operates under a dual economic structure, public services that are provided by the government are concentrated mainly in cities. This has created a situation in which the economic burden on rural farmers is tremendous, even as they lack financial and technological support to move ahead.

Rural infrastructure and the provision of social undertakings lag demonstrably behind the situation in urban areas. If we want to turn around a situation in which rural and urban disparities are growing wider, we must go further with our economic reforms, and put in place mechanisms that reinvigorate our systems. The *Report* of the 17th National Congress expressly enumerated several key points to focus on in our rural reforms, both at the current time and into the future. These included 'deepen comprehensive reform, further innovative approaches to the financial system, and reform the [existing system] of collective ownership of forests.'

First in this general category of 'deepening comprehensive rural reform' is the process of promoting reform of township and village organizations in a proactive but also stable way. The key to this process lies in changing the fundamental functions of government at the local level. It lies in putting more effort into strengthening social administration and improving public services. It involves reforming the system of rural public finance, strengthening the capacity of grassroots-level government to provide services, streamlining organizations, developing professional staff, and setting up rural administrative systems that are highly capable and efficient.

While reducing the tax burden on farmers as a primary condition, it involves growing the rural economy and gradually creating the conditions for more equal access to public services between rural and urban areas.

Second in this category is speeding up the process of making sure that public finance coverage extends to all rural areas, and making sure that public services in rural areas are improved. This involves going further in adjusting the allocation of our national income and the structure of our public-finance expenditures. It involves setting up long-range effective mechanisms that support farmers through stable and gradually increasing public outlays, as a part of the effort to have 'urban areas bring along rural areas.' Most of the additional State expenditures every year on such things as education, public health, and culture, and most of the increased investment in fixed assets, should be spent on rural areas.

In addition, we should gradually increase the percentage of money derived from the government's revenue from 'land transfer fees' that is then spent on rural areas.

We should make every effort to address those issues that farmers feel are most in need of attention with respect to both their work and their lives in general, and we must make sure that their situations in both areas improve. We must set up the conceptual understanding [among cadres] that provision of basic public services between rural and urban areas must be equalized. We must consolidate the results of free mandatory education in rural areas, expand the 'new-style cooperative health system coverage' in rural areas, gradually set up a public cultural facilities system that covers both urban and rural areas. We must lift poverty-alleviation standards, and the level of expenditures on poverty alleviation, and thereby accelerate the pace at which destitute people in rural areas are able to extricate themselves from poverty. We should institute a minimum living allowance system on a universal basis in rural areas, improve rural emergency relief systems, and explore setting up a rural old-age pension system.

The third category involves promoting financial innovation in rural areas. Financial services in rural areas have improved to a degree in recent years, due to the following actions. [We have] deepened reform of rural credit unions, promoted structural reform of the postal savings institutions, expanded the functions of the Agricultural Development Bank, expanded the ability of rural people to get small-sum loans of money, loosened the conditions for entering the field of banking in rural areas, and instituted pilot programs in extending policy-type insurance for agriculture. Nonetheless, the outlook for changing what has become a long-term trend of an outflow of money from rural areas still does not bode well. Rural areas still get very inadequate support from financial institutions. At the end of 2006, the sum of loans being made to farmers by financial institutions nationwide came to RMB 1.32 trillion, which was only 5.6 percent of the sum of all loans. This was less than half of the contribution that value-added processing of primary products contributed to the country's GDP.

Severe imbalances in financing resources between urban and rural areas, and the lack of financial services in rural areas, are already serving as a serious bottleneck to rural development. We must formulate reform measures that are truly feasible as we continue to push for innovative solutions to the rural financial system. We should increase the social responsibilities that financial institutions should bear in supporting agriculture and rural development; we must cultivate a 'new type' of rural financial organization, standardize and properly guide the flow of what is called 'people's finance,' strengthen the functions of policy-type banks that serve agriculture, speed up the process of developing insurance programs for agriculture as well as a reinsurance system. We must go further in improving the systems that pertain to rural credit unions, including their governance and their property rights, and we must raise their quality of assets. We must dramatically improve the degree of financial support and services in rural areas, based always on a foundation of improving the operating efficiencies, operating results, and risk mitigation measures of financial institutions.

The fourth category in deepening comprehensive reform in rural areas involves reforming the collective ownership system that applies to forests. This will be the next major change in our overall 'rural operating system,' following on the changes that instituted the household contracting system. It should have the ability to release tremendous productivity in our forestry regions by motivating local farmers who are empowered to manage the resources.

Pilot programs that have already been undertaken in various areas show positive results. The system preserves collective ownership of the underlying land as per the requirements of our basic 'rural operating system,' which remains unchanged. On top of that, we set up operating entities that are based on rural households, and we clearly differentiate between 'usage rights' and 'ownership rights' to forests. We allow flexibility by loosening controls over operating rights, we make sure that rights of disposal are enforced, and we protect income rights, while at the same time advancing various associated reforms. These measures will contribute greatly to transforming our traditional forestry industry by taking it in the direction of modernization. They will also ensure that we have a more organic integration of ecological, economic, and social benefits.

2. Expand employment opportunities for farmers through diverse channels, with the core aim of increasing farmers' income

The fundamental problem when it comes to increasing farmers' income lies in insufficient job opportunities. The *Report* of the 17th National Congress of the Party has put forth the following demand: 'In order to increase farmers' income, [we must] develop town-and-village enterprises, strengthen county-level economies, and create multiple channels for shifting the employment of farmers [away from agriculture].'

In the past dozen or so years, there has been a rapid increase in the number of farmers who are employed in nonfarming occupations. Between 1996 and 2006, the percentage of 'wage-type' income taken in by farmers increased from 23.4 percent to 38.2 percent. In 2006, of the increase in net income per capita among farmers of RMB 332, some 60.3 percent was attributable to wage-type income. It is quite apparent that income derived from other forms of labor is going to be the main prop for increasing overall income among farmers. We must therefore continue to increase job opportunities via all kinds of nonfarming channels as we seek to increase farmers' income.

The first way to do this is to tap the inherent potential for increased income in farming itself. 'Farming' incorporates many different functions, and we should vigorously capitalize on those in order to enable more margin for employment and channels for increased income in the field of agriculture itself. In line with increasingly diverse demands from both our domestic and international markets, we should move to more intensive and 'meticulous' agriculture, accelerate the development of 'specialty' agriculture, of the 'biomass' industry, and of 'tourism' agriculture. We should promote the practice of having 'one village focus on one specialty product.'

The second way to do this is to promote further development of township-and-village enterprises and pump up county-level economies in order to enable further transfer of labor from farming into other jobs in the same locations. We should continue to support the growth of local enterprises that are low-energy consuming and modest in the degree to which they pollute the environment, but that also bring in good results and provide greater possibility of employment. Using policies that favor certain sectors and certain regions, within reason we should attempt to adjust economic activity between cities and neighboring rural areas, and among different regions. We must create the underlying conditions that enable rural populations to find employment in their own locale, and that enable a more rational distribution of economic activity. This involves integrating our various strategic-development policy objectives of 'greatly developing the western regions,' 'invigorating the old industrial-base areas of the northeast,' 'stimulating the emergence of the central regions,' and so on. In accord with the plans for 'major function-oriented zones,' it involves proactive industrial and regional policies that raise the level of economic activity in counties that are located in western and central regions. It involves encouraging, to a reasonable degree, a shift of human resources, projects, and capital into the interior parts of the country and into small- and medium-sized cities.

The third way to do this is to ensure that we protect the legal rights and interests of rural migrant workers, and that we provide services for those farmers who 'go out' to find jobs. In 2006, the number of such people 'going out' to find jobs reached 132.12 million. Their average per capita monthly wages were RMB 946. This has become a major path to changing employment and improving income among farmers. All of our large- and medium-sized cities must enforce policies that pertain to protecting the legal rights and interests of these rural migrant workers. We must improve employment services and social services that assist these people. We must improve the level of training provided to those who engage in trade, as a way to improve their skills. We must strengthen measures to ensure legal rights to proper labor contracts, wage guarantees, work safety, and participation in social services. We must provide compulsory education to the children of rural migrant worker families, as well as basic health services and basic social security.

3. Create a new integrated pattern of economic growth in which urban and rural areas develop in tandem, which means simultaneously undertaking our policy objectives of 'urbanization' and 'building a new countryside'

One of the salient characteristics of our country is that not only do we have a large population but a large percentage of it is rural. Changing this is going to be very long and arduous process.

From the rural perspective, it is clear that 'enriching farmers' must involve lowering the number of people in rural areas who are engaged in farming. This process is also necessary as we modernize our agriculture. From the urban perspective, it is equally clear that a massive shift of population into cities is not only going to be one way to increase domestic demand in the country and help sustain rapid economic growth, but is going to place extreme pressure on cities to provide employment, housing, and social security systems. This process is going to continue over the next several decades.

Given these very real considerations in our country, we must recognize the need to undertake a two-pronged approach that both promotes urbanization while engaging in 'building up a new countryside.' On multiple levels, we must continue to raise our degree of urbanization by pushing for coordinated development of large-, medium-sized, and also small-sized cities. We must increase the 'absorption capacity' of cities as they take in large numbers of rural people. This means creating the conditions by which rural people can become 'city people' with stable jobs and residence once they have left behind their registered place of residence, the original location of their *hukou.*

In this process, we must understand quite clearly that we will not be 'urbanizing,' to the extent that America and Japan have urbanized their populations, anytime in the foreseeable future. We have a population that exceeds that of America by 1 billion. Our population is 10 times that of Japan. For quite a long time, measured in terms of 'history' rather than decades, we will continue to have a very considerable rural population.

This is simply the unavoidable fact of the matter. Consequently, even as we adopt policies to promote urbanization we must place considerable attention on the simultaneous need to 'build up a new countryside.' Our orientation in development policies must adhere to this realization if we hope to build a 'moderately prosperous society in an all-round way' and achieve modernization of the country. That is why the *Report* of the 17th Party Congress stipulated that we should

> 'take a path towards modernization that recognizes China's specific situation, that strengthens the fundamental position of agriculture, that develops long-range effective mechanisms to enable industry to stimulate agriculture and cities to "bring along" rural areas, and that forms a new pattern of integrated socioeconomic growth between urban and rural areas.'

Under the policy guidance of 'coordinated socioeconomic development between urban and rural areas,' in order to meet the needs of 'greater production, better lives, a more civilized environment, orderly communities, and democratic administration,' we must stick to the plan of 'building up a socialist new countryside.' We must do all we can to improve living conditions of farmers and gradually raise their level of education, which also will create the necessary underlying conditions for modern agriculture in our country.

Note

* This article was initially published in the Reading Guidance for the Report of the 17th National Congress of the CPC.

Major works by Chen Xiwen

1 *Systematic Probe into the Reform of Rural Economic System* (co-author) (China Social Sciences Press, 1984)
2 'Change in the Pattern of National Economy and Development of Township Enterprises,' *Economic Research Journal,* 10th issue (1985)
3 'Interim Plan for Rural Reform,' in *Grand Thinking for China Reform* (Shenyang People's Publishing House, 1988)
4 'The Key of Rural Economic Development: Treating Farmers Correctly,' *Development Research Journal,* Vol. 2 (1986–1989) (Beijing Normal School Publishing House, 1990)
5 'China Rural Reform: Review and Outlook' (monograph) (Tianjin People's Publishing House, 1993)
6 *Research on Fiscal Difficulty in Counties and Towns and Farmers' Income Growth* (chief editor) (Shanxi Economic Press, 2002)
7 *Research on Reform of Use and Management System of Chinese Government's Agriculture Supporting Fund* (chief editor) (Shanxi Economic Press, 2003)
8 *Research on China Food Security Strategy* (co-editor) (Chemical Industry Press, 2004)
9 *China Rural Public Finance System: Theory, Policy and Empirical Study* (chief editor) (China Development Press, 2005)

Index

For Product Safety Concerns and Information please contact our EU
representative GPSR@taylorandfrancis.com
Taylor & Francis Verlag GmbH, Kaufingerstraße 24, 80331 München, Germany

www.ingramcontent.com/pod-product-compliance
Lightning Source LLC
Chambersburg PA
CBHW050419280326
41932CB00013BA/1922

9 781138 595811